THE MILWAUKEE JOURNAL

THE MILWAUKEE JOURNAL

The First Eighty Years

Will C. Conrad
Kathleen F. Wilson
Dale Wilson

With a foreword by
Arthur Ochs Sulzberger

The University of
Wisconsin Press
Madison · Milwaukee · 1964

PN
4899
m37
J67

Published by the University of Wisconsin Press
Madison and Milwaukee
Mailing address: P.O. Box 1379, Madison, Wisconsin 53701
Editorial offices: 430 Sterling Court, Madison

Printed in the United States of America
by the George Banta Company, Inc., Menasha, Wisconsin

Library of Congress Catalog Card Number 64-19175

To Harry Johnston Grant (1881–1963)

Who built The Milwaukee Journal to a great and endur-ing institution, and created a lasting memorial through its Employe Ownership Plan; and

To Miss Faye McBeath

Niece of Lucius W. Nieman, whose firm beliefs and steadfast support were vital to the success of Employe Ownership of The Journal

Foreword

The Milwaukee Journal, lively as a golf ball and clean as spring water, is a newspaper with a chapter all its own in the history of American journalism, but I have a complaint to make about it. The complaint is that in the year I spent on the newspaper as a reporter I was kept so busy writing obituaries about freshly deceased Wisconsites that I did not have time to get to know enough of those still drawing breath.

Of course, other people have had complaints about The Journal, too. Government officials in Milwaukee complain that they cannot twitch a civic muscle without The Journal knowing about it. Politicians of every political party have complained that being flayed alive is a most uncomfortable sensation. And I imagine that there is hardly a reader of The Journal who has not complained at one time or another about having some of his favorite theories or prejudices or preconceived notions jostled so hard that he had to think them through again.

There are only a handful of newspapers in this country that have become synonymous with the cities where they are published. The Journal is one of them. To think of Milwaukee without The Journal is like trying to think of New York without Broadway, San Francisco without the Golden Gate, Washington without the Capitol—clearly impossible.

Perhaps more than any other newspaper in the country, The

Journal has become identified with the health and growth of its community. It has fought against its natural enemies—corruption and crime and civic lackadaisicalness. It also has fought just as hard *for* things—for civic integrity, for tolerance, for awareness.

But the story of The Journal is, I think, considerably more than the story of the relationship between a newspaper and a city. It is the story, most of all, of free thinking. The most important contribution of The Journal—a contribution that really goes beyond journalism—is that it has broken down shibboleths and clichés about the American mentality, most particularly the "Midwestern mind."

There is a caricature about the Midwest that is accepted as true portrait in many place in the world. In broad strokes, the Midwest is drawn as provincial, withdrawn, isolationist, stolid. By rights, therefore, The Journal should be interested only in its own backyard and have its mind made up in advance on political issues and candidates. Since the truth about The Journal is exactly the opposite, it has helped change some of the quick stereotypes about the Midwest.

The Journal is a great local paper—but it is not a provincial paper. The whole world is its beat. It is a paper with opinions as strong as hot mustard, but no politician and no party can assume support by The Journal in advance. It has a richness of heritage but has never been tied down by tradition—even when its own readers objected to its maverick qualities. Its story is worth reading, and remembering.

Arthur Ochs Sulzberger

Preface

The Milwaukee Journal: The First Eighty Years is the work of three former employes of the paper. The major part of the research was done by Will C. Conrad, chief editorial writer from 1943 to 1949, and contributing editor and historian from 1949 to 1959. Dale Wilson, formerly Sunday and feature editor, did further research, edited the manuscript, and brought the story up through 1962. The writing, for the most part, was done by Kathleen F. Wilson, who had been a feature writer and book reviewer.

The book is an effort to record The Milwaukee Journal's editorial policy on issues that were of major importance to Wisconsin or the nation, and to picture some of the men and women who helped guide the paper through the first eighty years.

The authors are indebted to the Journal library for aid in finding material; to Dr. Frederick I. Olson of the University of Wisconsin-Milwaukee for help on the chapter on the Milwaukee Socialist movement; to The Journal's editor, Lindsay Hoben, and to Paul H. Ringler and John Reddin, of The Journal's editorial writers' staff, for background information. Courtland R. Conlee, promotion manager, was of great assistance. All pictures in the book are by Journal photographers unless otherwise credited.

September 20, 1963

Contents

Illustrations

THE MILWAUKEE JOURNAL

1

The Young Editor

In the annals of success, one sometimes encounters the happy circumstance of a strong man appearing at a time of great need. There is often poverty, struggle, and, as the driving force, an immediate challenge. The story of The Milwaukee Journal and its founder repeats the familiar pattern. On the scene was L. W. Nieman, young, courageous, dedicated. And very soon there occurred the stark tragedy of a hotel fire to point the need, in the Milwaukee of 1882, for a newspaper with the daring, knowledge, and wisdom to print the truth.

The entire American press of that day was ripe for reform. The newspaper that catered to special interests was losing its hold on the reader. In its place was to appear the independent paper, conscious of its obligation to serve all the people. This transformation made journalism a power in an America which was awakening from the period of benumbed democracy following the Civil War—an era of exploitation in which Wisconsin with its vast natural resources had offered the exploiters great opportunity.

In the southern half of Wisconsin a rural and commercial civilization was developing, led by the metropolis that was building up around Milwaukee Bay. Beginning in the 1830's and continuing for fifty years, a vast stream of migrants from our own Atlantic seaboard and from Europe had poured through the port of Milwaukee. Out of the city radiated ship lines, plank roads, and then railroads. It was the market for wheat from the central part of the state and for lead ore from the southwestern part. Its commercial activities had produced a distinct aristocracy of wealth. To the north, in the woodland counties, the lumbermen were harvesting—some called it destroying—the forest resources. There, also, an aristocracy was developing, marked by the lumber baron's "castle" on the hill, above the lumberjack's shanty at the edge of the woods.

Milwaukee in 1882 was a city of cobblestone and wood block pavements, horse-drawn streetcars, and gas lights. Of the county's 130,000 inhabitants 38,000 were German-born, and probably an equal number were second generation Germans. The important leadership was held by those families who had profited from the manufacturing and commerce the city had developed. They were a class apart. The common people worked long hours to have enough money to support their small homes, drop in at the beer garden now and then, go to the new Exposition Building, join in the ever-popular torchlight parades, watch the drill exercises of the elegant military units the city supported, and go humbly to church on Sunday. They had little connection with the sparkling cultural activities that centered in the *Turnvereins* and the music clubs. Nor did they participate in formulating the civic programs by which the city was developed.

There were three German-language daily newspapers, and German was the classroom language in many schools. Two English-language newspapers, the *Sentinel* and the *Evening Wisconsin,* dating back to Solomon Juneau and Byron Kilbourn, were still politically powerful. Then there was the newborn infant, The Daily Journal, begun November 16, 1882, by Peter V. Deuster, Democratic congressman from Milwaukee, who was editor of the *Seebote,* a leading German daily.

Deuster had just been elected to a third term in Congress, following a hotly contested battle during which he had put out a campaign sheet in English to combat his Republican opponent. To that sheet, and to a slight trend away from the years of Republican rule, he attributed his victory, and thereupon decided to start an English-language newspaper of his own. He asked

4

Michael Kraus, publisher of the *Seebote,* to be a partner, and M. Almy Aldrich, formerly of the old *Daily News,* to be editor. They set up a cubbyhole office, 10 by 10 feet, in the Seebote building at 96 Mason Street and used the Seebote presses. It was a brave start but the little band soon ran into difficulties. They had no money for wire news services, a necessity in the days before press associations; and in the local news field Aldrich's editing was no improvement over that of his rivals. The Daily Journal, a four-page paper, measuring 13 by 19 inches, had a circulation of 1,000. At two cents a copy, and with little advertising, it was losing money. Representative Deuster decided he would withdraw.

This was the situation when young Nieman became editor, on December 11, 1882, just twenty-six days after The Daily Journal was founded. The times were auspicious for the rise of a great newspaper and Nieman brought great gifts to the endeavor.

Lucius William Nieman was born on December 13, 1857, in the Bear Creek country of Sauk County, south-central Wisconsin. His father, Conrad Nieman, was of German ancestry; his mother, Sara Elizabeth Delamatter, of French. When Conrad Nieman died in 1859, leaving the two-year-old son, Lucius, and a five-year-old daughter, Violette, the mother brought the children to Mukwonago to live with their grandmother, Susan Cupernall Delamatter. After a few years the mother, who had become a dressmaker, remarried, but the children were so attached to their grandmother that they stayed with her.

As a boy, Nieman talked of becoming a printer and urged his grandmother to let him get started in a newspaper plant. While she delayed, wanting to keep her twelve-year-old grandson in school as long as possible, he ran away. She caught up with him at Waukesha, ten miles from Mukwonago, but when he refused to return home she arranged with her friend, Theron W. Haight, editor of the Waukesha *Freeman,* an influential weekly, to give the boy a job. Young Nieman lived in the Haight home, and in the evening after his day of typesetting, he could listen to the wide-ranging and scholarly talk of the editor.

Grandmother Delamatter chose wisely when she entrusted the boy to Haight. The Waukesha *Freeman* had taken its name when it espoused the cause of runaway slaves, and Haight had carried on the tradition of freedom. For example, as a lawyer he had defended in court a group of Holy Rollers, a religious sect that was being driven out of town. Haight's library of early rare books was a treasured collection which the University of Michigan once attempted to buy, and Haight himself was a writer of distinction. He is represented in university libraries both in Europe and in America by his book *The Divine Weeks,* which traces the source of John Milton's inspiration in writing his poetry to the work of Guillaume Salluste du Bartas, sixteenth century Huguenot. Haight had been principal of the Mukwonago, Wisconsin, school and at all times was active in community betterment. Who can appraise the influence of this man on the energetic, fatherless boy in his years between twelve and fourteen?

At fifteen, proud of himself as a printer, Nieman got a job in the composing room of the Milwaukee *Sentinel,* the leading newspaper of Wisconsin. Before long he asked to be a reporter, but the *Sentinel* editor advised him to get more education. After a year he entered Carroll College at Waukesha, living again with his grandmother, who had moved there.

"If there is any good in me, I owe it to Grandma Delamatter," Nieman often said in later years.

While in school at Carroll, the sixteen-year-old boy began sending Waukesha news to the *Sentinel.* The dispatches were so well done that the editor offered him a job as a reporter in Milwaukee. He accepted. He had been at Carroll a year and a half. After one year of reporting, Nieman, not yet eighteen, was sent to Madison to cover the 1875 session of the state legislature. There he observed what was going on in Wisconsin politics, then under control of powerful men who had made fortunes in timber lands, railroads, and banking. Some of them, he suspected, did not hesitate to compensate legislators who voted their way.

The legislative session over—a session in which reporter Nieman had been denounced on the floor of the senate because of his tendency to pry into situations that appeared corrupt—he returned to the *Sentinel* news room, and within a year became city editor, one of the youngest men ever to occupy this responsible position on a metropolitan paper. He now had his first opportunity to try ideas that placed him in advance of his time. A news story must have a direct approach with its significant facts placed first, it must be told in an interesting way and be of reasonable length. Long, rambling stories, so characteristic of the time, began to disappear from the *Sentinel*. Nieman was promoted to managing editor. In a little over eight years he had come from printer's devil to the second most responsible editorial position on an American newspaper. He was now just under twenty-one.

But blows were to fall. Soon after Nieman started the job of making the paper brighter and more informative, there were important personnel changes on the *Sentinel*. Restraints were put on him, and he began to look for a new job. In St. Paul, Minnesota, the *Dispatch* was in need of rejuvenation. Nieman was offered the opportunity to breathe new life into the paper. During his year and a half in St. Paul he curbed the wordy writers, gave the paper a new dress, and, most important, restored readers' confidence by his independent handling of the news. The *Dispatch* was growing in circulation, and Nieman was given one-third interest in the paper, but his heart was not in St. Paul. The lure of Wisconsin was strong. He sold out and returned to Milwaukee, where he once more became managing editor of the *Sentinel*, whose owners and editor, impressed by the St. Paul venture, now seemed willing to give him a freer hand.

Then a second blow fell—one harder than the first. The *Sentinel* was sold to a group of politicians, promoters, and bankers. About a year and a half earlier this group had formed a syndicate to start a Republican newspaper in Milwaukee. To get press services they bought the *Daily News,* a solid paper that had once been edited by C. Latham Sholes, inventor of the typewriter. The new paper, called the *Republican and News,* appeared in January, 1881. Its editor was Horace Rublee, former Wisconsin chairman of the Republican party who still had ties with the political ring that controlled the state.

The *Republican and News,* dull and patently a political newspaper, failed to take root in the Milwaukee field. In May, 1882, its owners, with political money still available, tried to save it by buying the *Sentinel* and merging the two papers. Again Managing Editor Nieman was in difficulty. Under the editorship of Rublee he would have to return to the conventional way of handling news stories, and in serving the new owners he would be helping a political clique whose machinations he had seen when a reporter in the legislature.

How much fairness in the news columns could be expected in a paper whose first consideration was party politics? Before long this question was put to a test. When a Democrat was elected to Congress from the rock-ribbed Republican Walworth district, the editor refused to print the fact because he did not like it. Managing Editor Nieman at once began plans to have a newspaper of his own: he first considered starting a paper in Milwaukee through an arrangement with James E. Scripps, the Detroit publisher, and member of the family which already had newspapers in Cleveland, Cincinnati, St. Louis, and Buffalo. Their plan undoubtedly would have gone through—a location had been picked for the plant—if Deuster, Kraus, and Aldrich had not come out that November with The Daily Journal. Scripps decided to withdraw, and Nieman's only course was to try to buy into the new paper. The fact that The Daily Journal was faltering at the end of three weeks gave him his opportunity. Deuster was willing to sell his half interest. Nieman bought it two days before his twenty-fifth birthday.

2

The Newhall Disaster

It was characteristic of the new editor of The Daily Journal that he assumed his position without fanfare. Nowhere in the paper did his name appear; but Nieman's signature was there as truly as though it were printed in the masthead. It appeared in the telling headlines, the sparkling writing, and the human flavor of the stories. And soon his paper was to become a lone advocate for justice when tragedy struck Milwaukee and there was neither city official nor other newspaper willing to point the blame.

In the first edition of the paper Nieman stated his philosophy:

The Journal will be independent and aggressive, but always with a due regard for the sanctities of private life. It will oppose every political "machine" and cabal, venal politicians of every stripe, every form of oppression. It will be the people's paper, and will recognize that its field is Milwaukee and the state at large. The columns will mirror vividly the life of the metropolis which gave it birth, the humor and pathos, the scenes and incidents which go to make up the day and the year. Above all it will abhor dullness.

A few days later there was the colorful story "On The Avenue," the avenue now known as Wisconsin:

There was fine sleighing on Grand Avenue yesterday afternoon. The sport was fast and furious. Rosy cheeks; streaming golden hair; the flash of diamonds and gold mounted harness; horses tearing along like mad, men yelling like Modocs.

There is Mr. E. P. Bacon, president of the Young Men's Christian Association, and the man with the fast pacer is called Lucas. Mr.

9

E. H. Broadhead drives a magnificent span of bays, and they are much larger than the bay team near him driven by Miss French. George Peck's big roans are having it nip and tuck with the swill cart man, who is enjoying himself hugely. The nervous young animal which seems to think she hasn't room enough is Banker Hendee's property. "Darkness," the old pacer, is not there. The humane society threatened Mr. Hendee with arrest for speeding a horse over 20 years old.

It is said that several property owners on Grand Avenue object to the speeding and will take steps to prevent it. The horses go down at a thundering pace but experts handle the ribbons and the way cutters escape each other is a wonder to laymen.

To complete the picture, the article related that while all this was going on along one side of the street, a funeral passed slowly down the other side, with a carriage containing a weeping woman and her two fatherless children. Behind the funeral cortege was an old farmer in his wagon. He had sold his cord of stovewood and was homeward bound.

The Daily Journal was less than two months old when tragedy of undreamed proportions fell on Milwaukee. The tragedy began at 4 A.M. on January 10, 1883, heralded by an alarm from Box 15, downtown. The Newhall House, nationally known hotel, was on fire. There had been numerous small blazes in the hotel before, some of them occurring under mysterious circumstances, but this was the fire so long dreaded by those who knew the building was a firetrap.

Horse-drawn fire engines raced in over icy cobblestones. When firemen drew up around the great square building, six stories high, at the northwest corner of Broadway and Michigan, flames were shooting skyward. And inside were 180 persons, nearly half of whom would never escape.

The fire had started near the elevator and had quickly run up the shaft to all floors. Then, on each floor, it had spread around the big inner court. Sleeping guests and hotel employes, awakened by the roaring flames, tried to find their way to exits but were driven back to their rooms by the heat, smoke, and walls of fire. They began to appear at windows, pleading to be rescued. The firemen tried to raise ladders to take them down, but the building was so hemmed in by telephone wires that many of the windows could not be reached. Some ladders collapsed. The firemen who penetrated the halls and attempted to use the hose that was in the building found it so stiffened from age that it could not be unwound.

An attempt was made to use nets, but the nets were too small and some were rotten. Persons jumping missed them and crashed to the pavement. Some fell into nets only to go through. Others hit overhead wires as they leaped and were thrown off at an angle and killed. Some of the victims tried to escape through windows. At one time a bystander counted six persons hanging from ledges on one side of the building. Gradually their holds loosened and they fell to their deaths.

This heartbreaking scene was not without heroic action. One fireman laid a ladder from a building across the alley to a sixth-story window. Across this open work, high above the ground, he dragged six half-conscious hotel maids to safety. Nearly forty other girls jumped to their deaths or were burned. When the winter dawn came, the Newhall House was a gutted ruin. Around it and inside were eighty dead.

The Daily Journal swung into action to give a stunned city the full news of the disaster. The first edition, shortly after sunrise, had these headlines:

HORROR!

The Newhall House a Funeral Pyre
Eighty People Perish in the Roaring Flames!
Agonizing Scenes and Incidents of the Calamity

More editions poured off the presses and were sold on the street, for no one worked in Milwaukee that day. Crowds gathered around the ruins, or stood on street corners waiting for newspaper extras.

Editor Nieman began at once to unfold the appalling story of neglect, falsehood, manipulation, and concealing of truth that had preceded the tragedy. The Newhall House, of three hundred rooms, had been built in 1857 by Daniel Newhall and his associates. The exterior was of brick, but there were no fire walls inside. In the center was an enormous open court which in case of fire would act as a flue to ignite the whole building. Although the Newhall House must have been a profitable hotel, nothing was done, the Journal story pointed out, to correct the original construction faults or to remove defects that developed later. The chimney had cracked with age and set a fire or two, but the cracks were not mended. Modern heating pipes and plumbing were added without proper insulation.

What few fire escapes the building had were poorly placed and there were no signs pointing to them. There was no alarm system and no provision to awaken guests. The hotel's only night-watchman served also as porter and bootblack. Employes had not been instructed in fire fighting although the Newhall management had advertised: "The hotel employes are kept in training as a fire department on every floor, and every floor is supplied with water and hose."

Milwaukee insurance agencies had refused to underwrite the building. Newhall owners got their insurance through a Cincinnati firm which divided the risk among forty other companies.

The hotel's owners included some of the most prominent people of Milwaukee. The head of the Newhall House Association was a stockholder in the *Sentinel*. To print news about a fire hazard in a hotel would hurt business; so while numerous fires had occurred at the Newhall—thirty in less than eight years—they were not reported in the press.

There had been indications, said to be known to management, that an incendiary was trying to set fire to the building. After one blaze, which had been quickly extinguished, charred newspapers and kindling were found stuffed in a recess beside the elevator. Evidence of the deliberate covering up of facts was cited by The Journal. For instance, a La Crosse man, Stephen Martindale, said that the year before, when he was a hotel guest during a Civil War reunion, he was awakened by the noise of firemen in the alley bringing hose into the building to put out a fire. He gave the facts to a *Sentinel* reporter who wrote a story. It was never published. There had been six hundred guests in the Newhall that night.

As The Daily Journal printed these revelations it took a strong stand for punishment of those whose neglect had caused the fire. Its first editorial said:

> The Newhall House was a firetrap. This is notorious. Local insurance companies refused to take any risk on the building. They knew it was not safe. They knew, as does every newspaper man in the city, that the old shell had been fired time and time again, and that interested parties had sought to conceal the facts. Nothing rash should be done, but the responsibility must be fixed, and the guilty persons, whoever they may be, must be held to strict account. Bury the dead, relieve the suffering so far as possible, and then let stern justice be done.

This was the opening of a campaign that was to continue many days.

The *Sentinel,* by contrast, was to pursue a puzzling course. First day editions indicated that the paper meant to report the full facts behind the fire. Opening lines of its first extra said: "What has been dreaded as a terrible calamity for years took place early this morning." Other editions on that day and the next told how unsafe the building was and how there had been no effort to correct the hazards. But after two days a change came over the *Sentinel.* An editorial on the third day said that the Newhall "was no more a firetrap than hotels to be found in every city." It did lack heavy partitions, its halls were "narrow," and it had a limited number of stairways, but "these faults belong to many of the hotels of the country."

Next day the *Sentinel* had a still stronger editorial in defense of the hotel and its management. The hallways, which previously had been "narrow" were now "wide corridors." The means of escape were many. Guests could have walked out but they lost their heads. On the fifth day the *Sentinel* went all the way in its reversal: "It is not an exaggeration to say that among first class hotels there is not one in a score which, in case of fire, offers so many and so easy modes of escape as did the Newhall House, and yet, in the confusion and panic, it became a firetrap." Although on succeeding days there was still much news of the fire, with crews digging in the ruins to find more bodies, the *Sentinel* printed no more about the tragedy on its first page.

The *Evening Wisconsin,* leading afternoon paper, edited by

a blind man, William E. Cramer, who lived in the Newhall House and would have perished in the fire if a hotel employe had not rescued him and his wife, took what could be termed a "neutral attitude." The *Wisconsin,* whose subscribers were the "respectable" residents of the east side Yankee Hill, did not try to justify the management as did the *Sentinel,* but neither did it give any leadership toward bringing the guilty to justice.

The reading public, disgusted, turned to The Daily Journal in great numbers. On the Sunday following the fire The Journal's demands for a thorough investigation and punishment of the guilty were supported in nearly every pulpit of Milwaukee. A coroner's jury heard the full story and held that the owners of the Newhall House and its manager were culpably negligent in ignoring the hazards and in not providing better protection for the lives of guests. But this was only a finding of fact; it was not an indictment. The real test would come when the grand jury convened.

Meantime, there had been another development. George Scheller, proprietor of the Newhall House bar, had been arrested on the charge that he had started the fire. The evidence was circumstantial. He was in financial difficulty. He had quarreled with the management and might be seeking revenge. He said he had closed the bar at 1:30 A.M., but his wife said that he had not come home till after 4 o'clock. Friends explained that he had gone to a secret gambling house and did not want to betray the proprietors. In jail Scheller was silent. Frenzied crowds in the street were talking of lynching, and the sheriff spirited Scheller to another jail. The Daily Journal vigorously condemned all threats of lynching and stoutly maintained that Scheller must be given a fair trial. Nieman, it is apparent from his editorials, strongly suspected that Scheller was being exploited as a scapegoat.

When the grand jury convened it indicted Scheller on the circumstantial evidence, and virtually cleared the hotel owners and management of negligence. It pointed out that there were some defects in safety measures and some shortcomings in the way firemen and policemen handled the situation. That was all.

Lucius W. Nieman (*above*), about 1900.

Theron Haight (*right*), Waukesha editor and scholar, who gave the boy Nieman his first guidance in newspaper responsibility and independence.

THE DAILY JOURNAL.

VOL. 1—NO. 22.   MILWAUKEE, MONDAY EVENING, DECEMBER 11, 1882.   PRICE TWO CENTS.

THE MISSING GIRL

A Lively Interest Again Manifested in the Hennecke Case—Latest Developments.

WHO HAMILTON AND BROWN ARE.

FOSSILIZED FRAUD

The School Board Ring Engaged in a Death Struggle—The Meeting To-night.

MISMANAGEMENT OF SCHOOLS.

BAILEY'S BOMB.

Bill Price's Election to Congress to Be Contested by the Ex-Claim Mayor.

A GREAT EXPLOSION PROMISED.

PEOPLE AND THINGS.

THE FOOL AND HIS MONEY.

Nieman's first Journal, December 11, 1882, three weeks after the paper had been started.

The Journal's fearless coverage of the Newhall House fire in January, 1883, was said by Nieman to have given the paper its first important recognition. Drawing from *Harper's Weekly*.

Editorial notice, page 2, of Nieman's first Journal.

MILWAUKEE, MONDAY, DEC. 11, 1882.

THE public is familiar with the change in the management of The Journal, which goes into effect to-day. The paper has met a reception which makes success certain. Important improvements have been decided upon, and will be carried out as soon as the necessary machinery can be secured. The Journal will be independent and aggressive, but always with a due regard to the sanctities of private life. It will oppose every political "machine" and cabal, venal politicians of every stripe, every form of oppression, and at the same time give all the news for 2 cents. It will be the people's paper, and will recognize that its field is Milwaukee and the state at large. Its columns will mirror vividly the life of the metropolis which gave it birth—the humor and pathos, the scenes and incidents which go to make up the day and year. Above all things it will abhor dullness; it will have to do with the humorous and interesting side of life. Some of the best writers in the state are members of its staff. Cheap price does not mean cheap tone. Do not judge The Journal by what its friends or its enemies may say. Read it, and if you like it come again.

The Journal business office about 1892.

The Journal composing room about 1892. The man wearing the straw hat in the center of the photograph is foreman H. O. Cook.

Early home of The Journal, 92 Mason Street.

Mayor Dave Rose, at first supported, then denounced, by The Journal for his "wide open" policy.

The anarchist drawings depicting the Chicago riot of 1886.

The first illustration, a picture of Edward C. Wall, Cleveland's nominee for district collector of internal revenue, appeared May 12, 1885, on the front page.

THE DYNAMITE BOMB.

ranks and fled, before the officers, in all directions. It only proved for the thousandth time what they ought to have known, that a few well armed, determined, drilled men, who stand shoulder to shoulder, like a stone wall, can put to flight a hundred times their number.

The wounded from both sides were conveyed by the patrol wagons to the station house. The scene there was heartrending. The officers' legs were torn and

AFTER THE BATTLE.

their fingers shot away and their brave breasts the lodging place of bullets. "Don't touch me," cried one who dragged himself home to die; "Don't touch me; I am shot full of holes?"

MILWAUKEE DAIL

THIRD YEAR.   TUESDAY, MAY 12, 1885.

ED C. WALL FOR COLLECTOR

TO SUCCEED J. W. BEAN, OF THE MILWAUKEE DISTRICT

Mr. Wall Endorsed by Both Congressmen and by the Postmaster-General — The Original Cleveland Man in Wisconsin — A Well-Deserved Compliment.

COLLECTOR WALL

IN THE COURTS

A Damage Suit for $5,000—The Merrill Estate—A Slander Case.

In the circuit court to-day the case of Michael Burns against the North Chicago Rolling Mill company is being tried. The plaintiff sues for $5,000 damages for injuries received by being run into by a train in driving across a line of track in Bay View owned by the defendant. The jury accompanied an officer to the scene of the accident at noon to-day, and were carried in a wagon over the road traveled by the plaintiff on the night the accident occurred, crossing the track in front of an approaching train.

In the probate court to-day, in the case of Mary E. Merrill qualified as the guardian of Fred F. Merrill, filing a bond in the sum of $2,000, with Alexander Mitchell and Mary E. Merrill as sureties, and as the guardian of Richard Merrill, with a bond in the sum of $10,000, with Alexander Mitchell, John Plankinton and Mary E. Merrill as sureties. Letters of guardianship were issued. The wards are sons of S. S. Merrill, deceased, and the guardian is the mother of the boys.

In the county court to-day, in the case of Louisa Sammer against Helbing, an action to recover $5,000 damages for alleged slander, Judge Mann sustained the defendant's demurrer to plaintiff's complaint that sufficient ground for action was not shown, because the complaint did not translate to English the alleged slanderous words spoken in German.

In the county court this afternoon the case of Frank N. Hadschek, as administrator, against Eliza Hammersburg, an action to compel the defendant to turn over to the administrator certain money held by

THE ALLEGED DYNAMITERS.

CONCLUSIVE EVIDENCE IS GIVEN AGAINST CUNNINGHAM.

Failure to Connect Burton with the Treasonable Acts—Testimony of Edward Weeks, the New York Witness—The Intention of the Attorney-General

LONDON, May 12.—[Special]—When the court in which the alleged dynamiters, Cunningham and Burton, are being tried opened this morning, every seat was occupied, and many stood in the aisles. Interest in the case seems to have in no wise diminished. Judge Hawkins was the presiding justice, the Q. C. of counsel for the prisoners complained to the court of the conduct of the governor of Newgate jail, in refusing to allow either himself or his colleague to have a private interview with his clients. He stated they were much hampered in their efforts to defend the prisoners by not being allowed to have a private conference with them. The prosecution suggested the defendant's counsel be allowed a private interview, and the judge stated he would see that one was arranged. The taking of evidence was then resumed. The reading of testimony adduced at the inquiry into the explosion at Charing Cross station of the underground road, was resumed.

At the conclusion of the testimony concerning the explosion at Charing Cross, Edward Weeks, the witness from New York, took the stand and swore to Burton's

MARY DEFENDS HER TROUSERS

Why Women Have More Right to the Bifurcated Garment than Men.

Dr. Mary Walker has reached that point in life called an uncertain age. She is certainly getting old, however, although it is shown in the lines about her eyes and mouth, in the drawn appearance above the cords of the neck, and in the withered and yellow skin, and not in her heavy dark hair, which is still black and glossy, and untouched by time. She is a fluent speaker, at times illiterate. She says "cum" instead of "come," "yallur" instead of "yellow," "white" instead of "white," and gives other evidences of being a "down-easter." She is a woman's-rights worker, and insists that women should wear breeches, and declares the seen formerly wore gowns very similar to the Mother Hubbards of to-day.

"I've been arrested fourteen times for wearing men's clothes," said Dr. Mary last evening. "It's persecution. In the Biblical days men wore dresses, and the women were attired in garments nearer approaching to trousers than the men then wore. The change was made for convenience in laboring," and she went into an exhaustive argument to prove why women should be permitted to wear pantaloons if they desired, and attempted to prove why they should so desire.

Dr. Walker said she was not only a regular graduate of a medical college, but had taken a course in law in order to be able to act in cases where she was arrested for dressing in male attire. She does not think it beneath her self-respect to appear in museums; she is making money out of the business, and does not intend to receive $50

Senator Robert M. La Follette as a young man leading the Progressive branch of the Republican party.

The Journal newsboys brass band, organized in 1897, became particularly active in 1899 under the directorship of Bert Hall, Journal circulation manager. The boys were in demand at park concerts and toured the state, playing in many cities.

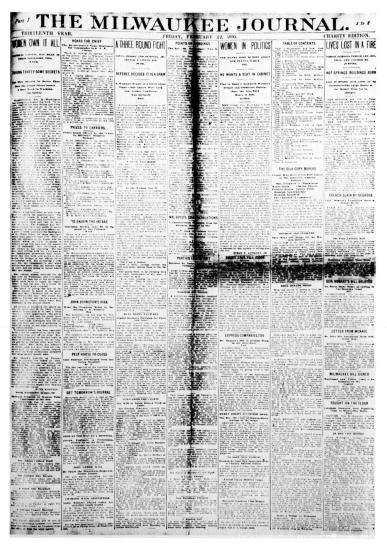

A limited number of copies of the charity edition of February 22, 1895, the work of Milwaukee society women, were printed on silk and sold for $100 each.

The Daily Journal was outraged. Here are the headlines that announced the news:

It Is Daubed on by the Grand Jury—Nobody Is Condemned
Guilty, but Didn't Mean to Be, You Know
A Thin Trashy Presentment
Happily the Victims Not Convicted of Committing Suicide
Now Let the Gods Weep and Milwaukee Hang Her Head
The World Points Its Finger at Us!

Next day The Journal had a story headed "A Great Farce," quoting Milwaukeeans who bitterly denounced the grand jury report. On the third day The Journal published in its editorial columns the names of the grand jurors, with a deep band of mourning around the list.

Tragic drama! The city was getting it. And in the center of it all was The Daily Journal. Its circulation had grown so fast that Editor Nieman appealed to readers to be patient. More newsboys were being put on as promptly as they could be found and trained.

Scheller was brought back, tried, and promptly acquitted for lack of evidence. The Daily Journal, supporting the acquittal verdict as just, printed another thundering editorial:

The great farce is ended.

The grand jury declared that only one person was in any way responsible for the slaughter of nearly a hundred human beings in the Newhall House fire.

Suspicion must now take its finger from him. . . .

But who is responsible for the loss of life in the Newhall House fire? Certainly somebody must be.

To say that nobody is, you must be prepared to admit that there is something wrong with our civilization. . . .

A landlord, unless he is criminally negligent, will not crowd people into his house with no other assurance for the safety of their lives than that the building does not catch fire.

He will not only guard against fire.

He will provide means by which his guests may escape in case of such an emergency. . . .

But the farce is over.

Everybody is acquitted of any responsibility for the slaughter on that January morning.

Justice is denied the dead.
It is denied the living.

Thus ended the Newhall House affair. In the public mind was the suspicion that the social and political leaders who controlled Milwaukee could go even behind the locked doors of the grand jury room to conceal their acts and their manipulations. The people had been awakened because they got their news, in this instance, from a little upstart newspaper that dared to turn a light into dark places and give the public the full report. The outlook for The Daily Journal was now bright.

Years afterward, L. W. Nieman, as he told the story of the great calamity, would always add: "Our handling of the Newhall fire made The Journal a newspaper."

3

Public Guardian

Milwaukee had responded to The Journal's courage in printing all the facts it could get after the Newhall House fire. The paper soon had three times as many readers as before the tragedy. To all it was apparent that if exposure of conditions at the hotel had been made earlier, the lives of eighty persons might have been saved. For future guidance, The Journal resolved that it would print the news, but it would also, to the best of its ability, go behind the scenes and sound a warning where warning was due.

The paper at once started a campaign for a new ordinance regulating building construction, for more fire-fighting apparatus, for an overhauling of the fire department, and for strengthening of the police force to handle all emergencies. This time the *Sentinel* and the *Evening Wisconsin* were in accord and the city was ready to make improvements.

The Journal next turned to conditions in the state. In campaigning for reforms there the paper was pretty much alone, because political considerations kept its rivals from cooperating. Rumors of deplorable conditions at state institutions had been heard for years. The Journal investigated and then charged that the state board of supervisors was manipulating funds. Specific examples were given of what went on inside the Northern Hospital for the Insane at Oshkosh, the Mendota State Hospital, and the state prison. Governor Jeremiah Rusk, when urged to make an investigation, said that the whole thing was a fuss stirred up by "the new Milwaukee paper." But when The Daily Journal's facts had been piled high enough, the governor ordered a public hearing on conditions at the Northern Hospital for the Insane. The Journal sent its best correspondent to Oshkosh to report on the hearing, which revealed shocking facts—tainted meat and rancid butter served to inmates, with demented old men doing the cooking; squalid quarters for the inmates; buildings so dilapidated that they were a menace to life. The Journal commented that conditions were much worse than it had known when it first called attention to the shortcomings of the board of supervisors.

Another issue The Journal examined was that of public lands. Madison had long been infested by men who were growing rich dealing in timber lands which had been granted to the state by congressional action for the support of the public school system. Wisconsin had arranged to sell these lands gradually so that they could be absorbed by private enterprise, then put the money into the school fund. But each time tracts were announced for sale the land grabbers would apportion the bidding among themselves to eliminate competition, and the land would be sold to them at about one-third of its worth. The Journal heard of one rigged sale in which the state school fund's loss was $150,000. Editorials and articles followed which fully exposed the abuse and compelled the state land commission to set up a new system to end the practice. Despite the loss of millions, there was still enough land left to give the fund the sizable total it now has. But for this exposure the school fund might have been much smaller.

Matters nearer home were not neglected. The Milwaukee school board, the paper learned, was being run by an "executive committee" behind closed doors. The story was printed and soon the power of directing Milwaukee public schools was restored to the full board of directors.

At the same time The Journal was developing more thorough coverage of national news. The big sensation out of Washington was the Star Route swindle in the post office administration, involving $750,000 fraudulently collected by corrupt politicians in return for big contracts for mail routes, some of which did not exist. The Star Route trials were held in an atmosphere of bribery and jury fixing. One juror was an habitual drunkard. Twice during the trial he fell off his seat. The day the verdict of acquittal was brought in he had an attack of delirium tremens.

The Journal gave full news coverage and dryly commented when the decision came: "The Star route jurors should remove to Chicago. They would be employed the year around on murder cases."

In addition to its political scandals, the year 1883 was a lively one for other news, most of it violent. Sioux Chief Brave Bear was hanged for murdering a Dakota settler; outlaw Frank James was tried in Missouri for train robbery, with the judge barring firearms from the courtroom; an Illinois housewife posed as a man and "married" a girl at Waupun, Wisconsin. In a statewide hunt for the elopers, a Journal reporter was proud to announce that he had found them at Stockbridge and had obtained a confession.

Most of the news was made by people, but the violence of nature found space in The Journal, too, as in this account of a Racine storm:

Last evening, about 6:30 o'clock, two clouds of inky blackness were seen approaching each other from opposite directions, one traveling in a northeasterly and the other in a southwesterly direction. They hung near the earth and were traveling with marvelous rapidity, like giants rushing together to try their strength.

They met a short distance west of the Western Union Junction, coming together with a report like the discharge of a heavy piece of ordnance, and for a second they remained stationary. Then they began to whirl about, assuming the shape of a wheel about a quarter of a mile in diameter, and started in a northerly direction, gradually descending to earth and assuming the form of an inverted cone.

There were human interest stories, too. The Ida Sissons Minstrels, with a lively chorus, played for a week in Milwaukee and upset the daily routine of a group of gay young sons of bankers, merchants, and other well-known businessmen. The chorus girls were wined, dined, and taken for buggy rides daily, and on the evening the company left, the young men appeared in a body at the Milwaukee Road station, each dressed in "three-button cut-away, high standing collar, closely fitted pantaloons, gloves and high hat. Each carried a dainty walking stick." They prolonged their farewell by accompanying the troupe as far as Oconomowoc.

One day in that first year of The Journal an advertisement appeared for the "Chicago Museum," which opened an exposition in Milwaukee. Its "wonders" included the Seven Sutherland Sisters, whose hair trailed the ground; the man with the transparent head; and the famed Zulu Warriors, who were "so wild they had to be kept in a cage." In their terrible warrior dress they struck fear into the spectators. The show was filling the house daily until a Journal reporter stopped in Roth's poolroom on Broadway and found the "Zulu Warriors" playing pool, fashionably dressed and behaving in the best Chicago manner. The Journal commented editorially, accepted no more advertisements from the show, and it soon closed.

Political news was shaping up for the presidential struggle of 1884. Here is the paper's thumbnail sketch of Grover Cleveland, who was the Democratic candidate: "He is a very unaffected man, very accessible to the public, a patient and courteous listener, a man of decision and tenacity, not in any respect a demagogue, an early riser, a hard worker, reticent or plain spoken as duty demands, and is very popular with all parties."

President Chester Arthur made a trip through the Middle West to try to mend his damaged political fences. When his train made an unscheduled stop at Madison, many people quickly gathered to greet him. He sat at a window of his locked car reading, but deliberately turned away from the onlookers. The Journal commented bluntly: "He turned upon them the part of his pantaloons which is sewed up."

When Wisconsin's senators and representatives left for Washington, The Journal announced that it would keep close watch on them in Congress. As a starter it published sketches of all members. Here is what it said of Philetus Sawyer, the lumber baron senator and unchallenged boss of the state:

Senator Sawyer is 67 years old and the most venerable looking representative from the Badger state. Mr. Sawyer's success rather than his ability as a statesman has won him distinction. He is an unscrupulous manipulator of political wires and a party boss of recognized ability, notwithstanding his dearth of education and transparent selfishness. Personally Senator Sawyer is a warm friend or an invincible enemy— one who works quietly and untiringly for either friend or foe. He is a corporation king, a railroad magnate and a bank bolster who may be depended upon to coddle the people in campaigns and roast them in the senate. He never makes a speech because he can't, and because he has a way of working which obviates the necessity of his learning how. He has, in his public career, accomplished something for the state, considerable for his locality, and much for Mr. Sawyer.

In this first year The Journal started printing letters from the people. "The columns are open to short, pithy communications on all live topics," the announcement read. "The Journal never refuses to give people a hearing, no matter how much they may differ with this paper on any subject."

As the first year drew to a close, Editor Nieman was able to announce that The Milwaukee Daily Journal had the largest city circulation of any newspaper printed in English. No mention was made of state circulation. He also added that his paper was a success financially.

During the year The Journal had engaged in five editorial campaigns for the correction of abuses in city and state, and had won four of them. As a result Wisconsin would give better institutional care to its unfortunate wards; the state school fund derived from land sales would be larger; the city schools would be free of clique control; and Milwaukee would have safer conditions in its downtown area. Chief Foley of the fire department announced that he had added new fire-fighting equipment, had developed a better alarm system, and had completed training of crews to meet emergencies. The police department also announced that it had put in effect a training program for the better handling of disaster situations. The city council was working on an ordinance for new building regulations and provisions for inspection of all existing buildings. There would be no more Newhall House disasters.

Only one abuse that The Journal had attacked remained uncorrected—that practiced by state treasurers in pocketing the interest from investment of Wisconsin state funds. But this situation was deeply involved in politics, and correction would have to await political changes.

4

Turbulence in Labor and Politics

The Republican party had been in office since Civil War days. "Had Lincoln lived," people were saying, "times would have been better." But Lincoln had not lived and corruption had seeped into politics and into business until the scandal of it was apparent to all. To Nieman, the presidential election of 1884 was crucial. The Journal was beginning its second year. What stand would it take on abuses such as government land grants to railroads and to various promoters that had stripped the public domain of an area equal to six times the size of Wisconsin? Among the issues challenging editorial decision was the high protective tariff that meant more wealth to industry and greater costs to the already poor. Rumblings about an unsound economy were heard. Labor began to organize and agitate for better wages and better working conditions.

Various cures for the economic ills were suggested. The silver-mining states advocated stamping silver at the mint at more than its worth. Some farmers favored the "Greenback," paper money printed without security behind it. The more level-headed thought it was time for a new regime in Washington; and among these was Editor Nieman. During the campaign he would be independent, he would speak his mind, and he would spare no one, not even the party he would choose.

As political convention time approached he began to prepare. He arranged for full telegraphic reports from the United Press.

He leased a private wire to Chicago where conventions of both parties were to be held. He expanded his staff. Three days before the Republicans convened on June 3, Journal writers were on hand.

The main contest in the Republican convention was between President Arthur, who was serving the remainder of the term of President James A. Garfield, killed in office, and Senator James G. Blaine. When the balloting began The Daily Journal set up a bulletin board in front of its office on Broadway. It was the first time such a service had been offered Milwaukee. Crowds gathered and cheered or booed the results. When news of the nomination of Blaine and his running mate, Senator John A. Logan, was flashed on the bulletin board, Broadway was jammed. Journal reporters buttonholed local Republican leaders for their opinions.

The Democratic convention of July 7 was covered as fully. It ran for three days, and there were six candidates. Grover Cleveland was nominated for President and Thomas A. Hendricks for Vice President.

The Daily Journal, making its first choice of a presidential candidate, endorsed the Democratic ticket of Cleveland and Hendricks. It gave its reasons: Cleveland was for lowering the tariff, a policy The Journal had previously advocated. Cleveland, it said, embodied the hope of political reform "more completely than any other candidate since Abraham Lincoln." The Republican candidate, Blaine, The Journal charged, was for centralization of political power, high protective tariffs for industry, subsidies for shipping, high taxes, land grants to railroads, and an aggressive foreign policy. Blaine represented theories, The Journal said, that had been dominant since the Civil War and now were under attack by Republicans as well as Democrats.

The campaign was bitter. From a political standpoint both candidates were vulnerable. Blaine had become entangled with a group of Arkansas promoters and, it was charged, as Speaker of the House had used his influence to aid a million dollar land grab by an Arkansas railroad. The Democrats said he had received railroad stock as a reward for his influence.

In turn, the Republicans brought up Cleveland's Civil War record which showed that he had hired a substitute to serve for him. (There was nothing illegal in the action, but it had often been abused by draft dodgers.) Cleveland explained that his two brothers were in the army and that he felt it his duty to stay home to support his mother and sisters. His opponents made the most of it. They also charged that Cleveland was the father of an illegitimate child. A popular marching chant ran:

> Maw, Maw, where's my Paw?
> He's in the White House,
> Haw! Haw! Haw!

Though The Daily Journal endorsed Cleveland, it criticized the platforms of both parties. The Republican document, it said, was designed as a "vote catcher" and its economic policies would lead the nation to disaster. The Journal supported the Democratic policy of lowering tariffs, but condemned the "claptrap" of the tariff plank verbiage that tried to show "that nobody would be hurt by withdrawing high protection." The Journal said that somebody would be hurt and should be.

As the campaign progressed, bitterness grew. The religious question was raised, with the Republicans calling the Democrats the party of "Rum, Romanism, and Rebellion." At La Crosse, Wisconsin, a businessman was shot and killed while arranging a parade for Blaine and Logan, and the murderer was hanged that night by a mob. Through it all The Journal kept on an even keel. It investigated the La Crosse murder and found that the killer had been a mental patient. It put its emphasis on issues— the high tariffs, the subsidies, the dishonesty in government—and it pleaded for return to the ideals of Jefferson and Lincoln. When Cleveland won, Editor Nieman had this to say: "How good and how pleasant it is to know on election day that you have misrepresented nobody, lied about nobody and scandalized nobody's family."

The Journal had worked hard for Cleveland, but it did not regard itself as the mouthpiece of the Democratic party. The day after Cleveland's victory had been verified, which also was The Journal's second birthday, the paper, ever the watchdog, said:

The editorial columns of this paper are independent of party, clique, or boss. The Journal is no party organ nor will it be. Infallibility is the baseless claim of partisanship; neutrality is the device of cowardship; independence, The Journal understands, is the honest endeavor to uphold the right and honest man whenever and wherever found. The maintenance of honesty in news columns a journal owes to its readers. The maintenance of honesty in opinion it owes to itself.

This independence did not please many Democrats. There was a group in Wisconsin who talked of starting a new paper, one that would be a loyal Democratic spokesman. Nothing came of it.

Cleveland was no sooner in office than the question of civil service versus the "spoils system" arose. Cleveland reappointed a Republican postmaster in New York City because "he has been a good postmaster." The Democrats howled. Keeping to his policy of independence, Nieman looked in Milwaukee and the state for evidence of the spoils system in operation. The paper had opposed Milwaukee Postmaster Henry C. Payne because, it charged, he had used his office to further his work as Republican boss in Wisconsin. Cleveland removed Payne. But when George H. Paul, the new Democratic postmaster, nudged out a veteran employe to make room for his own son, The Journal opened both barrels on Paul.

The Journal pointed out another aspect of the spoils system in Wisconsin in the case of Republican editors who were holding federal jobs as postmasters, port surveyors, or land office officials. Nine-tenths of the Republican editors in the state, it was estimated, were under political obligations either directly or through their relatives. A Democratic editor in Baraboo tried to start the same practice by applying for the job of postmaster. A few well-directed articles and editorials stopped that movement promptly.

Midway in Grover Cleveland's term events of a more serious nature thrust these lesser issues into the background. In 1886 anarchy threatened the nation. Erupting in violence in Chicago, it spread to Milwaukee where there was also a fertile field for the agitator. The industrial rise which followed the Civil War had saddled laboring men with long hours, bad working conditions, and low pay. There were thousands of jobs but no protection against exploitation or displacement. Wages were cut shamelessly when there was the least glut in the labor market. An employer would sometimes discharge half of his force and bring in contract labor from Europe.

The Journal had early pointed out dangers ahead. On March 6, 1886, it stated: "In shorter hours of toil, higher education, more attractive homes and more home life—in fact, in the enjoyment of the legitimate fruits of labor—are the freedom of the workman, the safety of capital and the strength of government to be found."

The labor union movement as we know it today made its first feeble steps in the 1860's. Some crafts, among them bricklayers, railroad engineers, and printers had become established before the Civil War, but it was not until 1869 that a national labor union of some permanence—the Knights of Labor—was organized. This was a loosely knit group seeking increased wages and an eight-hour day. By 1885 it had 700,000 members throughout the United States. Meantime, the American Federation of Labor, based on unionism by trades rather than by general classification, had grown to a membership of 300,000. Both groups were active in Milwaukee. The Knights of Labor, under the leadership of Robert Schilling, had its strength in the Polonia Assembly, a south-side group of 2,000 Polish workers, many of them recent immigrants.

The Journal was not a "labor paper" but almost from the beginning it had supported the labor union movement, because it recognized the need for improvement of the appalling working conditions. The prevalent ten-hour day was often stretched to twelve hours with no extra pay. Many Milwaukee workers had to get up at 4 A.M. Because of the inadequate streetcar service a man might have to walk three or four miles to his job. He got home at night after his children were in bed. He seldom saw them except on Sunday.

Most labor leaders over the country were sincerely trying to solve the problem, but their organizations were infiltrated by anarchists, nihilists, extreme Marxists, and preachers of foreign doctrines for overthrow of government. The head of the anarchists was Johann Most, a Bavarian who had come to America after a career as a revolutionary agitator in Europe. A group of his confederates cultivated the movement in Chicago. From there it spread to Milwaukee.

Paul Grottkau, leader of the Milwaukee Central Labor Union, which included the American Federation of Labor group, had been on the staff of the Chicago anarchist newspaper, the *Arbeiter Zeitung,* but had split with its editors over methods. Grottkau wanted to bring about a social revolution by calling a paralyzing strike, but he opposed terror and violence. These ideas he brought to Milwaukee, and when the upheaval came the one in Milwaukee was not so violent as the one in Chicago.

In the spring of 1886 a recession threw thousands of workers out of their jobs. Other thousands struck for an eight-hour day. In Milwaukee, as May Day approached, 5,000 men were on strike. On May 1, 7,000 more walked out, mostly brewery workers, carpenters, and sewer diggers. On Sunday, May 2, a huge parade was held, with Labor Leader Grottkau on a big horse. The line was alive with red flags and red banners. After the parade a mass meeting took place at the Milwaukee Gardens, on State Street, between Fourteenth and Fifteenth streets. Speeches were so inflammatory that Sheriff Paschen and Police Chief Ries appealed to Governor Rusk for aid. The First Wisconsin Regiment of the National Guard was ordered out.

Next morning the big Polonia Assembly of the Knights of Labor marched to the shops of the Milwaukee Road and pulled 1,500 men off their jobs to join them. The Edward P. Allis ironworks (predecessor of Allis-Chalmers) barred its doors before the mob could get in. All that day and much of the night roving bands, estimated at 15,000 men, were on the streets, chiefly on the south side. The police, unable to control the crowds, ordered all saloons closed. Journal reporters were out until dawn listening to grievances of the strikers and trying to learn of plans for the future.

Strike leaders decided to direct the mob against the Bay View steel mill. Men marching four abreast halted at the plant and demanded that it close. The superintendent delayed his answer, knowing that the National Guard unit was on its way. When the unit arrived it fired over the heads of the workers and dispersed them. Next day, May 5, when the marching column made a second attempt against the steel mill it found six companies of national guardsmen there, including the Kosciusko contingent of young men who themselves were of Polish descent. It is uncertain whether the marchers were going to try to take the mill by storm, as some accounts say, or were just out to show the Guard that they were not afraid, as others put it. The Guard commander ordered the marchers to halt. They kept coming and the Guard fired point-blank into them. Seven persons were killed—five marchers, a boy who was following the excitement, and a nearby resident who was in his back yard. Scores of marchers were injured before the gunfire dispersed them. The Guard moved quickly now, not only at the mill but also in other parts of the city to break up crowds. By nightfall the danger was past.

In the Chicago anarchist uprising, even more direful events were happening. The aim seemed to be, not just to promote a general strike and paralyze the community, as in Milwaukee, but to seize political power through a reign of terror. The 50,000 men on strike in Chicago were mostly overworked, underpaid factory employes demanding rights. Anarchist leaders persuaded them to raid the McCormick reaper works, although workmen there had returned to their jobs. A clash with the plant guards took place without loss of life, but the anarchist newspaper, the *Arbeiter Zeitung,* printed a false news account titled "Revenge," reporting that demonstrators had been shot down in cold blood by company guards. Would the workers take that? The time had come to answer such inhuman acts! Chicago workers were to come to Haymarket Square that night and come armed!

At 10 P.M. on May 4, after Haymarket orators had whipped the crowd into a frenzy, Mayor Carter Harrison ordered a contingent of 400 policemen to move in. As they started, a bomb was thrown into their midst, killing eight and wounding forty. Other police riot squads then rushed up and in a terrific battle cleared the square. In the resulting trials, seven anarchists were condemned to death. Four were hanged, one committed suicide, and two had their death sentences commuted to life imprisonment.

In Milwaukee, thirty-seven labor leaders were arrested. Many were fined or sentenced to prison. An aftermath of the Milwaukee riot was a sharp division of opinion over the parts played by the Polish workers and the Wisconsin Guard. Some critics condemned the Polish people as a whole because the Polonia Assembly had led the rioters. Other citizens, chiefly from the Polish districts of the south side, favored boycotting everyone who had any connection with the Wisconsin Guard.

A third group was for denouncing all organized labor. Because The Journal had been friendly to labor, the paper was included in the condemnation. There were suggestions that The Journal be boycotted. Editor Nieman faced this condemnation by citing The Journal's record. The paper had recognized the rights of labor to organize to improve conditions, but it also had on every occasion warned against violence and against acceptance of alien doctrines. It had told the Knights of Labor and the Central Trades Council many times, and now it repeated, that their future depended on the saneness of their approach to labor problems. Two editorials highlighted The Journal's position. One, printed when red flags were flaunted in the big parade, was titled "The Union Flag Will Do." It said cuttingly:

The flag under which the brawn of American labor fought and freed the African slaves is good enough for American labor to fight its battles under. We do not believe that the bawling blatherskites who have gathered their knowledge of freedom from monarchial tyranny are qualified to teach individual liberty to American citizens, or are needed to swell the ranks of those who flatter labor that they may rob it. The men who froth at the mouth under the red flag of anarchy are misfit comrades, much less leaders, for those who offered their heart's blood for the emblem of citizen sovereignty.

In another editorial The Journal summed up the after-riot situation:

Labor has been the object of attack, the chief sufferer from the mobs. . . . The trouble is the natural outgrowth of allowing America to become the refuge for the Mosts, the Schwabs, the Spies, the Grottkaus and other lawless fag ends of foreign society whose animal proclivities Europe would no longer tolerate. . . . It is bread, not blood, which labor needs; just laws, not the abrogation of all society, which it asks.

The Journal stoutly defended the Polish people, saying that it was a great injustice to try to punish a race because some of its members had been misled. With equal vigor The Journal condemned the prejudice against the Wisconsin National Guard, the police department, and the sheriff's deputies for their part in curbing the riots. Answering the argument that the Guard fired hastily, the newspaper pointed out that the Chicago massacre of police the night before had made the Guard fearful that the Milwaukee rioters might use bombs. In a campaign to end incrimination and bring together various parts of the community, The Journal counseled labor to use moderation in seeking to regain ground it had lost. At the same time editorials did not let employers forget that their shortsightedness on wages and hours had prepared the soil into which seeds of anarchism were sown. As the public mood grew more receptive to such counsel The Journal emerged more respected and stronger than ever.

In these turbulent times in Milwaukee, Editor Nieman did not slight the national or state scenes. On its editorial page the paper applauded President Cleveland when he drove trespassing cattlemen off Indian lands, just as it did in his second term when, in behalf of sound money, he asked for repeal of the Silver Purchase Act, a scheme designed to enrich silver mine owners. It stood with him in his vetoes of Civil War pension bills that were tainted with fraud, even though denial of any pension claim was sure to react politically against the President.

In its coverage of state news the paper learned that the state fair, held at Madison, was poorly managed and was losing money. Reporters sent to other state fairs found them better than Wisconsin's. The paper advocated moving the fair to Milwaukee. When this was done, in 1886, the first exposition paid off Madison's past debts and left $4,000 in the treasury. Milwaukee became the permanent site of the fair.

5

Forsaking Independence

In the history of The Milwaukee Journal, 1889 might be termed the year of the great departure. On October 14, Nieman removed from the masthead the words "An Independent Newspaper" and announced that henceforth the paper would be the spokes-man for the Democratic party. For the next seven years The Journal remained a Democratic party organ.

In view of Nieman's earlier assertions that a paper best serves its readers through freedom from all political ties, why, one may ask, did he change his stand in 1889? One reason was the frustra-tion he felt over national and state politics. He believed that un-der the Democratic party banner the paper could help bring about many of the reforms he had long worked for.

Grover Cleveland, in his four years in the White House, had tried hard to put honesty into government, to lower tariffs, to end the spoils system through civil service, to do away with fraudu-lent Civil War pensions, to "make public office a public trust." Now, in 1888, Cleveland had gone down to defeat. The victor, Republican Benjamin Harrison, had been an attorney for the trusts and railroads, and was a believer in high protective tariff. In Nieman's view this meant a return to uncontrolled power for the special-privilege group in America.

The situation in Wisconsin was equally alarming. Lumber and railroad interests had continued to rule at Madison no mat-ter who was governor. In 1888, William Dempster Hoard, the

Fort Atkinson publisher and agricultural leader, had been elected governor on the Republican ticket. A man of high ideals, Hoard was, for instance, aware of the fact that state treasurers had no legal or moral right to pocket the interest from state funds on deposit. But he was such a novice in politics he could not force even his own state treasurer, Henry B. Harshaw of Oshkosh, to give up the long-established abuse.

To Editor Nieman, a complete political overturn in Wisconsin seemed the only answer. Such an overthrow would be no ordinary achievement in a sate which had elected only one Democratic governor since the Civil War (William R. Taylor, 1873–75). But a serious controversy over the exclusive use of the German language in schools had arisen which gave the Democrats new hope of victory.

In his first message to the legislature, Governor Hoard had recommended that the compulsory school law be revised and strengthened. The state superintendent did not know how many pupils were enrolled in schools because private and parochial schools were under no obligation to make reports. It was estimated that 50,000 children were attending no school at all. The method of instruction in the private and parochial schools was of equally great concern. In some of them, it was shown, classes were conducted in the German language, with not a word of English spoken. Some schools did not have a single teacher who could speak English. The law requiring instruction in public schools to be in English (with one hour a day for the teaching of a foreign language if the parents wanted it) did not apply to private schools.

Governor Hoard asked that parochial schools be obligated to teach the main subjects in English and to report their statistics, giving the state a complete picture of school attendance and future needs. In compliance with his request two bills were introduced in the legislature. One, by Senator L. E. Pond, would have required full reports on enrollment, age of children, attendance, subjects taught, and language used in the classroom. The other bill, prepared by Assemblyman Michael J. Bennett, required every child between the ages of seven and fourteen to attend some public, private, or parochial school and added this provision: "No school shall be regarded as a school unless there is taught therein . . . reading, writing, arithmetic and United States history in the English language."

Private and parochial school interests attacked the Pond bill, arguing that it would virtually put their schools under the thumb of the state superintendent. It was defeated. They seem to have paid no attention to the Bennett bill, which moved quietly along through house and senate. They did not awaken to its significance until Governor Hoard signed it into a law. Then the rumblings began. The law was denounced in German religious meetings as an invasion of the rights of parents and a blow aimed at the destruction of parochial schools. Racial groups took up the cry. Governor Hoard, who was expected to be a candidate for re-election, stood his ground. He said: "The duty of the state to require, and the right of the children of the state to receive, instructions in the language of the country shall be insisted on."

The Journal, meantime, had come out against the Bennett law, calling it a foolish statute, an interference with parental rights, and a blow at parochial schools. Follow-up editorials indicated that Nieman's belief in a maximum of individual liberty had led him to that conclusion. As for Americanization, he was confident that it would be taken care of by natural processes working on the immigrants in their new homes. What he did not realize was that many Wisconsin communities built around a church and a school under the leadership of a German-speaking pastor remained as strongly German in language, customs, and thought as many villages of the Old World. Little that was American touched their daily lives.

In addition to the prospect of defeating a law in which he did not believe, Nieman had a much sounder motive in supporting the Democratic party. His best hope of getting rid of the treasury abuse in the handling of public funds lay in a Democratic state administration. He had been the first editor in the state to condemn this long-established corrupt practice. However, the Bennett law question immediately became the stronger of the two issues from the voters' standpoint. A big meeting was held in

Milwaukee at which all German-speaking religious bodies united to fight the statute. Christian Koerner, a Milwaukee leader in German circles, pictured the law as "war on the people of German descent, an attack on their mother tongue, their parochial schools, their religion, their personal rights to educate their children as they saw fit." The Journal commended his report.

Most of Milwaukee's four German daily and three German weekly newspapers joined in the campaign and helped stir people of German descent into an emotional fervor. One, the *Columbia,* went so far as to say: "Perhaps it would be well for German blows to be felt in Wisconsin." *Der Herold* standing out against its colleagues, spoke up for the Bennett law and for the teaching of English. It circulated largely in that group of German-Americans who were followers of Carl Schurz and believed strongly in the Americanization of immigrants.

The first test of strength came in the Milwaukee municipal election in the spring of 1890. The Democrats nominated George W. Peck, journalist and author of *Peck's Bad Boy,* for mayor on an anti-Bennett platform.* In a bitter struggle in which the church school question superseded all civic issues, Peck won over his Republican opponent, Mayor Thomas H. Brown. Peck thus became the logical political leader to head the anti-Bennett forces in the state. German clubs blossomed everywhere. The Bennett law was denounced as paternalism, socialism, despotism.

When the Republicans held their state convention, on August 20, in Milwaukee's West Side Turner hall, there was much shaking of heads, but Governor Hoard was renominated and the Bennett law endorsed. The Journal installed a telegraph wire to get the fastest possible reports. For the Democratic convention a week later The Journal used two telegraph lines to cover the news. Mayor Peck was nominated for governor, and the platform de-

---

* "The distinguished looking Peck, with his pince nez and Prince Albert beard, was a highly popular humorous journalist, publisher of the comic newspaper, *Peck's Sun.* His reputation was made principally on his 'Bad Boy' serials, later published in book form. A native of New York, Peck came to Wisconsin with his parents in 1843, at 3 years of age. Later he learned the printer's trade at Whitewater and published papers in La Crosse and Ripon."—H. Russell Austin, *The Wisconsin Story* (Milwaukee: Milwaukee Journal, 1948).

34

nounced the Bennett law as "unnecessary, unwise, unconstitutional, un-American and un-democratic."

The Journal, endorsing this platform, started the campaign
for Peck by inventing a slogan "Peck and ALL the Schools," to
match the Republican slogan, "Hoard and the Little Red Schoolhouse." As the weird campaign developed through all its stages of
frenzy, tempers flared. Governor Hoard, attempting to speak at
Hales Corners, was pushed around and heckled by a crowd from
Milwaukee. That same evening a pro-Bennett group was attacked
in the city. The "Little Red Schoolhouse" that was mounted on
a wagon was demolished. A drunken mob in Madison kicked in
the door of Governor Hoard's house and shouted insults at the
governor.

Enthusiastically supporting Peck, one Journal editorial concluded: "Democrats, are you ready? You are to save or lose your
personal liberty and every interest of freedom. Upon you rests the
great responsibility of redeeming the state. Work! Work!"

As had been expected, the Democrats swept the state, winning
not only the governorship, but the legislature and seats in Congress. Among the Republican members of Congress who went
down before the avalanche was a young man from Madison then
serving his third term—Robert M. La Follette.

When Governor Peck was inaugurated, on January 5, 1891,
The Journal ran a special train to Madison carrying practically
all of Milwaukee's officials and many high members of the Democratic party. Forty-five thousand copies of a 24-page inaugural
edition of The Journal, striped with red and blue bars—the first
known example of color printing in the paper—were distributed
free in the capital. On the front page was a five-column eagle
crouched on the United States shield. From the eagle's beak
flowed two streamers. One said: "The Americanism of the Constitution is enthroned in Wisconsin today." The other said: "An
elective despotism is not the government we fought for—Thomas
Jefferson." The main story on page one broke into poetry:

> Hail, happy day, since from the darkening gloom
> Cast by intolerance o'er all the earth,
> Fate's magic fingers from life's mystic loom

Resolves a fiat that declares men free,
Proclaims the reign of true democracy
Upholds the right and deprecates the wrong,
And e'en to justice yields a second birth.

When the legislature convened, the first measure introduced called for repeal of the Bennett law. Repeal was completed within a month. Three days later The Journal was made the official state paper, the usual reward for being a leading party organ. The words—"The Official State Paper"—first appeared on the masthead on February 6, 1891. The Journal now published the new laws as they were passed, the proclamations of the governor, and other official state news. For this service it received about $3,000 a year. It also got $4,000 yearly from insurance companies, which were compelled by law to print their reports in the official newspaper.

The Journal was prospering. In two years it had more than doubled its circulation, and it now had a press that could print 28,000 papers an hour. It was the most talked of paper in Wisconsin, and for the first time in its existence it had "political power." But it also paid a price by losing much of its independence and objectiveness. Its editorials promoted a pre-chosen point of view. Its news stories, especially its political stories, often mixed editorializing with reporting. A paragraph from an editorial which ran just before the Milwaukee municipal election illustrates this point: "If there is a Democrat in the city of Milwaukee who will refuse to vote for the nominees of the party next Tuesday because of any fancied defect in the platform, he has either not read the platform understandingly or else it is a queer kind of democracy he believes in."

Nieman seemed to have forgotten things which he had told the state editorial association at Madison in 1887 on one of the rare occasions when he appeared as a public speaker. He said then that the American newspaper was advancing because of the rise of the independent press. He warned against the stultifying effect of being a party organ, concluding: "The true newspaper, although it is built up by private effort is, nonetheless, a public institution."

6

Scandal in the State Treasury

On the day in 1882 that Lucius W. Nieman bought the three-week old Journal, he began hammering away at state treasurers for pocketing interest money on Wisconsin state funds. And for the following eight years he printed an article every two or three weeks on the scandal. Not until 1890 when George W. Peck was elected governor on the Democratic ticket was the illegal procedure stamped out.

This practice by state treasurers of keeping the interest for themselves or for the political party probably began in 1858. These treasurers, who had been elected to office, said they were merely taking compensation for the low salaries paid them by the state. The legislature of 1876, however, passed a law raising the treasurer's salary from $1,200 to $5,000 a year, and labeled the salary "in full." All fees, perquisites, and other sums coming into the treasurer's hands were to be credited to the state. But, in a misguided effort to lock the door, the legislature decreed that there should be no more state funds deposited in banks. All money should be kept in the state capitol vaults, and counted every three months.

In 1878, however, Richard Guenther, the first treasurer to serve under the new law, found the treasury vaults at Madison so old and unsafe he could not get a bondsman to cover him if he used them. He said nothing, put the money in banks, pocketed the interest, and was back in the same nefarious business of previous treasurers. Edward C. McFetridge, 1882–87, and Henry B. Harshaw, 1887–91, continued the practice.

It was during Guenther's tenure of office that Nieman learned what was going on. On Nieman's first day as editor he heard of a letter written by a political lieutenant of Senator Sawyer saying that, despite the new law, Treasurer Guenther had put state funds in banks and had appropriated the interest. Nieman made a hurried inquiry and went into action. The next day he ran a front-page story with the headlines:

State Funds
Sawyer's Man Osborne Exposes Guenther
Trust Funds Loaned on Treasurer's Personal Account
Legislature Asked to Order an Investigation
Guenther's Jump into Wealth

The immediate effect was to call down on The Daily Journal the wrath of the state's Republican press. The Milwaukee "upstart" was a "yellow sheet" that could not be believed. There were threats of violence. The Journal came back with this challenge: "Richard Guenther, The Journal dares you to deny that you appropriated to your own use the interest on state funds." The dare was never answered. Instead, a policy of silence was adopted, not only by Guenther but by those newspapers that had reacted so violently to the first disclosure.

The Journal refused to let the treasury case die. It assigned a staff man to dig out facts and write a story every few weeks for the next eight years. One story, appearing in 1888, showed that the average monthly balance in the treasury bank accounts over a ten-year period was $802,498.56. Throughout that time the treasurer had taken the interest for himself. The Journal estimated that the state had been cheated of $35,000 a year. Since the treasurer's regular salary was $5,000, this extra bonus made his job eight times as lucrative as the governor's.

One month after George W. Peck became governor in 1891, he directed Attorney General James L. O'Connor to prepare cases against those earlier treasurers who had kept the interest on public funds. At the same time the governor read to the assembly the first month's report of the new treasurer, John Hunner of Eau Claire, showing that $1,027.40 in interest money had been received from banks and had been credited to the state. The assembly cheered.

The long fight was over, the illegal practice was ended, but recovery of the money due the state proved to be another matter. The cases scheduled for trial first were those against Guenther, McFetridge, and Harshaw, who had served after enactment of the 1876 law which banned the treasurers' graft. The trial began in Dane County circuit court with Judge Robert G. Siebecker presiding. McFetridge was charged with owing $159,166; and Harshaw, $133,204. Guenther's case was still being investigated. The preliminary hearing had barely begun, however, when Judge Siebecker announced he was withdrawing. He gave no explanation. He simply summoned the attorney general and the defense attorneys and said that matters had come to his attention which made it impossible for him to continue in the case.

Here was a mystery. What were these matters that had caused Siebecker to withdraw from so important a case? There were rumors of a secret visit from Senator Sawyer to Robert M. La Follette. Three days after the trial was halted, Senator Sawyer came to Milwaukee and gave an interview to the *Sentinel*. He said he supposed that, in withdrawing, Judge Siebecker had in mind his (Sawyer's) meeting with La Follette in the Plankinton House during State Fair week. Sawyer said he had offered $500 to La Follette as a retainer fee to study certain aspects of the Harshaw case. Sawyer was bondsman for Harshaw and stood to lose thousands, he said, if the treasurers had to pay. Sawyer said La Follette refused the fee, declaring that he wanted no connection with the case because he was related to Judge Siebecker by marriage. Sawyer said he had no previous knowledge that La Follette was a brother-in-law of Siebecker.

When Sawyer's interview was printed in the *Sentinel*, La Follette responded, telling what he said were "the facts." Senator Sawyer tried to bribe him, he said, to influence Judge Siebecker to dismiss the treasury cases. Here are Sawyer's words as La Follette quoted them in his statement: "Now I came down here to see you alone. No one knows I am here to meet you. I don't want to hire you as an attorney in the case, and don't want you to go into court. But here is $50. I will give you five hundred more or a thousand, or five hundred more and a thousand (I am uncertain which he said) when Siebecker decides the case right." The Journal ran the quotation six times in one day on the editorial page, interspersed with other material.

Judge A. W. Newman of Trempealeau County was called to Madison to hear the cases. The first three ran through December, 1891. The defense admitted that the treasurers had kept the interest, but had an ingenious explanation. When a treasurer gave his bond, the defense argued, that bond really took the place of the funds for the state. The money then, in effect, belonged to the treasurer to do with as he liked. If he lent it out, the interest belonged to him as long as the bond ran.

For the summing up, the state had Attorney General O'Connor, R. M. Bashford, and Senator William F. Vilas, who came home from Washington to make a powerful closing plea. The defense had Joseph V. Quarles, Charles W. Felker, and Joshua Stark. These were probably the six top lawyers in Wisconsin. Judge Newman studied the evidence for a month. He then ruled that the money in the treasury was, and remained, the state's and that the state was entitled to any interest earned. The verdict held that Guenther owed Wisconsin $102,000; McFetridge, $175,000; and Harshaw, $117,000.

The next step was to start collection cases against Henry Baetz and Ferdinand Kuehn, earlier treasurers who had taken interest on state funds. Judge Siebecker, who heard these last two cases, not only adopted and commented on the viewpoint of Judge Newman that the law of 1876 bound the treasurer to turn in all money he received, but added that as a matter of public policy, even in the absence of a statute, a treasurer must not pocket the interest on public funds. This nailed the door shut. The judgments against Baetz and Kuehn amounted to about $100,000.

The re-election of Governor Peck and Attorney General O'Connor in 1892 had enabled them to get all the treasury cases through the courts during their terms of office. But the appeals to the Supreme Court were still to be heard when The Journal exposed a new sensation in the case—the discovery of a plot among Republican leaders to stall further court action on the treasury cases. Republicans, expecting to win the 1894 elections, planned to forgive whatever sums remained unpaid by the convicted treasurers and their bondsmen. There would also be a resolution "to set the record straight" so history could not blame the Republican treasurers. Indignant at the exposure, Republican leaders and the Republican press once again charged The Journal with being a "yellow sheet."

The Supreme Court in 1893 gave a unanimous opinion sustaining Judge Newman's decree in the Guenther, McFetridge, and Harshaw cases and raised the assessments against all three. Guenther would have to repay $188,060; McFetridge, $207,652; and Harshaw, $129,738. When this momentous decision was announced, The Journal printed a facsimile of the front page of The Daily Journal of December 12, 1882, showing its first story written on the treasury frauds. Over ten years had elapsed from the day of that first exposure to the final decree of the Supreme Court.

The 1894 election intervened before the Baetz and Kuehn cases had cleared the Supreme Court. The Republicans won the governorship and control of the legislature. And one of the first acts of the new legislature was to pass a bill dropping the cases against Baetz and Kuehn. The lower court had decreed that Baetz and Kuehn owed the state nearly $100,000. The unpaid balance of $50,000 which the Supreme Court said McFetridge owed was also forgiven.

The Republican legislature had ended the treasury cases just as The Journal's story of a few months before had predicted. Editor Nieman, chuckling long afterward about how the legislators had proved him correct, said that some Republican leaders tried for years to find out how he learned about the plot to forgive the treasurers. He never told them.

The results of the victory for honest management of public funds were not confined to Wisconsin. The movement which The Journal had fought for spread to other states and resulted in the correction of similar abuses. The part played by The Journal was to Nieman one of the deepest satisfactions of his career. Its place in the history of American journalism has been commented on by many writers.

7

Fourteen Years of Growing

During the first dozen years after its founding, while The Journal was establishing a reputation and even playing a part in the shaping of history in the state, it was undergoing certain changes of significance in its own history. In its first seven weeks the paper had outgrown its little office and press facilities in the Seebote building. Fortunately just around the corner, at 433 Broadway, the *Herold* had extra space which it could share. The Journal moved in on January 29, 1883. Two days later the paper was incorporated as The Journal Company, with $15,000 capital stock, held chiefly by Lucius Nieman and Michael Kraus, though a small block was owned by Andrew F. Gruelich, member of a family long connected with Milwaukee newspapers.

The rapid growth of the new paper was not to go unchallenged. The *Sentinel* announced a program of expansion, which involved more mechanical equipment, an increased staff, and more state correspondents. With its eight pages, seven columns to the page, the *Sentinel* had the appearance of a metropolitan newspaper. It was more than twice the size of The Journal. The *Sentinel* had a leased wire to New York and another to Washington. It had the telegraphic services of two news gathering organizations which were forerunners of the Associated Press. It had special correspondents in Chicago, and its local news staff was large.

The *Evening Wisconsin,* also, announced that it was adding reporters and mechanical equipment. These two leading newspapers were strong where The Journal was weak—in facilities and size of staff—and they proposed to become still stronger. But they were weak at the points where The Journal had its strength. They still were dull, and they had undermined public confidence in their news handling.

In contrast to its rivals, The Daily Journal could afford only four or five reporters. But there was at the plant now, in 1884, an aura of success, the lure of freedom to write the truth; and competent volunteers appeared. Theron W. Haight, the Waukesha *Freeman* editor who had given Nieman his start, was now retired but he could not stay away from The Daily Journal. J. E. Follette, economist and expert on railroads and tariff questions, worked unpaid. Other volunteers were Nellie Bartlett, book reviewer; Robert Johnson, experienced writer; Sandy Dingwell, drama critic; and Colonel Jack Watrous, who knew earlier Milwaukee and Wisconsin.

To meet the growing demand for news space The Daily Journal enlarged to a seven-column page. With room for more type across the top of the front page, the name was changed to *The Milwaukee Daily Journal*. The paper took on a livelier appearance from the sprinkling of short stories on page one. Headlines became informative and to the point, replacing the simple labels such as "The Old World," "The National Capital," "Railroad News," and "Politics" that had been in use. A home department, forerunner of the women's sections of today, was added, and sports and financial news coverage was enlarged. On May 12, 1885, the paper printed its first front-page illustration—a picture of Edward G. Wall, newly nominated collector of internal revenue—in the new halftone engraving process just coming into use.

Perhaps more significant, the paper acquired its permanent title in 1885—*The Milwaukee Journal*. The new title was evidently the name the founders wanted to use in the beginning instead of *The Daily Journal* but there was another *Milwaukee Journal,* printed in German. In fact there had been four previous newspapers bearing this masthead, two in English and two in German. Through combinations, the *Freie Presse* as late as 1884 carried this masthead: *Sonntagblatt, Milwaukee Freie Presse,*

Banner und Volksfreund, und Milwaukee Journal. The present *Milwaukee Journal* had no connection with this German paper but when, through shifts in the newspaper field, the name "Milwaukee Journal" became available, Nieman took it.

By 1885 The Journal again needed larger quarters. Fortunately, one of the most up-to-date newspaper plants in Wisconsin was available. It was the four-story building at 92 Mason Street which had been equipped for the syndicate owning the *Republican and News.* The syndicate, however, had bought the *Sentinel* and moved into its plant, leaving vacant its former building with fine pressroom, composing room, and business and editorial offices. The Journal moved in May 11, 1885.

In the earliest days of The Journal, Michael Kraus, Nieman's partner and business manager, counted the pennies of the newsboys to meet the payroll, but by 1890 the paper was prospering, and Kraus decided to retire. On the day he left he visited each floor and shook the hand of every employe, many of whom had been there from the beginning.

In seven and a half years of frugal management and rapid expansion Nieman and Kraus had taken little money for themselves. Profits went for new presses, more reporters, and better news services. Further expansions were ahead. Nieman bought 5 per cent more of Journal stock from Kraus's half interest to assure himself of control, then divided the remainder between John W. Schaum, who was an officer of the firm, and Lloyd Tilghman Boyd, a newcomer. Capital stock was increased from $15,000 to $20,000. Officers after the realignment were: L. W. Nieman, president and editor; L. T. Boyd, secretary; J. W. Schaum, treasurer.

With the new business management came wider circulation, more advertising, and greater need for mechanical equipment. In three years the rotary press which had been so proudly acclaimed for its speed of 28,000 copies an hour was inadequate. An additional press was needed but since there was no space for it at 92 Mason Street, The Journal moved to the Montgomery Building, at Milwaukee and Michigan streets. By June 1, 1892, it could boast of a press capacity of 48,000 eight-page papers an hour. Another change, a revolutionary one, was the shift from hand-set type to machine composition. The Journal ordered eight Linotypes, the speedy typesetting machines which Ottmar Mergenthaler had patented in 1885 and was now beginning to manufacture. "The most complete printing office in Wisconsin" was promised for public inspection "as soon as our new machinery is in place," but that reception was delayed more than a year to give Mergenthaler time to make and install the Linotypes. These eight machines, the first used in Milwaukee, were curiosities to the visitors who went through the Journal building in a packed line for two and a half hours.

With mechanical problems out of the way, Nieman turned to strengthening personnel. He already had a good organizer in his new business manager, L. T. Boyd, thirty-year-old son of Dr. Frederick Boyd, a Waukesha minister. In 1891, he hired E. A. Belda as an advertising clerk. Over the years Belda advanced to assistant bookkeeper, cashier, paymaster, and eventually secretary of The Journal. His integrity and efficiency were stabilizing forces in the business office.

A twelve-year-old office boy who came to The Journal in 1890 attracted Nieman's attention by his willingness to work and his knack for getting on with people. He was William Wallace Rowland, of Welsh descent, who had quit school to help support his widowed mother. To give the boy some educational background, Nieman arranged for him to "go to school" each afternoon; Mary Stewart, an editorial writer, was his teacher. Before long he was known as "Brownie," a name which, with the coming of the horseless carriage and good roads, became familiar to all Wisconsin. Brownie's Tour Club, of the first quarter of the 1900's, issued maps and route guides which were invaluable in those days of unmarked highways. From office boy Brownie rose to sports editor, city editor, assistant managing editor, and in his late years vice president. He became Nieman's most trusted advisor. Brownie is also credited with introducing sports comments in the newspaper. The practice of the day was to print only the results of games and contests. When Brownie became sports editor in the early 1900's he wrote a daily column, "What Brownie Says," which gave terse descriptions of current sports events as well as comments on players.

In 1894, Henry Colin Campbell, an outstanding newspaper

man on the *Evening Wisconsin,* joined the Journal staff, first as city editor, then as managing editor, and finally, until his death in 1923, as assistant editor. Campbell and Nieman complemented each other well in editorial guidance. Both believed in complete newspaper integrity. Nieman was of a retiring disposition and little known to the general public; Campbell liked to mix with people and developed a large acquaintanceship. Nieman was a direct writer, economical with words and inclined to the barbed shaft; Campbell's writing was more polished, more subtle, and more wordy. The two men even balanced each other in politics. Nieman was personally a Jeffersonian Democrat; Campbell, a Republican. Campbell did a great service as managing editor by insisting that each day's news, in those times of sketchy telegraphic reports, have enough background written in to make it intelligible to the reader who did not remember earlier stories on the same subject. Campbell was a leader in state forest conservation and in the forward-looking City Club of Milwaukee.

In 1895, Isaac Newton Stewart, teacher and scholar, with a vital interest in public questions, joined the paper as an editorial writer. For ten years he helped steer The Journal's course through the difficult period of the rise of La Folletteism. Stewart was assisted by his sister, Mary Esther Stewart, who wrote book reviews and human interest editorials and in her spare time tutored office boy Rowland. Miss Stewart remained on the Journal payroll until her death at the age of ninety-one.

In 1896, Jacob John Schindler came to The Journal after graduating from the University of Wisconsin and making a round of state newspapers for training. He could not decide whether he preferred to work on the St. Paul *Dispatch* or The Milwaukee Journal, and was on and off each staff at least three times before choosing The Journal permanently. His conscientiousness over details of his work when he became managing editor probably hastened his death in 1923.

This group of Campbell, Stewart, Rowland, and Schindler, plus Boyd and Belda, carried much of The Journal's burden as Nieman steered the paper into the most dangerous editorial storm it had faced—the Bryan campaign of 1896.

46

8

What Price Freedom!

The golden voice, the stage presence, and the eloquence of William Jennings Bryan were casting their spell over the voters in the presidential campaign of 1896 when Editor Nieman concluded that The Journal could no longer remain an organ of the Democratic party. Seven years earlier Nieman had decided that only by clearing Wisconsin of Republican rule could flagrant abuses in government be wiped out, and had chosen to espouse the Democratic cause. Now he was to return to his original concept of a paper free of all political ties.

The important issue of the campaign to Nieman was free silver. In the summer of 1893 the country had been thrown into one of its worst financial panics. Then followed a depression of three years. Leaders who thought that all money troubles would be cured by the free coinage of silver had captured the Democratic party and had been joined by the Populists, who in the desperation of the depression advocated not only "free and unlimited coinage of silver" but the printing of vast amounts of paper money with no security back of it.

The sentiment reached an all-time high at the Chicago Democratic convention when Bryan made his famous Cross of Gold speech. "You shall not press down upon the brow of labor this crown of thorns; you shall not crucify mankind upon a cross of gold," said Bryan. A Journal writer described the scene:

Bryan stood with a smile playing on his face and an uplifted arm waiting for silence (from the thundering ovation). While he stood there, hundreds had their first view of the man whose political life in congress and afterwards had been identified with the movement for free silver. He was in face and figure a Roman on the stage. He had a clean-cut, firm mouth, a strong Roman nose and black hair, brushed back from his forehead and falling on his collar in short curls. His apparel was that of a plain westerner, a short alpaca jacket, a low-cut vest, a white lawn tie. With breathless eagerness the thousands peered forward to catch the first sentence of this young man whom many westerners appraise as their foremost orator.

But as early as 1884 Nieman had taken a stand against "the cheapening of currency through the unlimited coinage of silver." He said that there could be only one standard for money: "the metal that fluctuates least—gold." And as the 1896 convention time approached he warned once more against the free silver fallacy and against Democratic fusion with Populist groups "alien to true Jeffersonian democracy." Now the spell that Bryan was casting over the convention was alarming. Nieman decided that he could not endorse the Democratic ticket with Bryan as its presidential candidate.

The Republicans, meeting in St. Louis, had declared for sound money but they had nominated William McKinley, heir of the notorious James G. Blaine as the high priest of protective tariff. The McKinley tariff law, in the opinion of Nieman, had done much to bring on the panic during the second Cleveland administration. The Journal could not support McKinley.

Then those Democrats who believed in the gold standard and were opposed to Bryan and free silver called another national convention in September and nominated Senator John M. Palmer of Illinois for the Presidency. Nieman endorsed Palmer on the gold standard ticket as "representative of true Jeffersonian democracy." "The support of Democrats of the nation can be cheerfully given to Palmer," a Journal editorial said.

Then the storm broke. Milwaukee and Wisconsin Democrats were enraged. The newspaper's circulation department was overwhelmed with cancellations. Letters of protest piled high on the editor's desk. "I am sorry I must cease to read The Journal," wrote one subscriber, "but I am no sympathizer with the doctrine it now advocates. And the only way I have of showing my disapproval is by stopping my subscription." Printing this letter, The Journal replied editorially:

Our reader must remember that The Journal has a character as a newspaper to sustain. It has never consciously deceived its readers on public questions, nor taken ground that it did not approve. Now, on this question it has a strong and abiding belief that free silver is a mistake. . . . What would our reader think of The Journal if it should abandon this belief and plunge into the defense of what it thought to be harmful?

Still the cancellations poured in.*

Years later, commenting on this harrowing time, Nieman said:

I knew that free silver was wrong and I knew I would be in hot water if I repudiated the ticket and opposed the party. But what else could I do? If I cut loose from the thing I believed right I had nothing left to go on. We came out against Bryan and free silver, and in three weeks lost half of our circulation. People said we'd been bought by the Hanna crowd. Just as years afterward politicians invented the story that we'd been bought with British gold. Somebody will always say you've been bought if he doesn't like what you do. But we weren't bought, and, to tell the truth, for some time it looked as though nobody'd ever want to buy us. But we came through it all stronger than ever. It was the best thing that ever happened to us, and ended all idea of doing anything as a party paper does.

On the day The Journal repudiated the Bryan ticket, it returned to independence, resolved never again to be a party organ.

* The Journal's experience in this 1896 rebellion of readers was not unique: Joseph Pulitzer's New York *World* and Henry Watterson's Louisville *Courier-Journal* also bolted the Democratic party, opposed Bryan, and suffered a great setback. The Journal's circulation in 1895 was 15,000. Some of the big losses of the Bryan campaign were regained soon, and by the end of 1896 circulation was up to 12,500. In the presidential election Wisconsin voters paid little heed to The Journal's advice. Palmer got only 4,500 of the state's 438,000 total vote. McKinley carried the state, 268,000 to Bryan's 165,000.

9

The Ladies Get Out the Paper

Amidst the grim struggles of the 1890's was a delightful episode known in Journal tradition as "the day the ladies got out the paper." This event was the publication, on February 22, 1895, of the Charity, or Silk, edition of the Journal.

Victoria still ruled Britain, women did not have the vote, and the image of the feminine ideal was the clinging vine. But there were stirrings. Perhaps it was these stirrings that prompted a group of women prominent in Milwaukee society to approach Editor Nieman and Business Manager Boyd with the suggestion that their group take over publication of The Journal for one day for charity. Milwaukee, as well as the rest of the country, was in the throes of the depression following the 1893 panic, and funds in the city's welfare department were exhausted. The women were sure they could make a lot of money.

Nieman demurred at first; perhaps he was having enough troubles as it was. The women persisted. They would come to The Journal several weeks in advance to learn how to gather news, solicit advertising, write editorials. Only the pressmen and other mechanical departments would be required. And a limited number of papers would be printed on silk to be sold at $100 a copy. It had been done before, in San Francisco, Atlanta, and Memphis, with success. Nieman and Boyd gave in.

The list of women working on the edition is impressive.* Their

* The names follow: Board of editors, Mrs. John W. Mariner, Mrs. Thomas

accomplishments were even more impressive. They solicited enough advertising to fill a 56-page paper, a size unheard of in that day. No businessman could refuse to buy an ad. Even the city's physicians were approached. They cited their code of ethics which banned the use of advertising. But this was for charity! The physicians bought the advertising.

Susan B. Anthony, the suffrage leader, was asked to write a special article. She responded with a story, "Women in Politics," that made the front page. It was an account of how New York City Boss Tom Platt was rigging plans to control the next Republican convention. The cure for such nefarious schemes, said Miss Anthony, was woman suffrage. Miss Anthony also submitted an editorial telling of her plan to build a Woman's Temple in Washington to seat representatives of six million women—not to set up a separate government but to support women and their cause.

A Washington correspondent, Ruth Kimball, sent a news story, "Women Own It All," telling how two conventions, the Daughters of the American Revolution and the National Council of Women, had taken over the capital. Notable Wisconsin women

---

H. Bowles, Mrs. Guy D. Berry; managing editor, Miss Ida May Jackson; city editor, Mrs. William McLaren, assisted by Mrs. Herbert W. Underwood; drama editors, Mrs. Abbott Thorndyke and Mrs. George Nash; music editor, Mrs. George H. Russell; society editor, Mrs. John H. Tweedy, Jr.; children's department editors, Mrs. Charles F. Hibbard, Mrs. George W. Peckham, and Mrs. J. B. Oliver; sports editor, Mrs. Howard Morris; art editor, Mrs. Andrew A. Hathaway; exchange editor, Miss Annie L. Ilsley, aided by Misses Adelaide Steele, Anna M. Gibbs, Sybil Schley, and Maud Ellis; fiction and verse, Mrs. William D. Kimball, Mrs. W. O. Goodrich, Miss Upton; women's clubs, Mrs. Pierpont E. Dutcher; charities department, Mrs. Frank L. Vance, assisted by Mmes. John Johnston, Oliver Clyde Fuller, T. W. Spence, A. D. Seaman; men's department, Mrs. Francis B. Keene; literary editor, Miss Anna Hazelton.

Reporters: Mmes. G. H. Yenowine, R. A. Cole, O. Z. Bartlett, T. E. Camp, Frank Falk, H. Anderson, C. H. Hamilton, Charles Moses, M. W. Sherman, J. H. Pereles, Ernest Post ,and the Misses Young, Whitney, Jacobs, Terry, Dahlman, Ormsby, Leedom, Knox, Day, Mallory, Spangenberg, French, Graham, Scott, Green, Wahl, Merrill, Seaman, and Alice and Fannie Foster.

Advertising: business manager, Miss Elizabeth Black; advertisement solicitors, Mmes. George W. Peck, Jr., Samuel Adler, E. P. Vilas, and the Misses Jones, Pierpont, Bellows, Alsted, McCord, Brigham, Douglas, Bigelow, Winkler, Dickens, Cary, Wardner, Flanders, Wiswell, O'Neill, Hilbert, Hansen, Hopkins, Uihlein, and Camp.

who contributed articles included Ella Wheeler Wilcox, the widely known poet; Elizabeth Jordan, the novelist; and Elizabeth Banks, who became a *New York Times* reporter and later in London created a sensation by exposing a "racket" connected with presentation at court of wealthy American women. Among other contributors were Kate Upson Clark, author and educator; and the actresses Julia Marlowe and Beatrice Mansfield.

There was an editorial on the woman of tomorrow, "a type of noble woman who never forgets that she is a woman, and who yet has that strong, clear mind and keen intellect that the world will count among its greatest forces until we shall agree with Dr. Holmes that 'nature is in earnest when she makes a woman.'" Shorter editorials advocated the appointment of women to the University of Wisconsin board of regents, the establishment of a woman's gymnasium at the university, the founding of a country club in Milwaukee—all of which did come to pass.

The leading news story was the account of a fire in Hot Springs, Arkansas, which swept through a large hotel and took three lives. There were local stories on the movement for a children's hospital; on society events; on fashions, including comments from New York and Paris; on the season's dramatic offerings. A page was devoted to woman's work in the home. Financial news, sports news, the day's run of events, all were carefully covered.

At press time the women gathered to watch the printing of the edition. Accounts differ as to who had the honor of pushing the button to start the presses. Some said it was Mrs. Thomas H. Bowles, member of the board of editors. Others said it was performed jointly by Miss Ida May Jackson, managing editor, and Miss Elizabeth Black, business manager.

Newsboys had been told of the size of the edition, so they were at the Journal plant or at the distribution centers with push carts, coaster wagons, even baby carriages. It was long after dark before they completed their rounds.

In addition to the regular run, the women printed a number of copies on silk, which were priced at $100 each. The silk in each copy cost $22. Bidding for the silk copies was brisk and, as they became scarce, the price rose, some selling for as much as $150.

One was bought by Richard Mansfield, who was appearing in the play *Napoleon* at the Davidson Theater.

At least two well-preserved silk copies of the Charity edition may be seen by the public. One is in the State Historical Society library at Madison, donated in 1953 by Polly Mariner Stone and Constance Mariner Patton. The other copy is owned by the Milwaukee County Historical Society. It had turned up in 1929 at the Goodwill Industries, and was presented by that organization to The Journal. The Journal repaid them with a cash donation and later gave the copy to the County Historical Society.

The newspaper accounts of the Charity edition the day after its publication included some comments by the women. Mrs. Bowles was quoted as saying she "nearly died when told that it would run 56 pages," but she added, "I think the newspaper business is decidedly interesting. There is an immense amount of detail about it that would preclude a woman from following it as a steady vocation unless she is of strong constitution."

Mrs. John Mariner, who was on the board of editors with Mrs. Bowles and Mrs. Guy D. Berry, said: "We had great fun over the selection of the sporting editor, and one or two others, whose vocations are so much at antipodes with these little refinements which are at least credited to our sex."

Mrs. William McLaren, city editor for the day, told how they did it: "We gagged several sources of information and are in hopes that we have scooped our contemporaries—isn't that nice?—across the street." Another woman, in describing the scene at press time, said: "Women in silks and satins knelt on the bare floor and counted out papers for the grimy newsboys."

Despite their silks, satins, refinements, and hypothetical frailty the ladies had earned $3,775.90 for the Milwaukee welfare fund.

10

Rising Star of La Follette

So dominant was the influence of Robert M. La Follette in Wisconsin as governor and United States senator that his philosophy was given the label "La Folletteism." It had its beginning in the early 1890's. At that time La Follette said, "We have rested so comfortably in this country on the assumption that because our form of government was democratic, it was therefore automatically producing democratic results." He concluded it was not producing such results.

Editor Nieman applauded. For ten years his paper had been fighting a continuous battle inspired by the same view. Nieman watched La Follette closely as he began to blossom out as a state leader.

La Follette had been Dane County district attorney for four years, and had served three terms as Republican congressman in Washington. In 1890, when he was defeated in the Democratic landslide precipitated by the Bennett school law, he opened a law office in Madison. Here he could observe at first hand any abuses in government; and it was about this time that political boss Philetus Sawyer offered him "a retainer fee" to influence Judge Siebecker to dismiss the state treasury cases. This "bribery attempt" set the iron in the La Follette personality. He decided to re-enter politics, and he spent the next two years building up the liberal wing of the Republican party through speeches at county fairs and community picnics.

Free railroad passes to officials and men of influence had become a major political evil. Passes were held by governors, legislators, judges, sheriffs, mayors, councilmen, city and county attorneys, political bosses. And with the passes often went free railway express, telegraph and telephone service. These evils furnished La Follette a ready theme. Another theme which seldom failed to win the applause of state audiences was the charge that railroads, public service corporations, and many private corporations escaped their just share of taxation. On both these charges The Journal supported La Follette. It had been backing Assemblyman A. R. Hall of Dunn County for five years in his fight to abolish railroad passes.

In 1894, La Follette had wanted to run for the Republican nomination for governor, but his controversy with Sawyer over the bribery charge stirred so much criticism that he felt he could not win against the old Sawyer-Payne-Spooner machine, which backed William H. Upham. In the election Upham defeated Governor George W. Peck; and the political organization which for many years had held the state in its grip, through patronage and at times corruption, was again in power. Two years later La Follette once more sought the Republican nomination for governor. He came to the Milwaukee convention in 1896 believing that he had enough delegates to win, but his support melted away; whether by bribery, as he charged, or for other reasons, remains an unanswered question.

Would La Follette quit or would he go on? The Journal asked: "Is Robert M. LaFollette a rising star in the Republican firmament, or is he simply a comet whizzing its erratic way through political space . . .?"

La Follette answered the question in 1897 in a speech at the Waukesha County fair, in which he hurled one accusation after another at the state Republican regime, charging it with repudiating Republican pledges and with using the party for selfish purposes. He said there was only one way to correct things: Smash the machine. The Journal, warmly commending the speech, said: "He holds substantially the platform of The Journal on state affairs." A little later another editorial added this explanation:

The Journal has given some aid and comfort to the cause of Mr. LaFollette and has spoken well of him personally, notwithstanding he was an intimate of McKinley and prominent in the measures and methods which made McKinley's reputation. It has done this in a firm belief in his honesty of purpose, even when on a wrong track, and more than all because what he proposes as the policy of his following is undoubtedly for the advantage of the state.

A reporter was assigned to accompany La Follette on his round of county fairs. One article, entitled "Robert M. LaFollette the Orator," gave this word picture of him in action:

Infinite in facial expression and gesture, every inch of his solidly built frame is brought into play. . . . Disgust, hope, honor, avarice, despair, love, anger, all the passions of man he paints in strong words and still stronger gestures. . . . There is no joking, nothing frivolous. He is in earnest and gives himself up wholly to the work he is doing. He impresses even the unbelievers among his hearers that he believes in himself and in the truth of his statements.

To win the Republican nomination for governor in 1898 would be very difficult. His opponent, Governor Edward Scofield, had proved to be an able executive. He was beholden to the bosses, but he had succeeded in getting concessions that had pleased the liberal wing of the party. Besides, America was at war with Spain and there was the traditional inclination to keep incumbents in office.

The convention struggle was bitter. Finally, Scofield won the nomination, but the La Follette men wrote a major part of the platform. It included a pledge to end the free railroad pass and franking evils; advocacy of a primary election law and an anti-lobbying law; a promise to stop the practice of paying salaries in advance out of the state treasury. This salary problem was so far out of hand that some officials were six months ahead in collecting their pay checks.

La Follette crowded into the next two years a nervous breakdown from overwork, a recovery, and a vigorous campaign to win the nomination for governor in 1900. The Journal, watching him closely, did not like all that he said or did. It condemned his tendency "to arraign class against class," to offer ready-made solutions to difficult problems, to assume that somebody was personally guilty for every wrong found in society and then jump on the person selected. "If Mr. LaFollette ever brings himself to a change of attitude," said one editorial, "if the necessity of a public servant standing on more conservative ground gets into his head, he may become a leader, not of a faction but of a party, and perhaps of the people of Wisconsin."

In an interview the next day La Follette thanked The Journal for the advice it had given him. He won the nomination in August and was overwhelmingly elected in November. At last, after an eight-year struggle, he was governor of Wisconsin. In his first message to the legislature, read "with all the arts of the orator and the politician," he demanded the strengthening of the state tax commission, increased taxes on railroads and corporations, a primary election law.

The Journal was sympathetic, but urged caution. For instance, a month after he took office, when he was slashing right and left at leaders of his own party because they would not accept his whole program without question, an editorial urged him "to adopt a steadier attitude, founded on fact instead of emotion, and to give Wisconsin the changes it needs without radicalism." The editorial concluded: "The Journal has no personal interest in Mr. LaFollette any more than in any other young, aspiring and promising man; he is a young man worth saving to the state."

But Governor La Follette was not one to whom it was easy to give advice. He was now working eighteen hours a day formulating his program. Much that he was putting forward had not been tried elsewhere, nor had the plans been thought through. Under the circumstances The Journal adopted a new policy which was less kindly toward La Follette but more helpful to its readers. It would gather all the material it could on each La Follette proposal, present it in news stories, and then analyze it editorially. In explaining its attitude it again defined its idea of the function of a free press:

The independent newspaper is not necessarily without convictions. But the independence consists in not being in any manner bound steadily to support any one party, faction, man or set of men, in all they may do or propose, nor yet to condemn all they do. Credit must

57

be given for good work and honest effort. Every proposed policy must be argued on its merits without fear or favor.

To report and interpret Madison news, Ellis B. Usher, a veteran La Crosse newspaperman thoroughly experienced in political affairs, was hired. He wrote a signed article daily.

La Follette, desperate in his battle with the old-line Republicans, now known as Stalwarts in contrast with liberal Half-Breeds, was accused of building up a political machine of his own when he accepted the support of Isaac Stephenson, a lumber king with political ambitions. Usher pointed out that this alliance had the dollar sign written all over it and was a departure from the acclaimed La Follette principles. The governor was greatly annoyed.

The key proposal of the La Follette program was the primary election bill. It provided for direct nomination by the voters in each party of all state, congressional, legislative, county, and municipal candidates. In the next two years The Journal gave more space to this subject than to any other: Should the primary election plan be substituted for the traditional convention and caucus system; and if so, what should be the provisions of the new primary law? The nation was combed for examples of how primary laws were working. No state had held primary elections on a statewide basis that included all offices, but there were several experiments on a limited scale. These were set forth in stories from Pennsylvania, which had primary county elections; from Minnesota, where there were municipal primaries; from several western states that were working out primary election systems.

The La Follette program faired poorly in the legislative session, due to Stalwart control. The railroad regulation bills were killed. A primary election bill was passed but it was so emasculated that the governor vetoed it.

La Follette refused to give up the fight and with that surprising vitality of leadership so characteristic of him won renomination in 1902. In the November election, he defeated the Democratic candidate, Mayor Dave Rose of Milwaukee, by 40,000 votes. La Follette hailed his second election as a mandate to put through his program, including much that he had added since he first took office. He had among his followers in the new legislature many members of the Populist party who urged him to advocate their half-socialistic schemes.

The Journal, sensing in this situation a danger for Wisconsin, urged restraint. It conducted no crusading campaign; it took no sides on most of the bills La Follette urged on the legislature. It realized that the governor was trying to correct a bad situation. But by continuing its policy of giving facts and analyzing them, it hoped to get him to make sure that his reform measures were sound. Although the governor was inclined by nature to resent criticism and to hold that anyone who was not with him was against him, he modified some of his demands when facts brought out by The Journal were called to his attention.

The struggle between La Follette Half-Breeds and the old-line Stalwarts in the legislature became known as "the war of 1903." In the end much of the La Follette program was enacted. A comprehensive, workable primary law was passed subject to approval by the voters in November, 1904. The bill to tax railroads on their property valuation, rather than on a fee basis, was passed, adding nearly a million dollars a year to the state treasury.

In the 1904 election La Follette won by a majority of 43,000, and for the first time his faction of the Republican party controlled both houses of the legislature. The governor asked for these sweeping reforms: civil service for state, township, and city employes; property tax on street railways and on telegraph and telephone companies; an appointive railroad commission to fix rates, prevent rebates, and control service; graduated state income tax; inheritance taxes; a new state capitol.

The message, embodying more major proposals than any other governor had ever submitted to a Wisconsin legislature, contained more than one hundred typewritten pages. The governor had gone into semiseclusion for nearly a month to prepare it. Reviewing it editorially, The Journal commented that it was a masterly presentation, that it settled any question of La Follette's ability, that it would add to his reputation not only in Wisconsin but throughout the country.

La Follette's purpose in speeding up the legislative program soon became apparent. The term of United States Senator Joseph

V. Quarles was about to expire, and there was talk of electing Governor La Follette to the Senate. If this should happen, the time was short to push through the remainder of his reform program. As it turned out he had served less than a month of his third term as governor when he was elected to the Senate, on January 25, 1905. In message after message to the legislature, he redoubled his efforts to get his program through. And The Journal redoubled its effort to give its readers all the information it could find on the new subjects that had been brought up.

Governor La Follette stayed in Madison through 1905, and even called a special session of the legislature in December to finish details. Then he resigned and left for Washington to become senator at the beginning of 1906.

His third-term accomplishments with the legislature included: enactment of a railroad commission bill; authorization of a new state capitol; an increase in University of Wisconsin revenues; the making permanent of the state tax commission; creation of a civil service commission. These measures, added to the primary election law, the railway tax law, and the anti-pass statute, represented the largest body of reform legislation ever carried through by one governor. And there would be more to come. Although La Follette was shifting the scene of his official work from Madison to Washington, it was certain, as The Journal pointed out, that he would remain the leader in Wisconsin.

The relationship between La Follette and The Journal has been described as antagonistic by persons who knew little of this early period. The Journal's attitude in the period of La Follette's rise to power and his three terms as governor was neither pro–La Follette nor anti–La Follette. Sometimes there were sharp differences of opinion over proposals or over methods the governor used. But always there was the underlying belief that La Follette was trying to give Wisconsin a better government. The assertion was made editorially that the paper would put nothing in the way of a reform proposal which it considered sound and well thought out.

As an independent newspaper, The Journal made its contribution in a dynamic period in which news research and editorial analysis were invaluable.

11

Dave Rose and the Socialists

In addition to the La Follette movement, The Journal faced other political developments at the turn of the century that tested its resourcefulness as a free newspaper. One was the steady growth of socialism. Another was the rise to power in Milwaukee of David S. Rose, a politically ambitious Darlington lawyer who came to Milwaukee in 1886 and in the next twelve years built a profitable legal practice and created a personal following.

In 1898, Rose was nominated for mayor by the Democrats on a "reform platform" which—surprisingly, in view of what was to come later—stated:

We demand that the gang of public plunderers and lobbyists who have infested our city hall during the last four years of Republican misrule be driven from places of public trust, to the end that the fair name of our beautiful city not be tarnished by the manipulation of organized gang rings, garbage scandals and attempted bribe giving.

Informed observers had not been aware of this "corruption," but Rose's campaign talk was loud and was effective among voters.

The Journal did not support Rose. It did not like his associates; it did not like his record as a lobbyist at Madison where he had helped to put through land transactions that were highly questionable; it did not like his apparent belief that expediency should govern over principle.

After his election, the unpredictable Rose in his first two-year term cut taxes, built up a reserve fund in the city treasury, and promoted Milwaukee as a trade and convention city. This pleased the businessmen. The Journal, which itself had often campaigned for trade expansion, was favorably impressed and supported him for re-election in 1900 on "the ticket of progress," declaring, "We believe the best results will be secured by the return of the present administration, as a guarantee of settled purpose and a clearing of the field for business advancement."

Overwhelmingly re-elected, Rose took off his mask. He was for "a wide open town" that would attract business and make things hum. A city carnival was staged at which gambling and other irregular activities were introduced. The mayor personally started a gambling wheel rolling at a bazaar in the Exposition Building. While he was letting in the gamblers and prostitutes, and relaxing saloon restrictions, Rose forestalled criticism by making speeches praising Milwaukee as the "most orderly city in America." Now undisputed boss of the city, he rode about in a stylish victoria drawn by spirited horses. He was immaculately dressed, with goatee and mustache trimmed evenly, and a gleaming silk hat set high on his shapely head. He had a smile and a nod for everyone. "No mayor ever gripped the imagination of the people more than he," Representative William H. Stafford once said of Rose.

Those were the days of great parades in connection with conventions and anniversaries. There was lavish official entertainment of notables who came to Milwaukee. It was a booming, laughing, happy time. When Mayor Rose announced for a third term The Journal again supported him "because he has widened and broadened Milwaukee to a metropolitan status." It admitted that he had "run a wide open town," but pointed out that the city was "free of major crime." It said that Rose "has some qualities to which major objection may be made," that "he has certain weaknesses in his private life," that some of his appointments "have lowered the public service," that he resorted to expedients. But, the editorial concluded, "he keeps the city moving."

The issue as The Journal saw it the day before election was: "Shall Milwaukee turn backward or continue its advancement?" The Journal had been hoodwinked by the Rose propaganda just as had the businessmen of Milwaukee. The paper envisioned Milwaukee as the leader of the whole area north of Chicago; it advocated the founding of a "Half Million Club" to prepare for the 500,000 in population the city hoped to have soon.

Rose was re-elected by a larger majority than ever, but in his third administration the inevitable results of the open-town policy began to appear. There were rumors of streetcar franchise deals, of graft in street-paving jobs, of protection money paid by gambling places and houses of prostitution. A grand jury was called late in 1903. The Journal, making an investigation of its own and becoming convinced that something was wrong, strongly supported the grand jury procedure.

On February 1, 1904, came indictments of twenty-three city and county officials. A month later the grand jury indicted two officials who were high in the Rose political organization. The Journal, now aroused, declared: "The Rose administration is as rotten as punk." It urged citizens to get together in a reform movement that would rid the community of grafters. It made this prediction that was to come true seven years later: "The city and county must be cleaned of harpies or we shall have a Socialist mayor."

Guy D. Goff, a rising young Republican lawyer who was assisting District Attorney Francis E. McGovern in the graft investigation, was chosen by a group of citizens to lead the reform movement. The Journal supported him vigorously, but Goff was no match for Mayor Rose as an orator and politician. Rose succeeded in disentangling his administration, at least in the popular mind, from the grafters. He cried out that the whole grand jury idea was a political trick aimed at him. The day after the grand jury had indicted ten more officials and private citizens, the voters elected him mayor for the fourth time. Rose received 23,575 votes to 17,603 for Goff and 15,343 for Victor L. Berger, the candidate of the Social-Democratic party. In the Berger vote, with its sharp rise in Socialist strength, The Journal saw significance. Citizens disgusted with Rose's corrupt regime were voting for the Socialists.

Meantime a second grand jury, after working seven and a half months, indicted thirty-nine more persons, twenty-seven of whom were public officials. Big name magazine writers, among them Lincoln Steffens, came to Milwaukee to find out what was going on. Steffens found a great deal. In *McClure's Magazine* of October, 1904, he wrote:

The great scandal of Milwaukee was the extension of street railway franchises, and the men who put that through were Charles F. Pfister, the Stalwart Republican boss, and David S. Rose, the Stalwart Democratic mayor. Money was paid; the extension was boodled through. . . . As for Mayor Rose, his friends declare that he has told them, personally and convincingly, that he got not one cent for his service. . . . Rose knew that his council was corrupt before it was proven so; he told two business men that they couldn't get a privilege that they sought honestly from him, without bribing aldermen.

Despite all this, Mayor Rose announced in May, 1905, nearly a year before the election, that he would seek a fifth term. He was unmoved when, a month after his announcement, a third grand jury returned twenty-one more indictments involving officials and ex-officials of city and county. Rose assailed all the grand juries as creating an impression of corruption that was "a great injustice to Milwaukee."

The 1906 election was held under the new La Follette law that authorized nominations in a primary. Rose emerged as nominee of the Democrats; W. A. Arnold, of the Socialists; Sherburn M. Becker, of the Republicans. Becker, thirty-year-old son of a Milwaukee banker, soon showed that he could capture the public imagination just as did Mayor Rose. He had been a supervisor and a leader in the graft investigation, but the 1906 campaign was not waged on a question of principles or individual fitness. It became an uproarious rivalry as to who could put on the bigger stunt. William Hooker, veteran newspaperman and publicity agent who conducted the campaign for Becker, demonstrated that he could outdo Mayor Rose's best efforts. Becker's precinct workers were given three hundred broad-brimmed hats, Texas style. Street parades and marching clubs were organized. Each marcher had an oilcloth cape, a helmet, a package of tobacco, a corncob pipe, and at night a torch.

Rose got his name in the papers by stopping the city hall clock because its striking at 10 P.M. disturbed the German play being given at the nearby Pabst Theater. At one political rally when he learned a group of deaf-mutes were in the audience he paused every few minutes to summarize his remarks in sign language, to the delight of all his "listeners," deaf or otherwise. News of the incident was spread by his press agents all over the city.

The Journal believed that Becker was honest and not likely to be involved in graft but felt that he was lacking in leadership qualities. It did not mention names in its campaign editorials. It stressed honesty in office and it strove especially to insure the election of good aldermen.

Becker won by 2,000 votes over Rose, to the great surprise of the mayor and his lieutenants. After Becker had been inaugurated, The Journal urged him "to be a leader," to take the political initiative away from the old Rose crowd and to take the so-called "civic improvement" initiative away from the Socialists. But Mayor Becker had no well-grounded civic program. His proposals seemed to be planned more for their publicity value than for community betterment. He was soon dubbed "the boy mayor," and with his immaturity went a continuous round of stunts, such as the night foray when he tore down all the jewelers' clocks which were on tall iron posts on sidewalks of Wisconsin Avenue in front jewelry stores. He said the clocks were an obstruction. Another venture was his widely advertised trip to New York in his Pope-Toledo touring car, the "Red Devil," with a side trip to Oyster Bay to call on Teddy Roosevelt. He had two professional publicity men with him.

Weaknesses of Mayor Becker gave the Rose backers in the common council opportunity to put the administration at a disadvantage. The Journal saw the chance for better government slipping away and predicted that if Rose and his cohorts again captured the city hall, voters, in disgust, would turn to the Socialists to clean house. Ignoring such warnings, the voters elected David Rose to his fifth term in 1908. And in second place was Emil Seidel, the Socialist candidate. The vote stood: Rose, 23,114; Seidel, 20,867. The Republican businessman candidate, Thomas J. Pringle, was third with 18,169.

Rose said, on taking office again, that he was going to weed out disreputable saloonkeepers and close disreputable bars. His announcement was prominently displayed in the press, but The Journal carried the news under a tongue-in-cheek headline: "Is Mayor an Enemy of Dives?" Some of the most notorious saloonkeepers were put out of business. In this move Rose had the support of the brewers, who felt that conditions had become so bad as to hurt the brewing industry and encourage the spread of the temperance movement.

But Mayor Rose's reforms were short-lived. Soon there were rumblings about council deals over public utility franchises. The mayor lost much of his popularity when he vetoed a greatly needed school building program. And he failed completely in his greatest test: he did nothing to close the notorious red-light district.

Rose, having become an investor in western mining property, was away from the city much of the time. The Journal spoke of him as "the absentee mayor." His lieutenants, without even his restraining hand, began to carry their graft to new extremes. As the election of 1910 approached, the setting was perfect for a Socialist victory. Rose, saying he intended to move West, was not a candidate. The Democrats nominated Vincenz J. Schoenecker, Jr.; the Republicans, Dr. John M. Beffel; the Socialists, Emil Seidel.

The Journal supported Schoenecker and his platform for home rule for Milwaukee. But no amount of effort could have turned the tide, with the non-Socialist vote split between the Republicans and the Democrats. The Socialists swept the city, electing Seidel major; Carl P. Dietz, comptroller; C. B. Whitnall, city treasurer; Daniel W. Hoan, city attorney. The Socialists also elected a majority of the common council, a majority of the county supervisors, and twelve members of the legislature. In comment, The Journal said:

Milwaukee has elected the Social-Democratic ticket. The election however, does not mean that Milwaukee has been converted to socialism. It is a revolt against both of the old parties. It is not in any way an adoption or approval of socialistic principles of economics.

True socialism, The Journal had pointed out previously,

is a complete system of government as different from ours as is the

66

old patriarchal system or the absolutism of an Asian despot. Its adoption in this country would require a complete change in our constitution and organization of government.

The post-election editorial recounted that "12 years of misrule" in Milwaukee had gradually driven the people to vote for men who advocated a foreign philosophy. It cited the steps that had led to this debacle:

1. Dictation of city decisions by the utilities.
2. Mayor Rose's alliance with the liquor interests.
3. The mayor's failure to support the school building program.
4. Municipal rule by big business.

Milwaukee was the first large American city to elect a Socialist government.

12

Victory for Nonpartisan Elections

The crucial test of independence as a newspaper was met by The Journal during the Socialist rule in Milwaukee, when it sought to steer a course between the extremes of party organs. After Emil Seidel was elected mayor in 1910, Victor Berger started the Milwaukee *Leader* as the Socialist party paper. In the opposing camp Milwaukee's Democratic and Republican papers damned the Socialists even when they accomplished some good. Nieman's course was to print the facts to the best of his ability.

Checking the day-to-day accomplishments of the party with its campaign promises was not difficult. The Socialists had publicized their program thoroughly during the campaign. They had promised:

1. A public slaughterhouse to lower the price of meat.
2. A municipal quarry for the production of cheaper building stone.
3. Municipal wood yards, coal yards, and ice plant to sell fuel and ice at cost.
4. City dispensaries where drugs would be sold at cost and free medical services would be provided for people of low incomes.
5. Work for the unemployed.
6. The suppression of vice.
7. Small neighborhood parks "where the laboring people could rest," not large parks for millionaires to drive through.
8. Slum removal.
9. Immediate improvement of utility service, with subsequent taking over of utilities.

These promises reflected pure Socialist dogma. Few of them, however, were fulfilled. Instead, Mayor Seidel and the council announced that they would go after tax dodgers and would provide better sewer construction; and they said they had found a way to reduce paving costs.

In the spring of 1911, unemployment became a grave problem and the Associated Charities were overwhelmed. Help for the unemployed had been a strong campaign promise of the party; back in 1908 when jobless men had appealed for help Emil Seidel, then an alderman, had said: "Put me in the office of the board of public works for a couple of weeks and I will find plenty of legitimate work for the unemployed."

The Journal quoted Seidel's words during the recession of 1911, commenting: "The Socialists are now in power. Where's the work?" In the end it was not the Socialist administration, but The Journal and the Associated Charities and other relief organizations that provided most of the aid for the unemployed. The Journal conducted a fund-raising campaign, and the Associated Charities used the money for relief of the neediest families. The program also included finding jobs for workers, until the Socialists finally established a free municipal unemployment bureau.

At the close of the first year of the Seidel administration The Journal recounted the Socialist promises and accomplishments. There had been progress in getting better utility service. One small city park had been added. Plans were under way to buy a large tract of the Milwaukee River bank in the northern area of the city: though an excellent idea this was in contradiction to the "small park" plan. But there were no movements for a municipal slaughterhouse, quarry, coal yard, or ice plant. The Socialists had not been the leaders in unemployment relief; slums were not being cleared; and vice was not being suppressed. Summing up, The Journal said of Socialist rule: "The Socialists have not given an administration marked in any particular degree for superior efficiency, but they have given the city an honest administration. There has been no suspicion of graft."

The first year of Socialist control gave rise to widespread belief that the Socialists were just another political party in power.

This gave The Journal opportunity to push with all its might for something it had long advocated: nonpartisan city elections. At the Milwaukee charter convention in 1907, the movement for nonpartisan elections came to the front, largely as a result of Journal articles. A legislative bill requiring all candidates to run without party designation was killed in the 1909 legislature, however, by politicians of both parties who wanted to keep control of their party machines.

When the Socialists won the Milwaukee elections of 1910, another nonpartisan bill was introduced in the 1911 legislature. It had the strong support of Governor Francis E. McGovern, a La Follette Republican. The bill passed the senate readily enough, but in the assembly the twelve Socialist members blocked it. Holding a balance of power between Democrats and Republicans, they tied up important appropriation bills and then engaged in logrolling, often lining up with representatives of special interests to attain their aims. In a vote-trading alliance with upstate legislators the Socialists passed a reapportionment bill which juggled Milwaukee district boundaries in a scheme to give Socialists additional strength in the assembly. Governor McGovern vetoed this bill.

Commenting on the Socialist manipulations at Madison, notably the political alliance which was blocking the nonpartisan election bill, The Journal said: "The Socialists place their party above the people. They wish to be guided not by what a majority of the people demand, but by their own dictates. Could there be any more intense partisanship than this?"

The struggle at Madison over the nonpartisan bill went on for weeks but in the end the Republicans and Democrats gave in to the Socialists and killed the bill. This left the Milwaukee opponents of the Socialists in a bad position as the 1912 election approached.

The Socialists grew bolder. When they attempted to oust Police Chief Janssen and Fire Chief Clancy, The Journal decided to try a daring experiment. It proposed that Milwaukee's non-Socialist voters voluntarily lay aside their party labels and unite in a nonpartisan election ticket of their own. The Journal announced that it would conduct a straw vote campaign for the 1912 spring election. When it asked for suggestions for candidates, thirty-two names, among them the most prominent men of the city, were offered.* Through withdrawals the list was reduced to the following twelve names, which were submitted to Journal readers for preferential balloting: Dr. Gerhard A. Bading, Sherman Brown, Joseph P. Carney, William J. Cary, Eltinge Elmore, Charles E. Estabrook, Fred C. Lorenz, F. C. Morehouse, Theobold Otjen, George W. Peck, Emanuel L. Philipp, and William Pieplow.

The balloting was brisk, with as many as a thousand votes coming in by mail in a single day. Soon three men emerged as leaders: Dr. Bading, who had been health commissioner under Mayor Becker; William J. Cary, the fourth district congressman; and Joseph P. Carney, the alderman who had led the opposition to the Socialists in the council.

To add to the interest The Journal conducted a slogan contest, with an award each day. One award went to Charles L. Aarons, the young lawyer who later became a prominent circuit judge, for his slogan: "Milwaukee Needs Men—Not Parties." The final winning slogan—"For Public Good, Not Party Gain"—became the battle cry of the nonpartisan movement.

A city-wide committee of Republicans, Democrats, and some nonpolitical civic leaders named the following nonpartisan ticket: Dr. Gerhard A. Bading, for mayor; Louis Kotecki, for comptroller; Joseph P. Carney, for treasurer. Republican and Democratic city committees endorsed this ticket unanimously and arranged a complete slate of nonpartisan candidates for alderman. All agreed to drop party politics and work to make the nonpartisan movement permanent. The Journal repeated that it was for nonpartisan

* The citizens suggested were Alvin P. Kletzsch, Frederick L. Pierce, Theobold Otjen, Emanuel L. Philipp, Albert F. Gallun, Adolph J. Schmitz, Eltinge Elmore, Frederic C. Morehouse, William J. Cary, William George Bruce, Dr. Gilbert E. Seaman, Archie Tegtmeyer, T. J. Neacy, William E. Pieplow, Nat Stone, Joseph Carney, George H. Benzenberg, Carroll G. Pearse, John T. Janssen, Fred C. Lorenz, Sebastian Walter, John C. Karel, Alonzo Pawling, Sherman Brown, Dr. Gerhard A. Bading, August Rebhan, Dr. John M. Beffel, Charles E. Estabrook, A. E. Kagel, C. A. A. McGee, George W. Peck, and Charles E. McLenegan.

elections not merely to oust the Socialists. It said that if the defeat of the Socialists was to mean a return to the Mayor Rose type of political rule it would not lift a hand to change the administration.

Dr. Bading was elected over Mayor Seidel, 43,064 to 30,200; Carney was named treasurer over Whitnall, 43,505 to 29,929; Kotecki was made comptroller over Dietz 43,506 to 29,701. The Socialist majority was swept out of the common council too. In a four-column editorial, The Journal said it was under no illusions. If the nonpartisans did not provide a superior government, the Socialists would again come to power. The Socialists' newspaper, the Milwaukee *Leader,* said that the nonpartisans had won "by the fusion of everybody who is crooked with everybody who is ignorant."

The nonpartisan victory received editorial comment all over the nation. The New York *Herald* said: "There is only one remedy for the ills of American cities and that is a nonpartisan city administration of municipal affairs by honest men trained in conducting large enterprises." The Baltimore *Sun* predicted that "Milwaukee will never see another city election fought out on the old party lines."

Steps to make that prediction come true were nearer than anybody realized. Governor McGovern had called a special session of the legislature to vote relief for northern Wisconsin counties hard hit by spring floods, and he had included in the call authorization for the legislature to change election laws. With the results of the recent Milwaukee election before them, legislators quickly passed the nonpartisan bill, and on May 6, 1912, Governor McGovern signed it. The pen used was given to Henry C. Campbell, managing editor of The Journal, as a memento of The Journal's fight which Campbell had led.

Not all credit for the victory belonged to The Journal, however. The *Sentinel* and the *Evening Wisconsin* had done effective work also; but their objective had been more the immediate defeat of the Socialists than the triumph of the nonpartisan plan. In any case, a basis for good city government was laid. City administrations would come and go, even Socialist administrations, but the partisan politics of Dave Rose's day and of the Seidel regime had been ended.

During Mayor Seidel's term of office he had as his secretary a young man with a bent for poetry who had been on The Journal two years as police reporter, labor news reporter, and city hall reporter, successively. Commenting forty years later, at his home in Flat Rock, North Carolina, on The Journal's role in freeing Milwaukee city government from party politics, he told a Journal interviewer: "It was then that I knew The Journal would develop into one of the great American newspapers—a point it has reached today. It had the right attitude of printing the news without slant. It did not color what the reader was to get."

The name of the former Journal reporter was Carl Sandburg.

13

Victim of Conspiracy

One of the earliest attempts in this country to conspire to put a rival out of business was launched against The Journal in 1900 by three competing Milwaukee newspapers. The ensuing litigation was to last more than three years and to take the case to the United States Supreme Court.

In 1899, to attract more readers, The Journal had reduced its price from two cents to one cent a copy. Within three months its circulation rose from the 1898 average of 12,500 to 22,294; and in the next three years it increased to 29,000. On January 1, 1900, advertising rates were raised 25 per cent, after the company had shown its books to a committee of advertisers, explaining that it could not meet the cost of this extra circulation without an increase in advertising rates. The merchants were satisfied, but not the other newspapers. The *Evening Wisconsin,* the *Sentinel,* and the *Daily News* got together and notified merchants that if they paid the increased rates to The Journal, they could not advertise in the three other papers without paying the same higher rate even though the other papers had not increased their circulations.* Moreover, if an advertiser wanted to use one of the other three papers, he would have to use all three. But if a mer-

* The 1899 circulation of the *Evening Wisconsin,* according to the *American Newspaper Annual and Directory* for that year, was 16,720, a decrease of 2,500 from 1898. *Sentinel* circulation for 1899 was about 21,000; and the *Daily News* reported 4,000.

chant would boycott The Journal completely, he could have all the advertising he wanted at the former low rate.

It was a difficult spot for the merchants. Each of the other papers had a smaller circulation than The Journal, but banded together they could not be ignored. Some merchants yielded to the threat, and Journal advertising revenue dropped. Fortunately, Wisconsin had an anti-conspiracy law designed to protect men and businesses from such maneuvers. Section 4466–A of the statutes read:

Any two or more persons who shall combine, associate, agree, mutually undertake or concert together for the purpose of willfully or maliciously injuring another in his reputation, trade, business or profession by any means whatsoever, for the purpose of maliciously compelling another from performing any act against his will, or preventing or hindering another from performing any lawful act, shall be punished by imprisonment in the county jail not more than one year, or by a fine not exceeding five hundred dollars.

The Journal swore out warrants against the business manager of the *Evening Wisconsin,* the business manager of the *Sentinel,* and the editor of the *Daily News.* They were arrested and taken before Judge Neele B. Neelen, who bound them over for trial. Then began a series of hearings and legal maneuvers that took the case through the Milwaukee County courts three times, to the Wisconsin Supreme Court twice, and finally to the United States Supreme Court.*

On November 7, 1904, The Journal won a complete victory, one that had far-reaching significance as the first effective step to prevent business conspiracy. Both Justice R. D. Marshall of the Wisconsin Supreme Court and Justice Oliver Wendell Holmes of the United States Supreme Court, the men who wrote the leading opinions, made clear that the right of a newspaper or of any other firm to business freedom and protection must be preserved. In his conclusion, Justice Holmes said:

There is nothing in this [statute] militating at all against the right of individuals to combine and associate together for the purpose of

* Cases involved in The Journal's suit were: Aikens v. Wisconsin, Hugein v. Wisconsin, and Hoyt v. Wisconsin, 113 Wis. 419, 89 NW 1135; carried to the Supreme Court in 195 U.S. 154, November 7, 1904.

promoting their individual welfare in any legitimate manner. It strikes only at the assertion of a right of combining . . . to wrongfully accomplish harm to another in the line of those things mentioned in the statute.

Justice Holmes also quoted an opinion of Baron Bramwell* in an often-cited case:

The liberty of a man's mind and will to say how he shall bestow himself and his means, his talents and his industry, is as much a subject of the law's protection as that of his body, and if any set of men agree among themselves to coerce that liberty of mind and thought by combination and restraint, they are guilty of committing an offense.

The defendants in the case were fined. The attorney who won the decision for The Journal was James G. Flanders, assisted by A. C. Umbreit and W. H. Austin. The case attracted national attention. So great was the demand for information that the paper printed a booklet giving the history of the conspiracy. In the offices of The Journal's rivals, however, resentment ran high. A publisher's notice in the *American Newspaper Annual and Directory* of 1903 said that the *Sentinel* had "achieved a circulation of the best sort—the Milwaukee, Wisconsin, kind of well to do, enterprising conservatives who won't stand for flashy fakes or flim-flam of any sort, but who want, and can afford, the good things of this earth in plenty."

During this period of far-reaching legal decisions, The Journal, in a lighter vein, was trying out carrier pigeons as news dispatchers. This was in the days of few telephones and no automobiles. A reporter covering the Wisconsin state fair, for instance, was hard put to get his story back to the paper in time for the afternoon edition. He had nothing faster than a horse and buggy. It was "Brownie" Rowland who conceived the idea of using carrier pigeons and accordingly bought about one hundred of them, including some from France and Belgium. The reporter would take a pigeon with him as he went to get a story, write his dispatch on the spot, put it in a capsule attached to the bird, and

---

* George William Wilshere, Baron Bramwell, helped set up the British Common Law Procedure Act in 1852.

send his messenger on its way. A story handled in this manner was labeled "Pigeon Dispatch to The Journal."

The record of one sensational use of the pigeons is in the paper's files. During a strike at the Allis-Chalmers plant, recalcitrant union members, determined to meet where no newspaper reporters could hear their discussion, chartered a ship of the Flint and Père Marquette line and embarked on a 25-mile cruise on Lake Michigan. But the strikers had not reckoned with pigeons and Sylvester Sullivan, a Marquette University student working part time for The Journal. Sullivan, a friend of Captain Peter Barry, boarded the ship as a crew member, carrying two baskets of "supplies." During the meeting Sullivan secreted himself where he could hear what was going on. When the ship docked a few hours later, the union members were greeted, to their amazement, by newspaper boys shouting the headlines of a "Pigeon Dispatch to The Journal" which contained the fiery speeches and the resolutions of their meeting.

The pigeon dispatch stunt was abandoned after a time. Some of the pigeons would return to the Journal roof only to perch just out of reach and no amount of coaxing could lure them into their coop. But they created a great deal of interest. The pigeon exhibit at the state fair of 1900 was a big attraction. That year The Journal had aided the fair, which was in financial difficulties, by promoting a guarantee fund among Wisconsin businessmen. The fair took on new life.

In 1902, The Journal installed a four-deck press with color printing attachment. In 1906, erection of a new plant—the first building of its own in The Journal's history—was begun at 734 N. Fourth Street, north of Wisconsin Avenue. It was a three-story structure designed by A. C. Clas and George B. Ferry. The paper moved in April 8, 1907, seven months before its twenty-fifth birthday. The Silver Jubilee edition printed the following account of the changes in those twenty-five years:

In 1883 the population was about 130,000; now it is 350,000. Then there were 20,000 wage earners; now there are 100,000 or more. Wages paid in 1883 amounted to $7,000,000; now they amount to more than

77

$57,000,000. At that time there were 800 manufacturing establishments; now there are 3,500. The product of manufacturing establishments in 1883 was worth $43,000,000; the product of the plants in Milwaukee today is worth $350,000,000 each year. In 1880, Milwaukee's jobbing business amounted to $48,000,000; in 1906 it reached $449,000,000. Bank deposits in 1883 amounted to $18,000,000; now they are nearly $70,000,000. . . .

The people are better fed and better clothed now than they were 25 years ago. They are better educated. Social conditions generally are better. There are more schools, more churches, more hospitals, more philanthropic enterprises. Milwaukee now has a fine system of public parks, with playgrounds for the children; then there were no parks. The "square deal" among men is given greater recognition now than it was then. There is more of kindness, generosity, helpfulness and brotherly love. And it is these things, after all, that really count.

On November 19, 1911, The Journal printed its first Sunday paper, which sold at the same price as a weekday edition. It was a paper of twenty-eight pages, containing about the same news coverage as the daily Journal, plus a limited number of features. Most of these features had been appearing in the Saturday edition. "We contemplate rounding out the week with a regular edition to be printed on Sunday morning, and to be delivered to our readers at the same cost as a week-day edition," Nieman announced. "Our aim is to give the news of the day, as on every other day, in condensed and readable form."

It was in the period soon after 1900 that there were on the staff three reporters who were to become famous in literature. Zona Gale of Portage, Wisconsin, came in 1901 from the University of Wisconsin, where she had received a master's degree. Later her novel, *Friendship Village,* was a national success, and she won the Pulitzer prize for literature in 1920 with *Miss Lulu Bett.* Edna Ferber came to The Journal in 1906 from the Appleton, Wisconsin, *Crescent.* She worked hard as a reporter until 1909 when she became ill. While recovering, she wrote *Dawn O'Hara,* her first novel. The prototype for one of its characters was "Brownie" Rowland. In her autobiography, *A Peculiar Treasure,* she wrote in detail of her reporting days on The Journal. Carl Sandburg, poet, Lincoln biographer, and Pulitzer prize

Edna Ferber (*above*), Zona Gale (*right*), and Carl Sandburg were Journal reporters in the early 1900's.

Henry C. Campbell, assistant editor (*above*); Jacob Schindler, managing editor (*left*); Lloyd Tilghman Boyd, business manager (*below, facing page*); and E. A. Belda, treasurer (*above, facing page*), helped Nieman in the troublesome years between 1890 and 1923.

J. Robert Taylor, The Journal's first and only photographer in 1909, covered his assignments on a motorcycle.

Journal artist's sketch of the pigeon loft. Pigeons were used in 1900 to carry reporters' copy to the city editor, but unfortunately often sat on the Journal roof just out of reach until after press time.

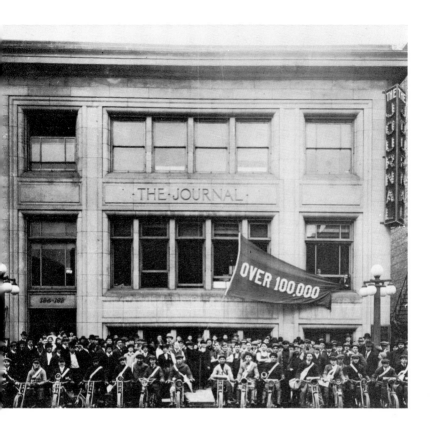

The Journal building on North Fourth
Street showing the circulation banner
hoisted on April 10, 1915.

Harry J. Grant in 1916, at the time
he came to The Journal.

Medal offered in 1914 by The Journal's Motorcycle Club to promote good roads and highway courtesy.

"Brownie" (Wallace Rowland, *right*) and "The Poor Cuss" (in this picture William Cuddy) on one of their Tour Club trips to report on Wisconsin roads.

Wisconsin's Thirty-second Division came home from World War I on June 6, 1919, proud of its fighting record against kaiserism.

Victor Berger, leader of Milwaukee Socialists.

This Pulitzer medal was awarded to The Journal in 1919 for the paper's stand against anti-Americanism in World War I.

winner, was on the staff from 1908 to 1910, as has been mentioned earlier.

Various editorial campaigns occupied The Journal during this period. The paper had not supported William McKinley for the Presidency but in the closing years of the 1890's it backed him fully in his effort to keep the United States out of a war with Spain. In the uprising of Cuban rebels against Spanish rule, William Randolph Hearst's papers were prodding America to go to the rebels' defense. When war was made inevitable, however, in 1898, by the blowing up of the battleship *Maine,* The Journal gave its support wholeheartedly. In 1903 the paper began one of the first movements in the nation to promote study of forest resources and to shape a program to stop depletion. Wisconsin forest lands at the time were being denuded by the lumber barons. Loan sharks were the next target of The Journal. In 1904 the paper began exposure of a group of economic cutthroats in Milwaukee who were as rapacious as any in the nation. In one instance a man had borrowed $100 to meet expenses of illness. In two and a half years he had paid $285 in interest and still owed the $100. Such exposures laid the groundwork for legislation correcting these abuses.

The Journal's Goodfellow organization was created about this time, and for more than twenty years under the sympathetic guidance of Florence Rowland, sister of "Brownie" Rowland, it raised funds and distributed toys to children and baskets of food to needy families. These relief functions were later taken over by the Community Fund and county relief agencies.

On November 29, 1900, this simple announcement appeared on the society page of The Journal:

The marriage of Miss Agnes Elizabeth Wahl, daughter of Mr. and Mrs. Christian Wahl, and Lucius W. Nieman took place last evening at the residence of the bride's parents, The Rev. Charles Stanley Lester officiated. The bride was attended by her sister, Mrs. Arthur C. G. Weld, as matron of honor, and by Miss Ilsa Wahl as bridesmaid. The little Misses Carola Berry, Elizabeth Bowles and Agnes Carpenter and Master Cyril Weld also attended the bride. Judge Joshua Eric Dodge was best man and the ushers were John I. Burke and Otto Falk.

Miss Wahl was one of the women who had worked on the Charity edition of The Journal, in 1895. She had studied music in Europe, and was interested in literature and art. Her father had long been a civic leader in Milwaukee, especially in developing the park system.

Nieman in his bachelor days had lived at the Milwaukee Club. The home of the newly married couple was at 930 East Knapp Street.

14

Hail Woodrow Wilson

Theodore Roosevelt stimulated the imagination of the country when he became President in 1901. His flashing teeth and his favorite expression, "delighted," were inspiration for cartoonists. His epithet, "malefactors of great wealth," and his slogan, "Tread lightly, but carry a big stick," used widely at the time, have enlivened the language. The voters were either wholeheartedly for him or violently against him.

When as governor of New York he made a speech in Milwaukee The Journal was impressed. "He has a development of citizenship out of the ordinary," it commented. "He is a man of conviction, courage and vim." But when he became President the paper noted that, while Roosevelt voiced disapproval of "unscrupulous moneyed interests," he was content to let the high tariff stand—a tariff which, according to a Journal editorial, was protecting these same interests and exploiting the public. The Journal found Robert M. La Follette, who became senator from Wisconsin in 1906, more nearly in line with its own thinking. The paper had criticized La Follette for helping the free-spending Isaac Stephenson get a Senate seat, but it did not break with him.

In the 1908 presidential race, The Journal was dissatisfied both with William Jennings Bryan, who was running for the third time, and with William Howard Taft, who had been picked by Roosevelt. Taft was called "a statesman representing progress and construction but bound to a reactionary platform." In refusing to endorse either Bryan or Taft, The Journal said: "One thing is certain, and that is that a sound progressive program must be adopted in state and nation and made permanent and secure, or real radicalism will in the end smash the things that should be smashed and smash things that should not be smashed."

Taft, when elected, did nothing to check the advocates of the Payne-Aldrich high tariff bill, though independent newspapers urged him to use his influence. In the Senate the battle against the tariff bill was led by La Follette and a small group of progressive Republicans from the Middle West. "It is a high honor to the state," commented The Journal, "to be represented in the United States senate by a man capable of advocating the right so intelligently, bravely and unswervingly as Senator LaFollette." The Journal sent Henry Campbell to Washington to write a series on the tariff struggle. These articles did much to arouse the Middle West and turn it definitely from Taft. But the fight was lost and the Payne-Aldrich tariff bill was signed by Taft.

The shock of the passage of the high tariff law had scarcely worn off when new troubles arose for Taft. His Secretary of the Interior, Richard A. Ballinger, was accused of letting private exploiters take forest lands that Teddy Roosevelt had set aside for conservation purposes. Taft sided with Ballinger, and a vigorous battle developed. Republican progressives in Congress—La Follette, Norris of Nebraska, Dolliver and Cummins of Iowa, Bristow of Kansas, Borah of Idaho, and Clapp of Minnesota—lined up against Taft, his Cabinet, and the tory managers of the Republican party.

In its 1910 election editorials The Journal urged that "without any regard to party lines, progressive Republicans and progressive Democrats should vote for progressive candidates and against tory candidates." The anti-reactionaries swept the field in the election, and La Follette was looked upon as the logical man to challenge Taft for the G.O.P. nomination in 1912.

Meantime, a new voice was being heard among the Democrats— the voice of Woodrow Wilson, historian and president of Princeton University, saying that "corporate greed has almost debauched the nation," and that a new program, not radical but following

82

principles of democracy, was needed. Wilson was elected governor of politics-ridden New Jersey. He soon put the grafters in jail and led the legislature in a progressive program. The Journal printed a series of articles on Governor Wilson's success and on his views of public questions, and he reciprocated by writing for The Journal an exclusive article containing this often-quoted sentence: "I have a very profound belief in the common people of this country." Wilson made two important speeches in Wisconsin, which The Journal printed in full, commenting: "He represents the people's cause."

Teddy Roosevelt, back from his African hunting trip, found cause for dismay in the reactionary moves of Taft and in the political and economic crises that were brewing. It was a time of unrest, particularly in labor relations. The radicals tried repeatedly to seize control of the American Federation of Labor, and did not scruple to use dynamite in battles with management. Among the violent events of the period was the bombing of the Los Angeles *Times* by the McNamara brothers. Regarding political conditions, it was symptomatic that in the United States Senate three men were suspected of buying their way to office.

Viewing this picture, The Journal asked: "How much strain can the American democracy stand?" Then, as the time for the 1912 national conventions approached, it suggested a way to end that strain:

In Gov. Wilson not only the Democratic party but the whole country has an opportunity of taking a long step forward. In LaFollette the Republican party has the same opportunity, but present indications are that it will name one of two other men (Taft or Roosevelt) who have been tried and found wanting.

In Gov. Wilson, however, the country has a man the main spring of whose action has been the restoration of the government to the people, who not only has said that injustice must cease and justice triumph, but has found a way to make injustice cease and bring the right to triumph.

In the Republican convention in Chicago, President Taft's backers, through control of the national committee, disqualified enough southern and western Roosevelt delegates to assure renomination of the President. The Roosevelt men bolted the party and nominated "T. R." as the Bull Moose candidate.

The Democratic convention in Baltimore was split between tory and progressive factions. Governor Wilson was nominated over Champ Clark on the 46th ballot after William Jennings Bryan asked Clark whether he was a "progressive" and Clark refused to answer. The Journal hailed the nomination of Wilson in an editorial that reflected all the pent-up emotions of the long, long search:

The Journal feels that Woodrow Wilson's nomination means as much as Lincoln's nomination meant. God gave this country Abraham Lincoln in 1860. The Journal solemnly believes that a never-failing Providence gives us Woodrow Wilson in 1912. During the Civil War, patriotism and sentiment were called forth and attained their highest point. After the war, materialism, naturally and from the very needs of the country, began to find a place and has gone on increasingly. The time has come when there must be a halt and we must give our attention and our effort to other things—to humanity and justice, to the social and moral needs of the nation, to securing all the equality intended by the founders of the republic.

For the first time since the campaign of Cleveland in 1884, the independent papers of the country will be united on a candidate. The men who see clearly the need, the issues and the political lineup of the day, and who are free to follow their convictions, will support Wilson with one accord.

The split in the Republican party made Wilson's election certain. He got 435 electoral votes, to 88 for Roosevelt, and 8 for Taft. Wilson carried Wisconsin for the Presidency, and McGovern was re-elected governor. The Journal said:

Wisconsin has helped to elect as president a man who bore the Democratic label but is a progressive above everything else; and in the state it has elected to power men who bore the Republican label but almost all of whom are progressive above everything else. The spirit and good judgment shown makes one proud of the state and of the electorate of the state.

There was only one cloud in the sky of an otherwise fair day. In the capitals of the Old World men were saying, not out loud yet but in a whisper, that soon there might be a general European war. If war should come, America could not hope to escape involvement.

15

Pro-Germanism

"It is for this vision we have been waiting."

With these words The Journal acclaimed Woodrow Wilson's leadership shortly after he was sworn in as President on March 4, 1913. Wilson, in offering his program of reforms, had summoned "all honest men, all patriots, all forward-looking men" to help him. Nieman answered the call. The Journal was also to stand by the President in the difficult years before America's entry into World War I when alienism was rife in Milwaukee, and pro-Germanism was an ever-present menace.

Wilson's "progressive" measures which he had promised during the campaign were passed in a long session of Congress, summoned three days after the inauguration. They included: (1) a new tariff law which dealt a heavy blow to monopoly; (2) the Federal Reserve Act which set up a banking system to serve all the country and broke up New York's control of the nation's money; (3) an income tax law, founded on the principle of ability to pay, which changed the direction of America's taxing power, and which was based on the newly ratified Sixteenth Amendment; (4) an amendment to the antitrust laws that closed a gap through which monopolies, by first lowering and then raising prices, had been able to drive small competitors out of the market.

In the fight for these reforms The Journal gave the President solid support. Nieman and Assistant Editor Campbell carried on an extensive personal correspondence with Wilson. The reform movement was just getting momentum, however, when it was interrupted by war in Europe. Archduke Francis Ferdinand of Austria was assassinated June 28, 1914, and thirty-eight days later war broke out. The Central Powers of Germany and Austria were arrayed against the Allies of France, England, Russia, Serbia, and Belgium. Woodrow Wilson was faced with problems no President had known since Abraham Lincoln. Anxious to keep the United States out of the war, he appealed to the American people to remain "neutral in fact as well as in name during these days that are to try men's souls."

Britain's control of the seas enabled the Allies to buy war supplies from neutral America. Germany naturally sought to stop this trade, and German sympathizers and propagandists in the United States urged Congress to put an embargo on munition sales. The President vigorously denounced such an embargo and it failed to pass. Germany then ordered a submarine blockade in which ships were to be sunk without warning, even though citizens of neutral countries might be aboard. Wilson warned Germany that such an illegal blockade might have "regrettable consequences." The Journal supported the President. It also backed him when he warned Britain that she was violating the trade rights of neutrals by bringing foreign ships into English ports and searching them for food supplies that eventually might reach Germany. A Journal editorial said:

Now the war is the concern of the nations involved; our neutrality is our concern. Call it strict, rigid, frigid, or any other name which means that as a nation we are not taking sides one way or the other, you cannot make it too strong to suit us. The contending nations are our friends, and for us the only proper policy, the only safe course to pursue, is to be as neutral as possible. This, we believe, is President Wilson's sincere desire and purpose, and in his efforts to play fair and to preserve our peace he deserves the earnest support of all citizens who think first of America.

On May 7, 1915, a German submarine sank the British liner *Lusitania* with loss of more than 1,200 lives. At least 100 of the dead were Americans. A wave of condemnation of Germany swept the United States and there was talk of entering the war.

The Journal urged calmness and support of the President, whose note of protest to Germany asked for official disavowal of the submarine commander's act, and for assurance that there would be no repetition. No ultimatum was issued.

Germany gave an evasive answer to which Wilson replied: "America stands for freedom of the seas without curtailment and will contend for that freedom, from whatever quarter violated, without compromise and at any cost." Screams of protest went up from German sympathizers in the United States. The German-language newspapers, as well as the pro-German papers which were printed in English and the German-American National Alliance echoed the same opinion. They justified the sinking of the *Lusitania* and approved Germany's unrestricted submarine warfare.

The Journal saw German propaganda in these reactions. To combat it, Nieman and Campbell prepared for the greatest battle of their lives. Their task would be, first, to examine closely pro-German newspapers, whether in German or English, and, second, to explain to German-Americans that the goose-stepping Prussianism of Kaiser Wilhelm II had destroyed the kindly, peaceful fatherland which they remembered.

F. Perry Olds, a Harvard graduate and student of languages, who had joined the staff in November, 1915, was put to work translating German newspapers, and in a few months he gleaned some startling information. On October 14, 1916, the first fully documented exposure appeared. Entitled "Disloyalty Flaunted in the Face of Milwaukee," an article nine columns long cited the record of the Milwaukee *Germania-Herold* during the two years when America was trying to be neutral. The Journal article concluded:

1. Day in and day out the Germania-Herold has preached division along the lines of race and war prejudices.
2. Day in and day out it has endeavored to weld voters of German descent into a powerful political weapon to be used against the government of the United States at the dictation of the German-American National alliance and other representatives of Germany here.
3. It has virtually without exception opposed the government of the

87

United States in every step that President Wilson has taken to protect American sovereignty and the rights of American citizens against the aggressions of Germany.

This article hit Milwaukee like a bombshell. Not in all the years since people of German birth and descent had become dominant in the city, had anyone dared to challenge the German-language newspapers. The Journal was denounced as "the tool of the Allies"; it had "sold out to Lord Northcliffe of England." Threats of reprisals and boycott were heard.* The Journal answered that it was not challenging the loyalty of a great body of citizens of German descent. It was condemning the propagandists who were trying to mislead these people.

The most aggressive of the pro-German newspapers in Milwaukee was not published in German. It was the Milwaukee *Free Press,* founded in 1901 as a political organ to help Robert M. La Follette. Later it was controlled by Isaac Stephenson, the lavish political spender, when he won the senatorship. Stephenson retired from politics in 1915 and sold the newspaper to a group of prominent Milwaukeeans, who were mostly of German descent. Ernst Kronshage, brother of the original founder, Theodore, was made editor, with a contract provision that he could be removed only by two-thirds vote of the directors.

The *Free Press* was a strident voice for Germany. In the submarine controversy it ridiculed America and President Wilson, and praised the Central Powers; it wanted an embargo on arms shipments; it blamed America for the *Lusitania* sinking; it attacked the United States for not forbidding a loan to the Allies, although Germany had floated a loan in this country a little while before; it charged that the administration had been "soft" to England. One editorial included the following: "English ruled and English led? If that were only all. But to be English bilked and English booted, and with a president to invite a repetition

* Despite threats against The Journal and sporadic efforts to boycott it, during this period and later, daily circulation climbed to 112,000 in 1917, and to 119,000 in 1918. It fell to 101,000 in 1919, but rose steadily thereafter. Company earnings for 1917 dropped to $65,000, from the $100,000 total of 1916; but in 1918, as the exposure of pro-Germanism continued, earnings shot up to $145,000.

with 'Thanks, awfully!' is to reduce the United States to something infinitely worse than an American colony before the Revolution."

Word of this pro-German stand by the *Free Press* of Milwaukee spread over the country. Before long Wisconsin was being called a "province of Germany." However The Journal's scathing denunciation of the entire pro-German press, together with Journal translations each day which exposed the exact content of these papers, told the world that there was also a loyal American element in Milwaukee.

The Journal's next objective was to bring out into the open the German-American National Alliance. This organization, which had been chartered by Congress for purely cultural purposes, was conducting an intensive campaign to swing Wisconsin German communities over to Germany's support, even to ensnare ministers and churches. The Journal exposed facts that eventually led to congressional cancellation of the Alliance's charter.

Investigation of the teaching of German in Milwaukee schools was started by the school principals' association. Professor Leo Stern, assistant superintendent of schools in charge of the teaching of German, was also head of the Wisconsin branch of the German-American National Alliance. An inquiry disclosed that the teaching of German in the public grade schools, begun many years before as an aid to immigrant families, had become a vehicle to bring up the child of German blood to be German-minded instead of American-minded. Study of German was begun in the first grade and was continued through the eighth. Much less emphasis was placed on English, with the result that many graduates were woefully deficient in the language of the nation.

Disclosures of this survey caused The Journal to make one of the few reversals in its history. In 1890 the paper had fought for repeal of the Bennett law, a statute which required all schools in Wisconsin to teach the basic subjects in English. The law was taken off the books after an emotional political campaign, in which The Journal, siding with the Germans, argued that parents had a right to decide how their children should be educated and what subjects should be taught. It thought then that home influence would complete the Americanization of school children and that no special effort was needed in schools.

Now, twenty-six years later, the paper reversed itself and summed up the situation in these words: "The teaching of German in the public schools of America has not only seriously retarded the process of Americanization, but it has been used to induce worship of Germany, even of kaiserism, and to deprive America of the love of many of her native and adopted children."*

The paper joined with the school principals' association and with the civic organizations in the fight, which succeeded, after several months, in having foreign language instruction removed from all grade schools. In explaining this move to Americans of German origin The Journal pointed out that the German-language press in America had changed from the days of Carl Schurz. In the earlier period it had the commendable objective of interpreting America to the immigrant. But now the objective was to keep Germanism alive in the descendants of immigrants. The staffs of most German-language newspapers were heavy with aliens. A survey showed that of the twenty-eight editorial employes of two Milwaukee German-language dailies (one morning and one afternoon), thirteen were aliens.

In the fight against pro-Germanism, Paul O. Husting, junior United States senator from Wisconsin, was a vigorous force. On one occasion, after he had made a strong speech denouncing the German-American National Alliance, he answered a question about the effect of such talk on his political career: "I am not asking anyone about my political future. All I want to know is if this is the right thing for an American citizen to say, and if this is the right time. I don't see how being for my country can hurt my political future, but if it can, and if we are all mad, then I don't see that my political future is worth very much anyhow."

* In November, 1919, Assistant Editor Campbell wrote in The Journal: "Recent events have clearly demonstrated that the repeal of the Bennett law was a grievous error from the standpoint of public policy." This was on the occasion of the death of William Dempster Hoard, the Wisconsin governor who had gone down to defeat in 1890 in defense of the Bennett law.

In contrast to Husting, Senator La Follette, who was an isolationist and not sympathetic to the Allies, soon fell in with many of the arguments of the German propagandists and became in effect if not in intent a supporter of Germany. La Follette's record included these stands: (1) for an embargo on arms, although that could only be an act partial to Germany; (2) for a Senate resolution which entailed the surrender of rights of Americans at sea, by bowing to German demands; (3) against a resolution expressing confidence in President Wilson at a time when our relations with Germany were so critical that the administration needed undivided support; (4) for a resolution which he introduced to forbid the arming of American ships endangered by the German submarine campaign.

Finally, La Follette aroused national resentment with an antiwar speech made in St. Paul, Minnesota, on September 20, 1917, five months after America had entered the war.* The break between The Journal and La Follette which occurred at this time was permanent. Not ever again did the paper support this man whom it had often aided when, in his younger days, he was fighting for the development of American democracy.

The German submarine campaign was slowed down by Wilson's firmness in the *Lusitania* sinking. But German agents in America carried on another kind of war. Factories had unexplained fires; bridges were dynamited. Ambassador Dumba of Austria was handed his passport when caught trying to promote strikes in American munitions plants. The continuing trouble the United States was having with Mexico was to some extent German-inspired.

After the French victory at Verdun in November, 1916, Germany saw that her one chance of winning the war was to shut off

---

* In the portion of La Follette's St. Paul speech which brought accusations of disloyalty and sparked a movement to expel him from the Senate, he was quoted as saying, "We had no grievances against Germany." In May, 1918, eight months later, the Associated Press acknowledged that its correspondent had erred and that the stenographic report of the disputed passage read: "I don't mean to say we hadn't suffered grievances; we had." A Senate investigation of La Follette's conduct was dropped shortly after the war ended.

all American-made supplies to the Allies. This meant resumption of unrestricted submarine warfare. On February 1, 1917, Wilson handed the German ambassador, Count von Bernstorff, his passport. As the sinking of American ships continued, Congress was called into special session, and on April 2, 1917, President Wilson delivered his war message:

With a profound sense of the solemn and even tragical character of the step I am taking and of the grave responsibilities which it involves, but in unhesitating obedience to what I deem my constitutional duty, I advise that the congress declare the recent course of the imperial German government to be in fact nothing less than war against the government and people of the United States; that it formally accept the status of belligerent which has been thrust upon it and that it take immediate steps not only to put the country into a more thorough state of defense but also to exert all of its power and employ all its resources to bring the government of the German empire to terms and end the war.

The Senate passed the war resolution on April 5; the House, on April 6. In the Senate, among six adverse votes was that of La Follette. In the House, nine Wisconsin representatives were among the fifty who voted against the declaration. This was a higher percentage of "No" votes than that from any other state. Only three Wisconsin members of Congress supported Wilson—Senator Husting and Representatives Irvine L. Lenroot and David G. Classon.

Because of the majority action of the Wisconsin delegation, some eastern magazines charged that the state had been won over wholly to pro-Germanism. The Journal replied in a blistering editorial which pointed to the thousands of loyal Americans in the state, including many citizens of German blood. It predicted that in the great test ahead Wisconsin would write a record for America second to that of no other state. It continued:

We go to war in defense of America, but we go to war also in defense of all human liberty, of the right of men everywhere to be free in their persons and in their lives. We fight against the principle that might alone gives right. We fight against the effort of a great and marvelously efficient nation to make armed force the only strength of any nation and military service the first business of every man. For that is the plain meaning of Germany's war on the world.

16

Wisconsin Stands the War Test

When America entered the war, pro-German leaders and pro-German newspapers were quick to declare their loyalty. Ridicule of American officials and the American way of life disappeared. Open support of Germany ceased; instead, a subtle approach was used. Doubt was raised as to whether we needed selective draft service. Wouldn't a volunteer system do? Was it necessary to float immense war loans? Did we need to pass restrictive wartime laws? As for our allies, hadn't we better watch them as closely as we did the enemy? Radicals among the Socialists of Milwaukee spoke out in opposition to "imperialistic war." In the Wisconsin legislature an attempt was made to put the state on record for something less than all-out support of a campaign against Germany. In the United States Senate, when the selective service draft bill came up, Senator La Follette proposed a national referendum. This would have delayed for many months the creation of an effective army.

The Journal, meanwhile, called for a vigorous prosecution of the war. An editorial on April 16, 1917, said characteristically: "This is a war of the whole nation. We are fighting for the things in which we believe and for nothing that is unjust or hurtful to any people. Because we make war in such a cause, there is a place for every American to fill."

The Journal undertook an even more intensive study of German-language newspapers to detect the new type of propaganda.

Hundreds of passages were translated and reprinted in articles which explained their significance. Many of these articles were reproduced in other newspapers. Translator Olds worked twelve to fourteen hours a day. Pointing out the technique for creating dissension, one editorial said: "They [the German propagandists] do not advise it, they do not condemn it. They simply predict it. They keep it eternally before the minds of their readers, encouraging them by repetition of their predictions to open rebellion against our authorities."

Exposure of such propaganda was, of course, the best safeguard against its effectiveness. The great majority of Milwaukeeans were not fooled by it. In the military draft the registration was as orderly and successful as anywhere in the nation. In the first Liberty Loan campaign Milwaukee's quota was $14 million; the subscriptions for bond purchases totaled $18 million. The Milwaukee County Red Cross campaign was equally successful.

"The result is new proof to the nation that the heart of Milwaukee is loyal and patriotic," The Journal commented. "There is disloyalty here, there is hostility to the nation, its cause and its government, and there has been and still is a tireless and determined effort inimical to America, but it has not made the progress for which those behind it had hoped. . . . It has been fought, it has been exposed to public gaze, and for the time at least it stands baffled and defeated."

But the battle was far from won. When Senator La Follette announced that he would work for repeal of the draft law, a front-page editorial said: "It is time for loyal people to organize." Out of this suggestion grew the Wisconsin Loyalty Legion. Under such men as Walter S. Goodland, Wheeler P. Bloodgood, Judson G. Rosebush, W. A. Hayes, and Morris F. Fox, it was to do effective work in combatting the propagandists.

The situation in Milwaukee was complicated by the pacifistic ideas held by Socialists. Many of the party's top men, including German-born Victor Berger, who was editor of the Socialist daily newspaper, the Milwaukee *Leader,* were pledged to the 1917 party platform adopted at St. Louis shortly after we entered the war.

The platform condemned "the war of the United States against Germany . . . as a crime against the people . . . and against the nations of the world," and further recommended "unyielding opposition to all proposed legislation for military or industrial conscription." It pledged "continuous, active and public opposition to the war through demonstrations, mass petitions and all other means within our power."

When Milwaukee's Socialist mayor, Daniel W. Hoan, elected in 1916, opposed the Socialist party's stand and performed well his mayoralty duties required by the war, Berger turned on him in an editorial in the *Leader* on December 28, 1917:

> Of all times this is the poorest time to hedge, to wobble or to try "a seat on the fence" when a question of vital principle is asked—for instance, a question about the St. Louis platform.
>
> Any man who cannot stand on that platform, any man who cannot accept our (Socialist) international position—be that man a mayor or a constable—must get out of the party in justice to himself and the party.

In speeches and in editorials in the *Leader,* Berger clung steadfastly to the Socialists' St. Louis platform, but when he was on trial in Chicago on a federal charge of conspiracy to violate the espionage act, he testified that he had done nothing to obstruct government efforts to win the war. The Journal called this testimony "brazen, impudent effrontery." "The case makes it very plain," an editorial on February 21, 1919, read, "that the right of free speech does not protect abuse of the right of free speech. It carries the lesson, too, that citizens owe some obligation to the nation and that it is the right as well as the duty of the nation to protect itself against words and deeds that menace its very existence." Berger was convicted and sentenced to twenty years' imprisonment, but the appellate court in 1921 reversed the sentence.

In 1917 an attempt had been made at a meeting in Milwaukee to found a "People's Council of America," a movement part Socialist and part German, which advocated a quick peace with the Kaiser. The Journal, publishing the full story of this maneuver, pointed out editorially that such an organization held great danger of interference with America's war effort. This exposure stopped Milwaukee's organizing campaign and aroused other cities and states against similar attempts. More German sympathizers organized under the names of the American Embargo Conference, the American Independence Union, the Teutonic Sons of America, the Friends of Peace, and the American Truth Society.

In the summer of 1917 a Journal reporter, touring the state to sample public opinion, found a number of Wisconsin newspapers thoroughly aroused to the dangers of pro-Germanism and speaking out vigorously for a united prosecution of the war. By the close of the year there were definite signs that the pro-German campaign had passed its crest and was beginning to recede. One factor in this awakening had been the Journal coverage of all phases of the European situation. The leased wire services of the *New York Times* and the New York *World* which had been used in the Sunday Journal were extended to the daily issues, and the foreign service of the New York *Sun* was purchased.

James W. Gerard's significant book, *My Four Years in Germany,* in which the former ambassador to Berlin told what he had learned at first hand of the Kaiser's plots against the peace of the world, was published serially by The Journal. Another book serialized was *The Tragedy of Belgium,* by Hugh Gibson, former ambassador to Brussels, telling the cruel story of the German invasion of that neutral country. This full coverage proved to be the best possible answer to the whispering campaigns.

In March, 1918, the Wisconsin legislature officially censured Senator La Follette for his record on the issues of the war. Passage of that resolution, marking another milestone in consolidation of the state's loyalty, would not have been possible a year earlier. The third Liberty Loan campaign in April was an even greater success than previous ones. Soon after, a rather amazing thing happened. The *Germania-Herold,* which had so long been in the forefront of the pro-German movement, admitted Germany's war guilt on the basis of documents released by the American State Department. The most persuasive of these disclosures was the memorandum written by Prince Lichnowsky while he was German ambassador to London, 1912–14. His notes showed conclusively that the Kaiser had plotted the war and forced its coming. Toward the end of May, The Journal, in commenting on the changing situation, said:

We judge from the cheering reports that come from all parts of Wisconsin that the end of Deutschum's power in the United States is in plain sight. It invited its own destruction when it showed its ignoble, treacherous purpose. . . . Before long Germanism in America will be dead—trunk, roots and branches—and with it, let us fervently hope, as we have good reason to hope, alienism in any and every form will pass away forever.

As the tide turned in Wisconsin, the state began to get words of praise in the nation's press. The Des Moines *Capital,* commenting on the fight, said:

The people of the nation must remember the loyal men in Wisconsin. No men in the trenches ever fought with more courage than they. . . . The Milwaukee Journal, in season and out, without apology stood by President Wilson and the United States of America. The Journal neither looked to the right nor to the left, but drove bravely ahead, and Wisconsin, so far as positive returns show, has been redeemed.

The Louisville *Evening Post* said:

All citizens will admire the fortitude and the determination of the great loyal element in Wisconsin which has had to face and overcome a situation more serious than that which the citizens of any other state have had to meet.

The Pittsburgh *Chronicle-Telegraph* said that Wisconsin had fought the attempt to lead it into disloyalty most courageously, thanks to The Milwaukee Journal.*

Then, with that perfect timing which a large swing of events sometimes provides, came the final loyalty test. Wisconsin's boys went under fire in France in the second Battle of the Marne. War dispatches with accounts of the valor and efficiency of the Thirty-second Division (made up of Wisconsin and Michigan contingents) stirred a glow of inner pride which swept the state to new heights. Many of the Wisconsin soldiers were sons of German immigrants. Some were from homes in which little English had been

* It was the fight against pro-Germanism and later the crusade for the League of Nations that "first attracted attention to The Journal" and "developed [its] international outlook," according to Edwin Emery and Henry Ladd Smith, *The Press and America* (New York: Prentice-Hall, 1954), p. 753.

spoken. They had parents who, remembering the kindly, enlightened Germany of old, found it hard to understand why their sons were fighting the Kaiser.

An insight into how these boys felt "over there" is provided by a letter from Claude Manly, a Milwaukee Journal reporter who had enlisted and then advanced to a captaincy in a machine gun battalion. Captain Manly, in answer to a question, wrote to George E. Ballhorn, a Milwaukee attorney: "Our friends in Milwaukee who are worried about German propaganda and what will happen after the war need have no fear. These men will vote as they fight—for America."

The Allied campaign of 1918 was difficult. The Communist revolution had taken Russia out of the war—Lenin and Trotsky had been smuggled into Petrograd with the aid of the Germans—and Russia's demobilization enabled the Kaiser to shift troops from the eastern front to Belgium and France. But even these reinforcements could not save Germany. The Kaiser now made a bid for a negotiated peace to avoid outright defeat. England, France, and America rejected the offer. The Journal supported the rejection, much to the annoyance of those small groups in Wisconsin that still sympathized with Germany.

Now that the end was in sight, Woodrow Wilson began to think of the future peace and of ways to avoid another such war. In a New York speech launching the fourth Liberty Loan drive, he proposed an international organization to be known as the League of Nations. The Journal endorsed the idea.

Because of the many problems that were sure to come up in Europe with the end of the war, the Allies agreed upon a plan to send abroad a group of American leaders of public opinion to study the situation at first hand. England offered to sponsor a tour by American educators and newspaper and magazine editors. Lucius Nieman was invited to be a member of the party; others were Ellery Sedgwick of the *Atlantic Monthly,* Dr. Albert Shaw of the *Review of Reviews,* Edward W. Bok of the *Ladies' Home Journal,* Charles H. Towne of *McClure's Magazine,* Dr. Edward I. Wheeler of *Current Opinion,* President Charles R. Van Hise of the University of Wisconsin, Duncan Clark of the Chicago *Eve-*

ning Post, F. W. Kellogg of the San Francisco *Call,* Alfred Holman of the San Francisco *Argonaut,* R. V. Oulahan of the *New York Times,* Mark Sullivan of *Collier's,* and James Thompson of the New Orleans *Item.*

The group visited England, France, and vital military spots on the western front. Its members talked with officials who were then trying to prepare a program to save western Europe from as many postwar troubles as possible. Nieman sent back a series of articles to The Journal. His most important conclusion—one which he tried hard to impress upon his readers—was that America's future was tied to Europe's future and that the United States could never safely return to its isolation.

By the time the editors got back home in late October, the end of the war was in sight. The German military situation was desperate; the Kaiser's throne was shaking; surrender might come any hour. Due to a misunderstanding of signals, the United Press on the morning of November 7 reported an armistice had been signed. Three Milwaukee papers put out extras announcing Germany had surrendered. Crowds gathered downtown. Factories and schools closed.

Meanwhile, The Journal, relying on the Associated Press, refused to report that the war was over until it had official confirmation. In the city's delirium of celebration, The Journal was roundly abused. It was charged with wanting to prolong the war "for the benefit of England." Insulting messages came over the telephone; reporters on the street were threatened. Toward the close of a day the staff would long remember, the paper was able to publish an official announcement from Washington that no armistice had been concluded. A conference with the German armistice delegation had been scheduled but no meeting had yet been held. The Journal promised its readers that when an armistice had been signed it would issue an extra, day or night.

The opportunity came early on the morning of November 11. It was still dark in Milwaukee when Journal newsboys came on the street crying, "Extra! Extra!" Soon whistles were blowing and church bells ringing. On that Armistice Day, 227,000 papers were sold, the highest circulation The Journal had ever had. The denunciations of four days earlier had given way to praise. The paper had enhanced its reputation for reliability.

On June 2, 1919, The Journal received the Pulitzer award for meritorious service, the highest honor in American journalism. Melville E. Stone, general manager of the Associated Press, who was on the Pulitzer committee, said in his summary:

The Milwaukee Journal was one of the first newspapers of the United States to recognize the absolutely uncivilized methods employed by the German government in conducting its war against civilization. It was the first newspaper of the country to employ an editor for the sole purpose of following German propaganda. . . .

In its editorials, from the very beginning of the war, it has followed an absolutely and unswervingly American attitude. In a city where the German element had long prided itself in its preponderating influence, The Journal courageously attacked such members of that element as put Germany above America.

It is estimated that The Journal printed, from November, 1915, to November, 1917, no less than 750,000 words not printed by any other newspaper in the United States. Some of the most important exclusive stories were sent out in proof to all the great newspapers of the country, and to members of congress and other influential Americans.

The Journal in its own editorial on the award said:

The situation in this country and here in Milwaukee and Wisconsin grew out of the exceeding boldness and insolence of men who put Germany before everything else in the world, and the stunned silence of men who did not think as they did. . . . With the outbreak of the war in Europe, the German propagandists made so much noise, they claimed such numbers, they threatened with such insolent confidence, that men were deceived with regard to their real strength. . . .

As the voice of a community and commonwealth, our duty was plain. No thought of courage came to us. A fight was forced on us and we had but the alternative of sinking into contempt. . . .

Your continued support said to all: "These are the things the real people of Wisconsin believe."

The Thirty-second Division returned to Milwaukee on June 6, 1919, to receive the acclaim of the city and the state. Led by Major General William G. Hahn, their commander on European battlefields, the soldiers marched down old Grand Avenue twenty abreast, with battle flags flying. A squadron of war planes, with engines throttled to the lowest possible speed, moved overhead toward the lake. It was a scene not to be forgotten, especially by those who knew what might have happened if the forces opposing the war effort had not been broken.

Perhaps up there in the blue of that June day, there also flew another squadron, outward bound—the ghosts of alienism, leaving Wisconsin forever.

17

Reaction, Isolationism, and Communism

Woodrow Wilson returned from Europe in July, 1919, bearing the Treaty of Versailles, which included the provisions for peace with Germany and the charter of the League of Nations. Wilson found the country war-weary and, to a great extent, disillusioned over involvement with foreign countries. The isolationist feeling was strong. In Wisconsin this movement was particularly active. Robert M. La Follette, who had opposed entry into the war from the beginning, was still United States senator, and the governor was E. L. Philipp, isolationist leader of the Stalwart Republicans. Wisconsin, like all the Middle West, wanted to crawl back into its shell.

Again The Journal assumed an unpopular role. In editorials it supported the League of Nations. It also published articles by Frank Simonds, one of the ablest writers produced by the war, and by William Howard Taft, former President, both of whom sought to show the need for the League. In September, Woodrow Wilson set out to carry his appeal for a peace treaty and for the League to the people. In three weeks he made forty speeches, and then collapsed. His physician, Admiral Cary T. Grayson, ordered him home and to bed.

The Journal redoubled its efforts for peace and the League. To show how one country with an unbridled leader could plunge the world into war, it ran serially several accounts by high-ranking Germans—Admiral von Tirpitz, General Ludendorff, and Count von Bernstorff. Von Bernstorff, who had been ambassador to Washington, exposed German propaganda in the United States. At the same time articles by Cardinal Mercier appeared, describing Germany's ruthlessness in Belgium.

Peace and the League were not the only vital issues in 1919, however. Another problem Americans were worrying over was the threat of communism. As a glance over the 1919 files of the paper will show, The Journal was very early concerned with Communist efforts to undermine labor unions, by infiltrating their ranks and by openly calling all workers to unite for world revolution.

On May Day, 1919, there were riots in American streets, the Communists and the radical Industrial Workers of the World standing side by side. Then in July, race riots over Negro housing broke out in Chicago. Postwar living costs had shot up, and a wave of strikes hit the United States, involving railroads, docks, automobile plants, and other vital industries. The Communists tried to seize control of unions but were defeated by a movement led by Samuel Gompers, head of the American Federation of Labor.

The Communist party met in Chicago in September and adopted a revolutionary manifesto. The Journal printed the text of the manifesto, which included the following excerpts:

The class war rages fiercely in all nations. Everywhere the workers are in a desperate struggle against their capitalist masters. . . . The Communist party of America is the party of the working class. The Communist party proposes to end capitalism and organize a workers' industrial republic. . . . The war is at an end but peace is not here. The struggle is between the capitalist nations of the world and the international proletariat, inspired by Soviet Russia.

The Journal said editorially that the aim of the Communist party was to convert strikes into revolutionary movements "which are equally a revolt against the bureaucracy of the unions and the capitalists. . . . The objective is the conquest by the proletariat of the power of the state. Communism does not propose to 'capture' the bourgeois parliamentary state but to conquer and destroy it."

The Chicago Communist manifesto was based on the Moscow manifesto of a few months before, signed by Lenin and Trotsky, and calling for a world revolution—which in the 1950's was to become "the cold war." From his sickbed Woodrow Wilson directed the Department of Justice to take action. More than 2,000 aliens were arrested and many of them deported. Commenting on these developments, The Journal stated its position on the immigrant problem in these words:

Work to combat agitation which threatens American institutions is needed. Violent radicalism constitutes a danger. . . . Many times during many years The Journal has emphasized the urgent necessity of taking in hand the newcomer to our shores and teaching and training him for the duties of citizenship. When he arrives he is a stranger, as a rule, to our language and institutions. He works. He is commonly regarded merely as a worker and not as a potential citizen. Nobody pays attention to his welfare or to the nation's interests so far as he is a factor in them. Those who do show an interest in his intellectual capacity are the agitators, and too often he becomes the prey of those who preach doctrines of discontent, of disorder, even of revolution.

The paper also reiterated its stand that with Communists bent on world revolution, the freedom-loving countries should band together in the League of Nations. But America's isolationists, working together in the Senate and led by Senator Henry Cabot Lodge, loaded the League charter with crippling amendments. Wilson said that "twelve willful men," of whom La Follette was one, had "cut the heart out of it." The charter was defeated in the Senate on November 20, by its own adherents, who would not accept the isolationists' shackles. The Journal commented: "Have they [the isolationist senators] listened to the voice of the country? They have not. They have listened, instead, to partisan counsels, with a weather eye for the votes of the pro-Germans, pro-anything but pro-America. They have missed the spirit and conscience of the American people."

President Wilson again submitted the League charter, and on March 20, 1920, it was again defeated in the Senate. The question was thus thrown into the presidential election. A measure of The Journal's concern for the fate of the League in the coming election was its action in sending eleven Wisconsin school teachers to Europe during the summer. The teachers toured the Continent, with all expenses paid, to observe conditions resulting from the war and to try to understand why America should take part in the councils of the world. When they returned they met with other teachers and led discussions on what they had learned from their travels.

At the Republican national convention, which opened June 6 in Chicago, The Journal had the largest group of contributors it had ever had at a convention. Besides its own staff members, Henry C. Campbell and J. C. Ralston, the list included: David Lawrence, noted Washington correspondent, Frederick William Wile, veteran writer on international subjects, Louis Seibold, Charles Michelson, Robert T. Barry, John J. Leary, Jr., Dorothy Dix, William Howard Taft, Ring Lardner, and Will Rogers. Artists to make sketches and cartoons included Robert Leroy, Robert "Believe-It-Or-Not" Ripley, and J. N. (Ding) Darling.

Of the platform provision dealing with the League, Campbell wrote:

> The Republican plank on the League of Nations is the result of cheap politics, alien influence and fear incredible. It is the final proof of the utter lack of courage and statesmanship in the Republican national convention. In saying this, one need not imply or feel sure that the Democratic national convention will take its stand on higher ground. American politics seems to be at a low ebb.

Senator Warren G. Harding, of Ohio, was the Republican nominee, and Governor Calvin Coolidge, of Massachusetts, was his running mate.

The Democrats, in convention in San Francisco, nominated Governor James M. Cox, of Ohio, and the young governor of New York, Franklin D. Roosevelt. The Journal praised both Democratic nominees and on September 19 printed a full page on the League of Nations. It contained the League charter; the Senate ratification resolution, with all the crippling amendments that were added to it before it was voted down; the Democratic plank which declared for ratification without reservations; the Republican plank which declared for rejection of the League covenant but said the Republicans were for "agreement among the nations to preserve the peace of the world" and would work for a new association of nations that would not compromise our independence. An editorial the day before election said:

Tomorrow every voter who goes to the polls will be called upon to pass upon the greatest moral issue that has arisen in our public life since the fate of human slavery was settled once and for all. The high purpose of the League of Nations covenant is to do everything possible to make war impossible—to prevent war and the sorrow, the suffering and the destruction of life and property which war causes.

In the election Harding and Coolidge were winners in an isolationist landslide which carried control of Congress and most of the state governments, including that of Wisconsin.

18

Harry Johnston Grant

The coming of Harry J. Grant to The Journal was eventually to mean ownership in the paper for all employes from the lowliest to the highest. Grant's own life is a story of scant means to riches. He was born in 1881 in Chillicothe, Missouri, the son of Ida Belle and Benjamin Thomas Grant. The family was moderately prosperous until the father died. Then the mother earned their livelihood as a dance teacher in St. Louis, and young Harry was forced to go to work after his freshman year in high school. His first job paid him five dollars a week.

Harry spent six years working for railroads and in stockyards, saving what money he could and tutoring himself in school studies at night. When he was twenty-two years old he was admitted to Harvard University as a special student, taking seven courses where four were the normal load. His money gone, he left Harvard but returned in 1905 for another year. To supplement his earnings he sold advertising for college papers and other publications reaching the students.

After this second year at Harvard, Grant went to New York to work for N. W. Ayer and Son, advertising agents. There he made contacts which took him to London in 1909 as European representative of the Rubberset Brush Company and the Celluloid Harness Trimming Company. It was while abroad that he met Dorothy Glyde Cook of Pittsburgh, whom he married in London in 1910.* Shortly after his marriage Grant was offered a job as manager of the American Viscose Company, manufacturer of the newly developed product, rayon. The couple returned to this country and Grant supervised the firm's first American rayon plant, which was in Pennsylvania.

The company prospered, but Grant's interest was in advertising and publishing. In 1913 he went to New York as vice president of the firm of O'Mara and Ormsbee, newspaper representatives in the national advertising field. He soon was made manager of the Chicago branch, and there one of his clients was The Milwaukee Journal.

In the meantime, Editor Nieman became ill. During the war years he worked twelve to sixteen hours a day and neglected the program of relaxation and physical exercise he had once set for himself. Nieman was still a handsome figure, in his well-tailored clothes and broad-brimmed black hat, the air of distinction accented by a black ribbon leading from his pince-nez to his coat lapel. But his ability to give dynamic leadership to The Journal was waning.

In 1914, L. T. Boyd, publisher of The Journal, was killed in an automobile accident. To fill the vacancy Nieman set up an office committee consisting of E. A. Belda, secretary; Paul C. Treviranus, business manager; and Herman Black, advertising manager. This committee was able to keep just one jump ahead of its difficulties. War circulation taxed the capacity of the presses and threatened to outrun newsprint supply. Publishing costs rose sharply as circulation boomed. On April 10, 1915, The Journal hoisted its "Over 100,000 Circulation" pennant on its flagpole. It was a Saturday, a busy day, with the Sunday paper coming up, but every machine was stopped, and every employe was present at the flag-raising ceremony. Then in 1916 the business committee lost Herman Black to the Chicago *Evening American*. Into this situation one day strode Harry J. Grant.

Employes of The Journal still smile when they recall Grant's progress down a corridor of the building on a mission to see some-

---

* Mrs. Grant died in 1923; the only child of the marriage, Barbara Anne, was married in 1936 to Donald B. Abert, a member of the Journal promotion staff.

one. Every muscle of his body was brought into the act and his coattails were flapping. Unconscious of his haste and oblivious of the impression he gave, he was out to get some result in a hurry and he usually succeeded.

Before Grant entered Nieman's office that June day in 1916, he was already known to the older man and admired for his ability and his vitality. Nieman had asked Grant to become advertising manager of The Journal. Upon taking the position Grant remarked that he intended to learn every phase of the newspaper business. It might take him five years, but it was his goal.

He soon began correcting flaws in the advertising department. Finding that the rates varied widely, he announced a schedule of uniform charges for all. Those who had been favored in the past groaned, but they soon complied. Some merchants previously had been allowed favored positions for their advertisements in the paper. "Hereafter," said Grant, "we will rotate the position of ads so as to be fair to all, but no advertiser will dictate his position."

A number of merchants refused to advertise in the Sunday Journal. When it had begun coming out, in 1911, the two newspapers already in the field had implanted in the minds of some merchants the idea that they should not be expected to support a third Sunday paper. In time Grant was able to dispel this notion and win over the merchants—all but one. "All right," said Grant to the recalcitrant one, "you will either end your boycott of the Sunday Journal or you will be barred from the daily, beginning right now." The advertiser fell in line. As a result of Grant's management, the advertising volume of The Journal grew, notwithstanding restrictions imposed by the war.

At the end of 1918, Paul Treviranus resigned to take a position with the Des Moines *Register and Tribune,* and Grant became publisher of The Journal. Soon after, he bought one-fifth of The Journal Company stock, from Judge J. E. Dodge and from George P. Miller, The Journal's legal adviser. In 1919, Grant's responsibilities were increased when Nieman suffered a breakdown so serious that it threatened his life. During the three years he had been with the paper, Grant had become thoroughly grounded in Nieman's policies—that the paper would have no outside ties, financial, political, or organizational; that it would cover news of the world, but would remain always a community newspaper, anticipating the needs of Milwaukee and Wisconsin, and fighting abuses; that it would formulate its own editorial policies, without the services of syndicated columnists. Though Grant's background had been in advertising he impressed his fellow workers in the editorial department with his quick and thorough grasp of the broader over-all viewpoint.

Under Grant's direction The Journal had begun to make enough money to warrant staff expansion, better salaries, and additional mechanical equipment. To strengthen the business office, Grant hired Leslie A. Webster, in 1917, as assistant advertising manager. Webster had risen to assistant publisher in 1939 when he resigned. Leon W. Robinson, an industrial engineer who came to The Journal in 1921, modernized the accounting system and increased the efficiency of the production departments. He was vice president and treasurer when he retired in 1954. Harry Gwaltney joined the paper in 1918 and soon transformed classified advertising—of minor importance before his day—into a principal source of revenue. An experienced circulation manager, Ottokar von Fragstein, who had helped found the Audit Bureau of Circulations, joined The Journal in 1919, when Leonard Bowyer was promoted to business manager. As circulation manager, Bowyer had contributed to the dominance of The Journal in home deliveries in Milwaukee by arranging for the paper to have its own carriers, independent of other newspapers.

Grant had long been an admirer of the Kansas City *Star* for its honesty, its independence, its thorough news coverage; and feeling that The Journal needed a managing editor who would give a fresh approach to the news department, he offered the job to Marvin H Creager, feature editor of the *Star*. Creager came to The Journal in 1920 and remained thirty-four years, becoming president and editor when Grant resigned those positions in 1938. Creager's philosophy was that of Nieman: the paper must serve no special interests. He once said in a speech:

We like to think of our paper as attorney for the people. Private interests can provide themselves with able counsel to man their watch-

Sports fans in front of the Journal building about 1920 watching the blackboard posting of baseball scores.

In 1926 the first baseball game was broadcast in Wisconsin by Journal sports writer Sam Levy.

Nieman and Grant laid the cornerstone for the new million-dollar Journal building on April 12, 1924.

Editor Nieman pressed the button to start presses in the new building on State Street. Mrs. Nieman came in for the celebration.

The Journal building shortly after its completion in the fall of 1924.

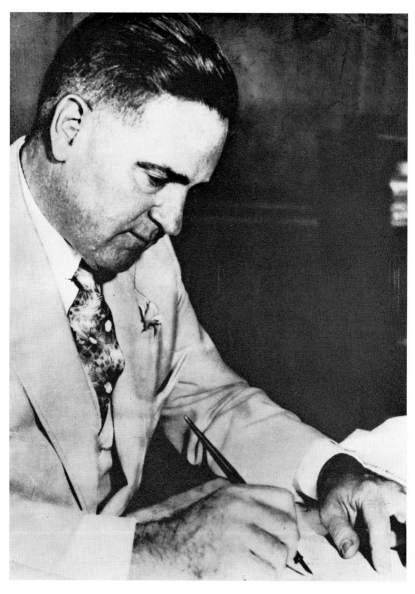

Harry Grant signing the National Recovery Act code in 1933. To increase jobs, mechanical departments of the paper and the radio station were at once put on a forty-hour week.

Sure, I'll Work for Both Sides

This cartoon by Ross A. Lewis of The Journal won the 1934 Pulitzer prize for cartoons.

Lucius William Nieman. Portrait by Carl von Marr.

Harry Johnston Grant. Portrait by Leopold Seiffert.

Marvin H Creager (*above*), president and editor, 1938–1943.

John Donald Ferguson (*left*), editor and president, 1943–1961.

Lindsay Hoben (*below*), vice president, succeeded Ferguson as editor in 1961.

owers. But the public business is everybody's business and what is everybody's business is too often left for George to do. Every community needs a disinterested newspaper on guard to sound the alert, with a plain statement of fact and its implications.

Creager was a strict advocate of separation of the editorial department from the business department. One reporter recalled a court case in which the judge reprimanded a south-side department store for prosecuting a shopgirl after she had been allowed to buy luxuries she could not pay for. The store's attorney warned the reporter not to print the story. "If you do, we'll cancel our Journal advertising," he said. The reporter turned in the story, with a note concerning the threat. Creager sent it back to the city editor with this memo: "Run as is. Page One. Must." The advertising was not cancelled, and word quickly spread that Journal news judgment could not be influenced by advertisers.

In this editorial freedom, Creager was vigorously supported by Grant, a man whose early training had been solely in business. Some outside observers have commented that this editorial dominance, in which the news department of the paper was entirely separated from the business office, was one thing that allowed The Journal to rise to the heights it later attained. There was the time, for instance, when an advertiser approached Grant with the suggestion that because of his $50,000 contract with The Journal the paper should print some favorable news on his product. "You mean the $50,000 contract you *had* with The Journal," said Grant. "Your contract is now cancelled."

In January, 1923, the deaths of Henry C. Campbell and J. J. Schindler, the mainstays of the editorial page, left The Journal in urgent need of editorial reinforcement. Grant sought the advice of Walter Williams, dean of journalism at the University of Missouri, who suggested the name of a former student, John Donald Ferguson. After graduating from the University of Missouri, Ferguson had worked for the Kansas City *Star* and later, when Grant approached him, was directing the editorial page of the Sioux City *Tribune*. He joined The Journal as an editorial writer in 1923. "Fergy" was well liked: he was kindly and understanding of his fellow workers, and he had a gift of lively intuition, which once enabled him to "scoop" the world on a presidential nomination.

It was while Ferguson was an editorial writer that Editor Nieman, still the adept political forecaster in spite of his failing health, sent him to New York in advance of the 1924 Democratic national convention with this instruction: "Get acquainted with John W. Davis. In a deadlocked convention Davis will likely be the compromise nominee." Ferguson called on Davis in his Wall Street office.

The convention, one of the longest on record, was tied up two weeks in the fight between Al Smith and William J. McAdoo; and sweltering delegates were running out of expense money. Ferguson each day asked Davis' headquarters at the Waldorf-Astoria about a possible break in the deadlock. On the morning of July 9, Davis' man said mysteriously: "Watch that side door." Ferguson did. Shortly afterwards, Davis stepped out of a cab, flanked by the managers of Smith and McAdoo.

"Congratulations, Mr. Davis," said Ferguson as they passed.

"Thank you," Davis replied. That was all.

The Milwaukee Journal that afternoon scooped the world in announcing that John W. Davis would be the Democratic candidate. The nomination took place that night, on the 103rd ballot.

Three years after coming to The Journal, Ferguson was made chief editorial writer. As head of the daily editorial conference in the next two decades he steered The Journal's course through the troublesome years of boom, panic, depression, the New Deal, recovery, and World War II. When failing health caused Creager to give up the presidency and editorship in 1943, Ferguson succeeded him. He retired January 1, 1961.

19

The Expanding Horizon

The decade following World War I saw a number of innovations in The Journal, both in the paper itself and in what went on behind the scenes. The daily editorial conference, so important in shaping the special character of The Journal, originated at this time. The editorial page feature took its place beside the editorials; women's features were greatly expanded; the "Green Sheet" was developed; sports coverage was enlarged; there were changes and improvements in the physical plant and in the mechanical department.

The daily editorial conference plan provided for a meeting of the editorial writers, the cartoonist, and often the editor of the paper, with the assistant managing editor sitting in as a go-between for news and editorial departments. Each editorial writer qualified as a specialist in one or more fields; none was asked to express an opinion that he did not believe in.

Editorials in The Journal have always been written by staff editorial men, the policy of the paper being to run no syndicated columnists. The principle behind this policy was the subject of a speech in 1951, before the American Society of Newspaper Editors, by J. Donald Ferguson, at that time The Journal's editor and president. The wide use by the press of syndicated columnists, Ferguson said, arose when newspapers in general had failed to predict Roosevelt's elections. Editors felt that they had lost the confidence of their readers and believed that by printing widely varying opinions, expressed by outside writers, they might more nearly satisfy the public. These syndicated opinions usually included the statement, "This newspaper assumes no responsibility for the views expressed in this article." Ferguson went on to say:

The editor soon found he not only had destroyed the character of his editorial page, but that the readers did hold him responsible for the gossipy and irresponsible columns. The columnists had taken over. No longer did subscribers say, "The Daily News says this," or "The Herald says that." It was "Pearson says" or "Lindley says" or "Pegler says." The editor had abdicated.

Ferguson cited the presidential election of Truman over Dewey when nearly every paper in the country, depending on the opinions of the "experts," predicted that Dewey would win.

They might not have been so sure if they had instead sent a dozen garden variety reporters from their staffs to barber shops, cross-road lunchrooms, baseball bleachers and factory eating spots to learn how the people with the most votes were going to mark their ballots. Even though it may sound sacrilegious to say it, we wouldn't trade one experienced reporter for all the syndicated columns that we could crowd into the editorial page of The Milwaukee Journal.

Marvin H Creager, as editor of The Journal, in 1939, told the American Society of Newspaper Editors, "A newspaper should have ideas of its own and express them without the help of syndicated writers who at the same time are expressing opinions for 50 to several hundred other newspapers over the country." When any event of great interest takes place, however, The Journal provides its readers with editorial comment from other newspapers. On these occasions a column or two of excerpts from editorials printed here or abroad is run.

In the same spirit of service to its readers, The Journal created the editorial page feature, which appeared alongside the two columns of editorials. This feature, usually written in the office, took its theme from some happening in the news—an obscure country that suddenly became a trouble spot, or an unknown person elevated to high position. In other instances, significant material in an important new book might be condensed to a thousand or so words by a staff writer. The accompanying illustration would be an appropriate line drawing, cartoon, or photograph, which, with the three- or four-column headline, gave the feature an attractive appearance.

This main feature supplanted some of the "exchange" material that had been used on the editorial page after Marvin Creager was appointed managing editor in 1920. Creager, coming from the Kansas City *Star*,* brought with him certain practices of that paper. The "exchange" material reprinted consisted of interesting excerpts from books, magazines, and other newspapers. The problem was, in the rapidly changing world, to find articles that were timely. Under Dale Wilson, who became feature and Sunday editor in 1926, exchange material gave way generally to staff-written articles, which in turn were widely reprinted by other newspapers and digest magazines. The Journal gave blanket permission to other papers to use these articles, the only condition being that they credit The Journal and the writer. Some of the names that became familiar to readers through circulation of these articles were Walter Monfried, Jessica Knowles, Frances Stover, Kirk Bates, Leslie Cross, Gerald Kloss, Alfred H. Pahlke, and E. C. Kiessling.

In 1921, "Betty Ann" was introduced to women readers of The Journal. When the paper was founded it was distinctly a man's publication. A home department was added in 1890, fashion news in 1900, and a spring fashion section in 1909; but it was not until twelve years later, when Elizabeth B. Moffett came to The Journal from the Kansas City *Star,* that distinctive progress was made in news of interest to women. Taking the pen name of "Betty Ann," Mrs. Moffett, accompanied by a sketch artist, visited Milwaukee's department stores and women's dress shops, looking for the new or unusual in women's apparel. When Betty Ann found an item of special interest, she asked permission to have it sketched. "What will this cost me?" was the invariable question of the store man-

* Two other staff additions of the early 1920's who came from the Kansas City *Star* were T. Murray Reed, who as city editor won staff loyalty by his vigorous backing of reporters, and Fred D. Moffett, who as Sunday editor made important improvements in the Sunday features.

ager, suspecting an advertising scheme. Betty Ann assured the manager that she and the artist were from the news department, and that the feature and sketches would cost nothing. No store names would be given, only a note telling the reader she might call or write Betty Ann to get the information. This personal service for the reader became an important feature in the paper.

Mrs. Moffett retired after five years, and Aileen Ryan, her assistant, took charge. Miss Ryan soon included furniture in the woman's page coverage, with Dorothy Dawe writing on that subject. So successful was Miss Dawe that when she died, in 1947, the Chicago Furniture Mart established in her honor the Dorothy Dawe Award, a golden cup trophy given each year to the newspaper or magazine that has done the best work in presenting furniture news.

In 1931, Miss Ryan went to the New York City apparel market, the first Midwest newspaper fashion editor to attend this buyers' convention. Soon she was going to New York twice a year with an assistant and two photographers, and the women's sections printed full pages, in color and in black and white, on their work.

Later there were many other features of particular interest to women. A weekly food section, making wide use of color printing, attracted nation-wide attention. Its director, Clarice Rowlands Nevada, has received awards from the Grocery Manufacturers of America, the American Dairy Association, and the American Meat Institute.

Another development of the 1920's was The Journal's "Green Sheet," a four-page daily supplement printed on green paper, which became a conversation-piece in Milwaukee. "Did you read that article in the Green Sheet?" was a question heard often when Milwaukeeans got together.

The first Green Sheet appeared as a two-page supplement in 1913, but ran only a year before it was dropped because of the war. The second came out in 1920 when Hearst's *Wisconsin News* was courting circulation through sensational stories. The Journal considered this second Green Sheet all right for street sales, but not suitable to be delivered to the home. The third Green Sheet, dating from 1927, was edited by Larry Lawrence, who was not one to abjure the sensational, but who preferred the more whole-some stories of everyday life. He had the knack of spotting the bright, the humorous, or the touching in little episodes of normal people. For more exotic tastes he included articles on such questions as "What is it like to be a pearl diver off an Australian reef?" or "How were the pyramids built?" He ran pictures and names of couples celebrating their golden wedding anniversaries, a reassuring antidote to the divorce stories appearing in the news columns.

The Green Sheet also carried the paper's daily serial, the comics, puzzles, word games, and the Ione Quinby Griggs column. This column was a brainchild of Lawrence, who gave this account of how it originated:

On a post not far from my desk was a loud speaker connected with the police circuit. I could hear the police desk man call the squad car and tell the officer to go to number so-and-so, street so-and-so. The desk man would add, "Family trouble—that's all."

I found myself repeating those words, "Family trouble—that's all." Then an idea struck me. There must be a story behind each of these assignments. From the frequency of the calls, there must be many personal and family problems.

I typed out a letter, presumably coming from a housewife, which told of a husband who was given to drink, who neglected his home and was suspected of playing around with other women. The housewife was inquiring what she should do. I handed the letter to Mrs. Griggs, who had come to us as a feature writer, and said "Answer that—tell her what to do."

Mrs. Griggs wrote out an answer which showed her ability to grasp and enter into other people's problems. We published the letter and the answer with an invitation to Green Sheet readers to write letters presenting their personal difficulties. The response was immediate and almost overwhelming. The Mrs. Griggs column was on its feet.

In the years that followed, Mrs. Griggs's work became known nationally, even internationally. It was the subject of articles in the *Saturday Evening Post, Pageant,* and *Coronet.* A Dutch publication carried an account of the Green Sheet column in an effort to promote similar activities in The Netherlands press.

The Green Sheet was now eminently suited to go into Milwaukee homes. In 1934, it was increased to four pages. During World

War II thousands of copies were mailed by relatives and friends to men in American camps and overseas. When The Journal discovered the extent of this practice, it added a weekly column of home news items written by Richard S. Davis, addressed to "Dear Joe."

Davis, a top writer on The Journal, was well qualified to give "Dear Joe" the assurance that his friends were thinking of him. He had been with The Journal since 1918, when he joined the staff as a reporter, after having first studied here and abroad as an opera singer. He soon was made drama and music critic. Then followed a long career of special writing on many subjects—political campaigns, prize fights, European travel, and human interest stories wherever they turned up. So good was his work that when he retired The Journal published a book of his selected writing, *The Best of Davis*. One item included was an editorial, of March 28, 1944, about Marian Anderson, written after Davis had attended her Milwaukee concert:

Last night in the Auditorium, one of the great artists of the day, a tall, handsome woman with sorrow in her face, sang for an audience of thousands, who whispered to themselves: "There simply couldn't be a lovelier voice than that one. Nor could there be a greater gift for singing."

And that was right.

Last night in the Auditorium, the tall woman with the almost tragic face—yes, of course, she was Marian Anderson—stood as she sang beneath a huge American flag. People commented: "There's meaning in that, her singing there against the background of the flag."

And that was right.

Last night in the Auditorium, when the woman sang "Ave Maria" of the tender Schubert and the hall was as hushed as a house of prayer, there were tears on hundreds of white cheeks, and tears on scores of black cheeks, and when the last golden note had floated away, the listeners said: "No song by any singer was ever more beautiful."

And that was right.

Last night from the Auditorium, the people poured into the crisp night and every face was lighted. The great majority hurried every which way to their cheerful homes, but those who belonged to the race of the incomparable singer had to carry their soaring pride into the ramshackle, tumble-down district where neither pride nor hope can long survive.

And what was right about that?

Another colorful writer, Lewis C. French, whose interest centered in farm problems and farm people, came to The Journal in 1926, when circulation had reached a high mark in rural areas. One of his early tasks was to learn why so many northern Wisconsin farm settlers were failing. He found, in numerous instances, that settlers had been sold cutover land unsuited for agriculture. There was good land in the state, but "colonizers" had to be experienced to find it. French wrote knowingly on the subject, exposing these "farm tragedies" created by unscrupulous land companies. The advertising department had been accepting without question "colonization" ads. When the misrepresentation was brought out by French, The Journal at once refused the ads and denounced them editorially. "It is not a question of soil, but of making the right use of soils," one such editorial said. "It is a matter of improper exploitation, of ill-advised colonization, of large land owners selling as farm land non-agricultural tracts from which timber had been taken."

Out of French's disclosures and The Journal's editorial stand grew the movement for the zoning of northern counties. French's work through the years was highly esteemed by the state agricultural authorities, and the farmers considered him an understanding friend. The farewell party given for him upon his retirement in 1959 was attended by twenty leaders from the state Department of Agriculture and the College of Agriculture, who came to Milwaukee from Madison in a bus.

The 1920's have been called "the golden age of sports," because of the towering sports figures that emerged. To meet the great reader interest, The Journal gave added space to sports and built up a strong group of writers. The sports editor was Sam Levy, whose specialty was boxing and baseball. Manning Vaughan, who came from the *Sentinel* in 1924, immortalized "Mrs. Hassenpfeffer's front porch" across the street from the baseball park as the place where Milwaukee Brewers' home runs landed. Billy Sixty, a protégé of Editor Nieman and once his golf caddy, not only wrote of golf and bowling, but was himself an expert golfer and bowler. Oliver Kuechle's field was football, track, and basketball. He was influential in bringing Green Bay Packer football games to Milwaukee. Russell Lynch, a newsroom man who succeeded Levy as sports editor, was a powerful factor, along with Levy, in changing the Boston Braves to the Milwaukee Braves. Lynch later returned to the Journal news staff and became a writer in the field of natural resources. Kuechle succeeded him as sports editor. The colorful writing of Gordon MacQuarrie and Mel Ellis on hunting, fishing, and other outdoor activities was favorite reading in a state where almost every other man is a fisherman or hunter.

In 1923, The Journal added a rotogravure section, printed in Chicago but edited in Milwaukee. A contest for naming it produced 11,000 suggestions, the winner being "Roto-Art," a name which in later years was changed to "The Picture Journal." The format of the section was also changed later from full page to tabloid. In 1927, the printing of pictures in color was a revolutionary step in the rotogravure magazine. Color advertisements followed. The first full-page colorgravure advertisement in Wisconsin appeared on December 11, 1927, paid for by the Electric Company and directed to the Christmas trade.

20

Grow! Grow! Grow!

By 1924 The Journal had outgrown its building at 734 North Fourth Street, erected in 1907. A better and a larger paper had meant increased circulation, more advertising and, fortunately, enough money for a new plant. Having enough money was all important. A basic principle of the paper was that it would incur no indebtedness. No bank, business concern, or individual would ever be able to suspend a Damocles sword over its head.

The cornerstone of the new building at 333 West State Street was laid April 12, 1924, by L. W. Nieman and Harry J. Grant. At the ceremonies Nieman said:

The Journal has grown up with the people of Milwaukee. It has lived close to them. It has never cared about classes but about people. . . .

One of its more important policies has been to get all the information it could about matters of importance to the public, giving them all sides of a question. It has never denied to any man who had a case the opportunity to state it. In its news stories it has kept up unceasingly the effort not to do injustice to anyone or bring into its stories what might hurt people innocent of all offense.

This we do not think of as something particularly virtuous, but simply as trying to be square—a policy which makes a newspaper trusted and wins it a place in the life of the community.

Moving day was Sunday, October 26. The movers came in as soon as the Sunday paper was off the presses. According to "best laid plans," all equipment from pencil sharpeners to Linotypes would be in place by Monday morning when the staff came to work in the new building. The moving started on schedule, but like new home-owners who discover that the grand piano will not go through the front door, The Journal had its troubles. Equipment was moving out of the old building in orderly fashion, under the supervision of John Keating, the resolute and resourceful head of the mechanical department, when word came that a hitch had developed at the new building.

On the scene in a matter of minutes, Keating shouted up to the fifth floor, "What's wrong?"

"The Linotypes are too big to go through the door," came the reply.

"I'll fix that!"

Keating grabbed a sledge hammer and began slugging at the bricks around the entrance. The Linotypes were moved through, and Monday's paper came out on time.

The new building was designed by F. D. Chase, of Chicago, in close association with Leonard W. Bowyer, Journal business manager, whose understanding of architecture was in advance of his day. It was five stories high and occupied a quarter of a block. The exterior, of pink Kasota limestone in a pleasing pastel shade, was decorated on two sides with a frieze of twelve panels depicting man's age-old endeavor to communicate with his fellows. An unconventional architectural feature, which was a source of curiosity at first, was that the windows were set flush with the outside walls instead of being recessed in the usual manner. The building had cost $1 million; it was equipped with the most efficient machinery available, at the cost of another $1 million.

Formal opening day for the public was November 16, 1924, The Journal's forty-second anniversary. In the four months following, 30,000 persons toured the new building. One of the striking features they found inside was a general absence of partitions, resulting in wide open areas which allowed quick and easy rapport between workers in the news, business, and mechanical departments.

The man who directed the selection and installation of mechanical equipment for the new building was the John W. Keating mentioned above. Keating had begun his printing career at the age of twelve, working seventy-two hours a week for two dollars at the Oshkosh *Northwestern*. He left Oshkosh a young man and, as an itinerant printer, worked in most of the large cities of the East and the Middle West until he joined The Journal in 1917 as foreman of the composing room. It was said of him that he had the respect of all men under him because he knew everything that they knew, plus a little bit more. He became the first mechanical superintendent of the paper in 1919—the same year, incidentally, that Harry Grant called in a type expert, Benjamin Scherbo, to redesign the paper. Grant had not liked the physical appearance of The Journal: some headlines were in capital letters, others in lower case; many unrelated type faces were used, and the over-all effect was often confusing and annoying. Scherbo adopted Cheltenham type for headlines, a conservative gray face, in contrast to the bold faces generally in use by newspapers. The new headlines, in lower case type, were dignified and easy to read. The Journal was one of the first American newspapers to do away with capital letter headlines.

Keating became production manager in 1938, and at the time of his death in 1952, at the age of seventy-six, he was vice president as well. Through all his promotions he maintained his membership in the typographical union. He kept abreast of progress in printing and encouraged the seven mechanical departments under his supervision to experiment in improved methods. Since these seven departments included artists and photographers in addition to the usual mechanical staffs, the development of color printing was facilitated. Color printing for newspapers had been handicapped by the sponginess of newsprint and by the necessity for high speed production. Keating's experimentation overcame these handicaps.

There had been a rule—almost an axiom—that color printing must be made from four copper plates. Journal engravers showed that zinc, at a lower cost, could take the place of copper, and that successful color printing could be done with three plates only. This three-plate development not only cut costs one-fourth but helped simplify the matter of printing each color in exactly the right place over the other two colors.

Experiments in the use of color had begun as early as 1921, when The Journal's Sunday magazine first appeared. Through use of the Ben Day process, the staff artists, engravers, stereotypers, and pressmen became more skilled in reproducing color. Then came The Journal's Screen-Radio tabloid, in 1935, which used four to eight pages of Ben Day work and offered still further challenge to improve full process color methods. Department stores reported exceptional results from their color advertising in the Screen-Radio magazine, and inquired about color possibilities in the daily news sections (run-of-paper) printed on regular presses. The first run-of-paper advertisement in full process color appeared May 16, 1937, promoting Journal fashion news. Others followed, and The Journal took national—and international—leadership in newspaper run-of-paper color printing in 1947, the first year figures were compiled, and maintained that leadership through 1960.

Encouraged by Keating, the photographic department made rapid advancement. It had been started in 1909, with J. Robert Taylor its sole member. With an 8 by 10 camera and a motorcycle he supplied the paper with the few pictures it needed. In 1926 he was succeeded by Frank Scherschel, under whom the department was greatly expanded and was provided with well-equipped laboratories. One important development under Scherschel's successor, Robert Dumke, was the three-color bromide print process which reduced the time required for reproduction of color from three weeks to about four and a half hours, and eliminated many hand corrections.

In 1940, the Photographers Association of America selected The Journal as the nation's outstanding newspaper in quality of pictures taken during the year. No other paper has equalled the record set by The Journal in 1954 for speed in getting a color picture into the paper. The record photograph—of a Milwaukee fire—was taken at 8:30 in the morning and reproduced in color in the 1 P.M. edition of the same day.

Further experiments in the mechanical department during Keating's time showed that magnesium was superior to zinc in engraving. The Journal was the first metropolitan paper to switch to magnesium plates for better register, cleaner etching, and lighter weight. Even after Keating's death his enthusiasm for trying new methods lived on. In 1954 The Journal became the first major newspaper to install a Fotosetter, the revolutionary machine which combined benefits of the Linotype with those of the camera. By 1960, more than one-eighth of the advertising and features of the Sunday Journal and many parts of the daily Journal were produced by Fotosetters.

Many press inventions initiated by the Hoe Company have been further perfected by The Journal, notably by Joseph McMullen, a pressman who succeeded Keating as production manager in 1952 and became a vice president in 1955. McMullen's death came suddenly in 1959 when he was in the midst of plans for modern mechanical expansion in the Journal building addition. McMullen was succeeded by Robert Dumke who had been chief photographer and like McMullen had developed many new methods for newspaper color printing. As head of the photographic department he had become aware of the need for a device by which the picture editor could see in advance how the color photograph would look when reproduced in the paper. A $15,000 machine called the Curtis analyst was built to Journal specifications. Through its use photographers could strengthen or weaken any of the three primary color prints and improve the finished product.

Incidentally, a pressroom process which never fails to intrigue visitors is the changing of the huge paper rolls without stopping the presses. A tension belt does it. As the press rolls along at 1200 feet a minute, two spinning rolls, weighing 1800 pounds each, come in contact at the same speed. In ninety seconds the automatic change-over is completed.

21

The Newspaper and the Community

After the presidential election of 1920, with its clear evidence of a popular return to isolationism, The Journal quite naturally found local affairs occupying more of its attention than during the war and the subsequent campaign for the League of Nations. The paper turned with fresh vigor, for instance, to a project which it had backed since 1905—a civic center for Milwaukee. The Center now looms large and imposing along Kilbourn Avenue, but acquiring it was a problem which occupied civic leaders from 1905, when A. C. Clas, famed Milwaukee architect, designed it, until 1929, when the first unit was built.

In 1907 the metropolitan park commission recommended that a civic center be built on Kilbourn Avenue. The city planning commission expanded the plan, but World War I stopped all action. For a year and a half after the war the city argued the merits of a proposal for building a courthouse and a public safety building and for purchasing an area for other structures in addition to a plaza. Early in 1920 The Journal called for adoption of the plan by direct vote. "Yes, we have talked and talked—talked too long," said an editorial. "Let us bring about a decision at the polls next April." The civic center referendum won, but objectors forced a second referendum, in which the project was repealed. It was revived, and in 1929 it became a reality with the erection of the first structure, the public safety building.

Meantime other movements for city expansion, beautification, and reform were vigorously supported by the paper. The Journal had a part in ridding the city of vice and gambling, in the expansion of harbor facilities to meet the world commerce that came with the St. Lawrence Seaway, in elimination of railroad grade crossings, and in the election of the best possible men and women to serve as school board directors. In the latter effort it prints, before elections, unbiased biographies of all candidates for the school board. The same biographical information plan is used for other public offices, too, even when long lists of candidates sometimes require two or more newspaper pages of closely printed type.

An unusual political situation developed at the city hall under nonpartisan elections. Daniel W. Hoan, who had been elected city attorney in 1910 as a Socialist, was elected mayor in 1916 under the nonpartisan plan and served twenty-four years. But the common council, under the nonpartisan system, was not controlled by Socialists. With the checks and balances of a Socialist mayor and a non-Socialist council, Milwaukee boasted a good government that few cities could equal.

Under Hoan's administration the Milwaukee police department became nationally famous for keeping out gangsters and hoodlums. Honest city elections were insured, an honest system of making city purchases was installed, streets were paved, stiff housing ordinances were enacted and enforced, a new sewage disposal plant was built, and the lakefront was saved from seizure by industry. Hoan was a prime mover in the St. Lawrence–Great Lakes Waterway project and was president of the United States Conference of Mayors. In Mayor Hoan's long rule, The Journal supported him in some elections and vigorously opposed him in others. The paper was for Hoan in 1928, strictly neutral in 1932, and bitterly opposed in 1936. In the 1940 election, in which Hoan was defeated, the paper opposed him, but not bitterly.

The Journal gave thorough news coverage to the city hall and courthouse. Several Journal reporters, among them Edward Harris and Lloyd Gladfelter, were said to know more about city and county government than did the mayor, the council, or the county commissioners. Editorial writers were quick to analyze any irregularities that were revealed. Civic watch-dog editorials were usually printed in the lower left corner of the front page, under the heading "Milwaukee," a feature introduced by Grant in 1920. Ferreting out motives behind official acts and praising or exposing them, the feature quickly gained the respectful attention of politicians and officeholders. "I want you to understand what is back of a measure I am going to introduce in the city council," an alderman would often come to The Journal to explain.

This thorough check that the paper made on the acts of officials has been praised by civic-minded observers as a factor in giving Milwaukee good government. Carl Sandburg, for instance, has said that The Journal shares the credit with the Socialists. The Journal's viewpoint was stated by Marvin H Creager while he was Journal president and editor:

> Much that a good newspaper contributes to a community is intangible. But the spadework, the alerting of public sentiment which makes possible the final stroke, usually is the result of a newspaper acting as counsel for the most powerful force in the world today—American public sentiment. One specific case: Milwaukee stands out as a model in the control of crime. The main reason it does is that everyone charged with law enforcement knows that he will have The Journal's full support in refusing to wink at even minor lawlessness. Some there are who think that it is straining at gnats to insist that pinball and bingo in the name of the Lord be stopped. But it was by tricks just as innocent that the camel got his nose into the tent and you know what happened once his nose was in. Also you know that the roots of commercialized crime spread like quack grass, as witness our lusty neighbor Chicago.

Because the "Milwaukee" editorials were of interest chiefly to Milwaukeeans, they were omitted from state editions. In their place appeared an "On, Wisconsin" column devoted to the paper's reforestation and conservation campaigns. Thoughtful persons, looking around Wisconsin in the early 1920's, were shocked by the thousands of acres of land, once proud forests, now denuded by loggers and forest fires. This was before the lumber interests had acquired a conscience, before Smokey the Bear had become a familiar figure reminding lovers of the outdoors to be careful with their cigarets and their camp fires. The Journal urged action.

128

"Now is the time," it said, "for state and private reforestation." The Journal recommended creation of a state conservation commission, a special tax for conservation, fire-fighting equipment for forests, the saving of such irreplaceable wildlife refuges as Horicon marsh, and many other measures to preserve and beautify Wisconsin.

Assistant Editor Campbell became one of the state's chief spokesmen on the subject of conservation. Traveling over northern Wisconsin he made many speeches in small communities, and wrote articles and editorials for the paper. When a state forestry conference was held in 1921 in Milwaukee he was chosen its head. In 1948, another Journal editorial writer, Fred W. Luening, was awarded a commendation plaque by Wisconsin conservationists, for the part he had played in the program.

Old-timers still talk about the bad roads of Wisconsin in the pre-concrete days. A motorist starting on a little journey could get stuck in the mud, get lost, or break a spring. The rough dirt roads were unmarked, and there were no maps. To call attention to the condition of these roads, and to help the motorists who traveled them, "Brownie" Rowland conceived the idea of driving an automobile over the state and of telling the truth about how he did it.

Brownie was by nature a friendly promoter. With him on his travels went the "Poor Cuss" whose identity changed from time to time, but who was always chosen for his ability to write graphically and with humor. These two made their first inspection tour of Wisconsin roads in 1916. By 1921 they were traveling 8,000 miles a summer, sending back daily dispatches to the paper with advice on how best to get from one town to another, what landmarks to observe, and what spots to avoid. They drove a new car of a different make each year and reported on its performance in their dispatches.

Before long Brownie and the "Poor Cuss" were known all over the state and crowds gathered when they arrived in a town. Brownie, a colorful personality, was deeply tanned, had sparkling black eyes, and affected jaunty sports attire. He shook hands with all who stopped to see him and inspect his car. Frequently, when he and the "Poor Cuss" stayed overnight in a town, Brownie would give a talk on natural beauty spots in the state, on conservation or wild life, while the "Poor Cuss" operated slides illustrating the talk. Brownie became very real to many people. There is a story that on one occasion when he entered the Milwaukee Auditorium to attend a lecture the other members of the audience broke into applause for him.

In 1920 the Journal Tour Club was established, with headquarters in the lobby of the Journal building. Here firsthand information about automobile travel in Wisconsin was available. All motorists were welcome, and for a dollar one could become a member and receive Brownie's kit complete with detailed maps. In 1932 the Tour Club received 125,000 calls and boasted 45,000 members. However, as new highways were constructed, with clear direction signs, and as filling station road maps became plentiful, the Tour Club was no longer needed, and it was replaced by the Travel Bureau. The last of Brownie's "Call of the Road" guidebooks was issued in 1933.

Wisconsin is credited with being an early leader in the Middle West in the construction of hard-surface roads. State highway officials say "Brownie" Rowland was the first to point out the great need for road improvement and for a highway marking system.

The Journal turned an unsentimental eye on the little red schoolhouse in the years following World War I. Editorial writer W. C. Conrad, with guidance from State School Superintendent John Callahan, went into rural Wisconsin to look over facilities for education. He found hundreds of one-room buildings having but five or six pupils. The system was costly and not productive of good education. Conrad then went to New York State, saw its advanced consolidated schools, and wrote articles about them. In later years another editorial writer, John Baker, took up a fact-finding search for better rural education. The little red schoolhouse, however, proved to be as hardy as it was inefficient. Not until after World War II was any real progress made in modernizing it.

The public schools of Milwaukee were, of course, a very different matter, but The Journal found occasion to be of service to its readers in connection with them too. In 1923 the "project" method of education had been introduced into the grades, and many parents were bewildered by the adventures in learning as related to them by their children. Reading, writing, and arithmetic had been good enough for them, they argued, so why change? In an effort to inform the parents, the paper sent Kathleen Wilson, a staff member, to enter kindergarten as a pupil and, in an article a day, progress through the eight grades, writing details of her experiences. The resulting articles were recommended as "must" reading for all parents by the president of the school board, Loyal Durand.

One of the most heart-warming experiences in the story of The Journal was a letter-writing contest the paper sponsored in 1920, inviting all foreign-born citizens to express themselves on the question, "What has America done for me which makes me glad I came, which makes me love it, which makes me believe that of all the lands on earth it is the best one in which to live?" The response was tremendous. Hundreds of letters poured in. The Journal said it never enjoyed a greater privilege than that of printing these letters. A committee of leading citizens, appointed to judge the letters, awarded first prize to E. P. Zimmerman, a German-born Milwaukeean who had come from Prussia in 1911. He wrote:

To The Editor of The Journal: I arrived in New York nine years ago, March 13, coming from Wessenfels, Prussia. Three months later I took out my first citizenship papers. I felt that this was the country for which and in which I wanted to live—my country. The American spirit was taking hold of me—that atmosphere of liberty, equality, helpfulness, generosity and cheerfulness that one encounters daily in so many ways.

America has given me a comfortable living, a good wife, happiness and contentment in my own small way. Nov. 13, 1916, gave me the right to call myself an American. To live in the spirit of my adopted country, to uphold her constitution and traditions, was the vow of my thankful heart.

Is there another country on earth that starts you out with so even a chance, that knows no distinction between rich and poor, that gives you the same educational advantages and opportunities, that provides for you so plentifully, if only you are willing to work and save? Would history want a better proof of America's spirit than blossomed forth during the world war, when the whole nation rose like one man in voluntary, unselfish support of the Allies to save this world for democracy? Let the Belgian people, the waifs of France, the sufferers in Europe, friend or foe, tell the tale of American generosity and readiness to help.

That's the country I love. That's the country I live for and would die for—the best country on earth.

The writer of this letter had become an American citizen at the very time alienism was making its most vicious stand.

22

From Harding to Roosevelt

The years following World War I were a time of political corruption that reached even to the President's Cabinet. The seeds of corruption were sown in the Harding-Cox presidential campaign of 1920. Alarmed by the political tactics being practiced on behalf of Harding, The Journal said editorially a few days before the election:

This great conspiracy to foist a political candidate on the country will, if it succeeds, have its day of reckoning in which all must pay. The Harding forces represent in our public life things that were supposed to have been disposed of in the time of Theodore Roosevelt. . . .

We don't ask you to vote for Cox. We do ask you to cut this article out and refer to it again, if the forces of special privilege, if the old crowd which has gone through the terrible experiences of the last six years without changing a particle, gets into power again.

Twelve years later, in the black days of the great Depression, one reader returned the article to The Journal with the comment: "You have indeed been prophetic."

The prediction had come true even earlier in one of the worst political scandals America had ever had—Teapot Dome. Before this affair, it should be noted, Harding had made two moves that were commended by The Journal as "a step in the right direction." He had attempted to lead America to membership in the World Court of Arbitration; and he had called a Washington conference of leading naval powers. The conference agreed on limitations of warship building, outlawed poison gas, and made new rules for use of submarines in war. The Journal analyzed these treaties in detailed articles and supported ratification. But these acts of the President faded into obscurity as the Teapot Dome scandal burst upon the unsuspecting Harding.

President Harding had in his cabinet such capable men as Charles Evans Hughes and Herbert Hoover. But he also had political cronies like Harry M. Daugherty and Albert B. Fall. As Secretary of the Interior, Fall leased to private friends two vast tracts of oil land that had been set aside as reserve for the United States Navy. They were Teapot Dome in Wyoming and Elk Hills in California. A full-scale investigation was just getting started when Harding died in 1923 and Coolidge inherited the scandal. The Journal urged the new President to denounce Teapot Dome and meet "a great opportunity for leadership, stand up for principle and make a straight fight" even though that meant going against some men in his own party. But Coolidge chose to be silent.

The investigation, directed by Senator Thomas Walsh, was front-page news in every paper. The shocking testimony included the story of "the little black satchel" in which $100,000 had been carried from oil promoter E. L. Doheny to Secretary of Interior Fall. Witnesses told how a fortune in bonds of Harry F. Sinclair's oil company had found its way into Fall's hands.

The Senate committee condemned Fall; and the United States Supreme Court, in returning the naval reserves to the government, held there had been "conspiracy, corruption, fraud and collusion." But federal juries, under pressure from highpowered attorneys for the defense, failed to convict Fall and Doheny and Sinclair. The Journal, greatly alarmed, said such an outcome "shook the faith of people in government."

There did come a brighter day for restoring that faith. Fall was finally convicted of bribery and sent to prison, and Sinclair was found guilty of contempt of the Senate and of "jury shadowing" for which he served jail terms. In the ten years that the oil bribery story ran, The Journal published more than 300 editorials on it, echoing repeatedly Grover Cleveland's dictum that "a public office is a public trust," and insisting that wrongdoers must be punished if democracy is to survive.

134

Just as the Teapot Dome investigation had started, a new fear swept the Midwest. The Ku Klux Klan, who had burned crosses from time to time to frighten southern Negroes, now put on their hooded nightgowns in earnest and, declaring for white supremacy and Protestantism, paraded into a strong political position in Indiana, Ohio, and Illinois. But when Ku Klux organizers invaded Wisconsin they were slowed down by exposure in newspapers of the state. Paraphrasing Lincoln, The Journal summed up the danger: "America cannot exist half masked and half open." The Klan returned to its more secretive tactics but was still powerful enough in the Democratic convention of 1924 to block a resolution condemning the hooded movement. It also succeeded in throwing the convention into a deadlock between William G. McAdoo and New York's Governor Alfred E. Smith, the latter a Catholic and advocate of repeal of prohibition. Eventually John W. Davis was nominated.

The Republicans selected as their candidates President Coolidge and General Charles G. Dawes; and they dodged the Teapot Dome issue. Republican insurgents, led by Senator La Follette, revolted and formed the independent Progressive wing nominating La Follette and Burton K. Wheeler, who also received the Socialist party's endorsement.

The Journal, weighing this complex political situation, supported John W. Davis, though it said it did not like the selection of his running mate, Governor Charles W. Bryan of Nebraska, a brother of the paper's old foe, William Jennings Bryan. Of the La Follette opposition to Coolidge Republicanism, The Journal commented:

The LaFollette gesture is like many others that have preceded it. It recognizes disgust with special privilege government, but couples with it revolutionary schemes which would so certainly lead to disaster that many voters who use their heads will have nothing to do with it.

In contrast, Davis was praised as

a man able to show, if anyone can, how all the sideshows of government ownership, of subsidy, of favors for first one group and then another, lead to destruction. . . . He will be able to show the people the difference between his party and the Coolidge ticket and the heterogeneous thought that is gathering in the LaFollette candidacy.

Coolidge and Dawes won the election in a walkaway. La Follette carried only his native Wisconsin, where Davis, with The Journal's backing, got a mere 68,000 votes in a state total of over 835,000. The Coolidge victory was a signal for full speed ahead on Wall Street. In the first nine days after the election the price of stocks increased three billion dollars. As the speculation frenzy spread, a Florida land boom pulled two and a half million "immigrants" to the state in a single year. At one time 600,000 were living in tents. Some real estate agents promised 2000 per cent profit in a few months. Richard S. Davis, who was sent by The Journal to report what was going on, called the Florida boom "one of the weirdest things" that had ever happened in American life.

Editorial after editorial in The Journal warned that continuation of the stock market speculation and the Florida real estate hysteria would lead to economic disaster. While millionaires were being made overnight, the nation's farmers were sinking further and further into debt. Two farm relief bills were vetoed by Coolidge.

In the international field, however, the Coolidge Administration made one serious effort for peace, with the Kellogg-Briand Pact, pledging nations to settle quarrels by peaceful means. The Journal, commending all moves to prevent war, pointed out that the Kellogg-Briand Pact contained no provision for enforcement and fixed no common meeting place for consultation when danger threatened. The paper predicted that the treaties would be completely ineffective, a forecast which proved true when Japan invaded Manchuria in 1931 and again when Italy attacked Ethiopia in 1935.

At the Republican convention in 1928, Secretary of Commerce Herbert Hoover was named on the first ballot to run on a platform that praised the Coolidge business and economic policies, offered no remedy for the critical farm situation, and pledged continued rejection of the League of Nations.

The Journal had esteemed Hoover ever since the war, for his relief work in Belgium, but said it could not now endorse him on a Coolidge platform. Instead, the paper supported the Democratic nominee, Al Smith, warning early in the campaign, however, that Smith's religion and his stand against prohibition would stir strong prejudices. On July 8, 1928, an editorial asked:

Are we American enough to be Americans in this campaign when men will assail us with their vivid pictures of the "danger" of a Catholic president? Alfred Smith and Herbert Hoover are figures of but a few years. Soon they will pass from the stage. But the principle of liberty to worship God is, we have always said, one of the great foundations of America. . . .

If you vote because of a man's religion, for him or against him, you are condemning the principles on which men came from the old world to find a new freedom and build a new country. . . .

Applauding Smith's straight talk on prohibition, in a day when most politicians were dodging the question of whether they were "dry" or "wet," an editorial on August 23 said:

Gov. Smith as president would urge submitting the [prohibition] question to the people. He favors amendment of the eighteenth amendment. That would have to go to the people. It ought to go to them. No one foresaw the conditions which have resulted from prohibition. We wanted to abolish the saloon. Gov. Smith again repeats his opposition to the saloon. No legislation which will permit return of the saloon will have his approval. But there are other questions. One of them is respect for law in the minds of youth. Another is temperance, of which we used to hear, but of which little is in evidence today.

When Smith spoke in Milwaukee, The Journal in an enthusiastic editorial asked: "Could any man or woman listen to the speech of Alfred E. Smith last night and not forever after be a better American?"

Smith made a hard-hitting campaign, but Hoover was elected by an overwhelming majority which also carried control of Congress. In Wisconsin, Hoover's vote was 544,000 to Smith's 450,000 Despite The Journal's support, Smith was unable to carry "wet" Milwaukee County.

The Hoover victory, regarded as pro-business, started the stock market climbing again. A headline of November 10, 1928, read: "Buying Orgy Shatters Stock Records." Thousands of people of limited means were closing out their savings accounts or mortgaging their homes to gamble in stocks. Congress, alarmed at last, called on the Federal Reserve Board to use its powers to stop the speculation. But the fever was too high to be controlled. On October 29, 1929, the bottom dropped out of the stock market. In a week securities shrank $25 billion.

President Hoover found himself facing a depression that was to run to the very roots of American life. The Journal was one of several newspapers which urged him to adopt a bold course through the full use of federal resources to meet the situation. Hoover, instead, tried to get business going again through consultations. He called this method "economic education." It was a failure.

The President then proposed creation of a government corporation to lend money to banks to "prime the pump." Congress gave a farm board money to finance marketing and to purchase crop surpluses. Millions were spent without improving the lot of the farmer. When Hoover asked that tariff duties be raised on a few farm products, the high protectionists in Congress pushed through the Smoot-Hawley tariff bill, with 888 increases, which had the effect of raising the cost of living in time of depression. The Journal called this act "the worst tariff bill ever put together." Despite protests, the President signed it.

Unemployment spread to appalling proportions. A news story reported 108,000 persons on relief in Milwaukee County alone, in January, 1932. Countless thousands of other jobless men had not yet applied for aid. The Journal said that America had only two courses from which to choose. It would have to let people starve when the rapidly dwindling resources of cities, counties, and states were exhausted, or it would have to say that relief, in such an emergency, was a federal responsibility. President Hoover had steadfastly refused to put the federal government into the field of individual relief. Such action was contrary to his political philosophy.

But among the Democrats had arisen a leader who talked differently. Franklin D. Roosevelt, then governor of New York, compared the situation to that of wartime, when politics and political philosophies must be set aside. He recommended the use of federal funds to feed and clothe people until earning and purchasing power could be restored through a plan for national recovery.

The Journal hailed Roosevelt as the one leader who offered hope of curing the nation's sickness. When the Democrats nominated him to run against Hoover in 1932, The Journal said: "The moral force of a situation nominated Gov. Roosevelt as it nominated Woodrow Wilson 20 years ago, as it nominated Lincoln 72 years ago."

Roosevelt, dramatically flying to the Chicago convention to accept the nomination, climaxed his speech with the words: "I pledge you, I pledge myself, to a new deal for the American people. Give me your help, not to win votes alone, but to win in this crusade to restore America to its own people."

The Journal called this speech the end of the "do nothing" period in dealing with the Depression. "Forward! Courage! Action! This is the spirit that makes Gov. Roosevelt's speech the opening gun of a campaign not merely to elect a party, but to attack depression," said The Journal.

Roosevelt won by a landslide that carried forty-two states, including Wisconsin. His victory called for action, but in the interim between November and March, when he took office, banks began to fail in all parts of the country. Frightened depositors surged in to withdraw their accounts. In Michigan the governor declared a bank holiday. Soon, in practically every state, withdrawals were prohibited or restricted by decree. On the day Roosevelt took office few banks were open.

Here was almost complete prostration. The answer to it came in the inaugural speech: "The only thing we have to fear is fear itself—nameless, unreasoning, unjustified terror which paralyzes needed efforts to convert retreat into advance. . . . This nation asks for action, and action now. Our greatest primary task is to put people to work."

23

The New Deal

That morning in 1933, in the depth of the Depression, when the National Recovery Act code blanks arrived in Milwaukee, Publisher Harry J. Grant was waiting at the post office to sign up for The Journal and its radio station WTMJ. His was the first firm in Milwaukee to accept the blanket NRA code.

Roosevelt had taken office March 4, 1933. His first act was to close all banks to stop further bank failures. He then called Congress into special session, March 9, and there followed the remarkable "Hundred Days" when Congress passed one emergency measure after another in rapid succession. There was not time to assess each bill for merit or defect: there were 10 million jobless in the country, and many of them were desperate. Groups of farmers in the Midwest, facing mortgage foreclosures, were dragging judges from their benches and threatening to hang them. Angry dairy farmers of Wisconsin were being led into strikes of violence. Jobless factory workers, brooding at home, became potentially dangerous; or they became so dejected that they were an easy prey to subversive agitators. A wave of kidnaping for ransom had developed that was a national disgrace.

Congress passed bills to take care of the banking situation, to save mortgaged farms, to rescue railroads, to protect investors in buying securities, to create a system of public works to take men off the dole. One of the most important measures passed was the National Recovery Act, known as the NRA, setting up a system of codes to govern business and industrial employment practices. Its object was to increase jobs.

When the specific code applying to the press was drafted, The Journal was one of the first papers in the country to put it into effect. The American Newspaper Publishers Association had counseled not to enter into the agreement for fear of endangering freedom of the press. The Journal said that freedom of the press was not involved and urged everyone to accept the President's recovery program.

Two days after Grant obtained the necessary blanks at the post office, he put the Journal recovery plan into operation. The work week of employes in the mechanical, advertising, general business, and circulation departments was shortened to provide more jobs. When Washington later ruled that the editorial staffs of newspapers were exempt from the forty-hour week provision, The Journal waived the exemption. The cost of carrying out these self-imposed codes was more than $100,000 a year. In accepting the blanket code a front-page editorial said:

The Journal, in full accord and sympathy with President Roosevelt's program for industrial recovery, is adjusting its operation to conform whole-heartedly with the plan. Operation under the recovery schedule will begin at the earliest possible time and will not be held off until Aug. 31, the date set in the president's proclamation. As soon as a survey can be made and the necessary changes worked out, The Journal will announce in detail how it is meeting each of the 14 points in the president's re-employment agreement.

The paper supported practically all of the recovery measures on the ground of national emergency. It pointed out, however, the dangers in some of them, and stressed that such proposals should be regarded only as temporary. For example the Agricultural Adjustment Act (AAA) and the NRA set up powerful agencies with authority to make rules which were in effect laws. An agency governed by a board of three, five, or seven members could move more quickly to meet critical conditions than could Congress, but the plan involved some abdication of power by Congress.

By the autumn of 1933, Roosevelt could announce that of the

10 million who had been jobless in the spring, 4 million had found employment. One factor which increased jobs in Milwaukee, home of the nation's leading breweries, was repeal of the prohibition amendment on December 5, 1933.

The Journal had originally favored prohibition and in preprohibition days had refused liquor advertising. It had printed the following editorial, on February 21, 1919, a month after ratification of the Eighteenth Amendment, in reply to a letter from a reader:

A correspondent . . . disagrees with The Journal's opinion that the prohibition amendment is the law of the land and should be respected and obeyed.

He states that the amendment was rushed through congress with no thought to the will of the people. He does not know congressmen. Many of them voted for the amendment, not because they believed in it, but because they knew their constituents. The amendment was not rushed through congress. It has been before congress for years.

Our correspondent ignores entirely the fact that some forty odd states, through their legislatures, ratified the amendment—a fact which is of far greater importance than the vote in congress. He ignores the fact too that some nineteen states were dry before the amendment was passed, to say nothing of the still larger number that were partly dry through local option laws.

Editors and preachers could not have passed the amendment. It would not have been passed unless a nation-wide sentiment had supported it. The amendment having been adopted, it is the law of the land, and the duty of every citizen is to abide by it. The only recourse which opponents of the amendment can possibly have is to secure its repeal through the same processes as those by which it was enacted.

Gradually, in the next decade, The Journal came around to the belief that prohibition would not work. On July 30, 1933, the paper said:

Prohibition failed. There can be little question of that today. It not only did not succeed in prohibiting, but it also permitted the development of illicit sources of supply which, except by most careful planning, are bound to persist after the eighteenth amendment is a thing of the past.

The editorial suggested strict regulation of the saloons, which were to become "taverns," and added:

The state of Wisconsin owes nothing to the liquor interests. It owes nothing to the fraternity which sees in the return of liquor merely a chance for private profit. When prohibition is repealed, citizens of the state will be interested solely in obtaining good liquor in decent quantities at reasonable price. They will not be interested in making some barkeep rich.

In 1934 several of the New Deal laws which had been passed in haste to speed recovery were revised to take out defects, and many new projects were introduced to increase work opportunities. One such project was the resettlement in Alaska of a group of Wisconsin, Michigan, and Minnesota farmers who found little chance of success in farming where they were. The Journal sent Arville Schaleben, a reporter who later became executive editor, to Matanuska Valley to follow this experiment. He remained four months, writing many informative articles on farming in the Far North.

In 1934, violence in labor-industry relations was rife, with labor sometimes striking to obtain unreasonable benefits, and industry sometimes refusing benefits where they were due. Ross A. Lewis' cartoon, with the evil genie "Violence" saying, "Sure I'll work for both sides," summed up the labor-industry situation and won Lewis a Pulitzer prize. Lewis had become The Journal's cartoonist in 1932, when the high collar of Herbert Hoover and the long cigaret holder of Franklin D. Roosevelt were meat for caricaturing. The paper had printed front-page cartoons since 1891, its first being a "Little Napoleon" sketch of William McKinley, drawn by S. Rigsby. The first staff cartoonist was James Steel, who was followed by Fred Bernau. Syndicated cartoons of J. N. (Ding) Darling were generally used until Lewis began his daily cartoon in the Hoover-Roosevelt campaign.

Encouraged by the progress in recovery, President Roosevelt was working in 1935 on a program designed to remove the causes of depression when the New Deal got its first setback. The United States Supreme Court ruled that the NRA was unconstitutional. The 557 recovery codes were thrown out. Chief Justice Charles Evans Hughes in the majority opinion held that Congress had acted unconstitutionally when it delegated to the President the power to make code rules having the force of law; and in setting minimum wages and maximum hours, as well as regulating local businesses.

The President was bitter. He said the "nine old men" sitting on the Supreme Court bench had taken America back to "the horse and buggy days." The Journal, on the other hand, said believed a new NRA code could be written within the limits laid down by Chief Justice Hughes if Congress would work carefully The paper announced in a front-page editorial that it would continue to observe all the wage and hour regulations to which had committed itself. It said that the most vital thing was to keep recovery going.

In 1935, Congress passed the social security bill, the Wagner labor relations bill, a $4 billion work relief program, and the utility holding company bill, all of which The Journal lauded In January, 1936, the Supreme Court invalidated the AAA. To this blow Roosevelt responded by directing Agricultural Secretary Henry Wallace to work out a substitute law based on soil conservation, and the farm program went ahead.

In the 1936 election Roosevelt was a candidate for a second term. The Republicans nominated Governor Alfred M. Landon of Kansas, with Colonel Frank Knox, editor of the Chicago *Daily News,* as his running mate. The Journal declared for Roosevelt rejecting Landon on the ground that the Republican platform if carried out, would take the country back to 1929. Roosevelt and Garner carried forty-six states; Maine and Vermont went to Landon and Knox.

Then to the surprise of his most ardent admirers, Roosevelt interpreted the election landslide as a rebuke to the Supreme Court He suggested that the Court review New Deal laws and hand down decisions in the light of election returns. The Journal reacted sharply against this suggestion by the President, pointing out that if the Court found that the national government did not have power to deal with national social and economic problems a constitutional amendment should be submitted. Many newspapers throughout the country opposed Roosevelt on this issue and many of his backers in Congress began to revolt. Despite the un favorable reaction, Roosevelt soon started his "war" on the Supreme Court. In his "Court reform" bill he proposed that whenever a Supreme Court justice reached the age of seventy and did not retire, the President should appoint a younger man to sit with him. Since there were six judges over seventy, there could have been, under the Roosevelt plan, a bench of fifteen, with all the younger members beholden to the President.

On the day after Roosevelt submitted this bill, The Journal said in an editorial:

This is a proposal to run around and nullify a fundamental principle of our government by a simple act of congress. . . . No such change, no change of one-tenth of this importance, should be undertaken by a congress which has had not one word of instruction from the people on this subject. It amounts to making the supreme court subject to the will, or the whim, of the executive. . . .

The proposal of Franklin Roosevelt, in a few words, is a proposal to pack the supreme court. And there is all too much reason to fear that it would prove a way to stack the supreme court.

A fantastic battle raged for five months. In the end the court-packing measure was decisively defeated. The Journal commented:

In the emergency days of the depression, congress of necessity had subordinated its judgment to the executive. The White House sent over to the capitol those measures it desired, and congress without questioning accepted them. We had one-man government, and by general agreement.

After an astounding election, with the Democratic party having in both houses the greatest majorities in the history of parties, President Roosevelt continued to demand of congress its subordination to the executive. He went further. He demanded that the judiciary, the supreme court of the United States, likewise be subordinated to the executive. And congress balked. It not only re-established its independence but protected the independence of the judiciary.

The Journal was not to support Roosevelt in his campaign for a third term as President. There were several reasons why the paper made this decision, but an important factor was Roosevelt's attempt to pack the Supreme Court.

24

Radio and Television

Radio, which figured so importantly in American life during the Roosevelt era, first came into homes as a plaything, following World War I. In those days a mechanically minded man with a crystal and a headphone could hook up a receiver and, in a pinch, use a bedspring as an aerial. By patient manipulation of a piece of wire on the crystal, he could bring in faint music. The game was to listen until the station call letters came in, then try for another station. If a skillful listener got KDKA of Pittsburgh, WWJ of Detroit, and KFI of Los Angeles the same night, he sent a post card to each station or wrote a letter to the paper.

But in 1920 when KDKA broadcast returns of the Harding-Cox presidential election, radio took on importance. The public began to see its potentiality and to like the idea of getting news bulletins without waiting for the papers. Factory-made sets now appeared, and the number of receivers in the whole country increased from an estimated 5,000 in 1920 to 2.5 million in 1924.

The first Milwaukee broadcasting station was WAAK, opened by Gimbel Brothers on April 26, 1922. It was installed in a corner of the department store and was equipped with a 100-watt transmitter and a 40-foot tower on the roof. It broadcast a few hours a week, using local talent or show people who were playing in the city. A bit of advertising, announcing that the store sold radio sets and other radio apparatus, was included. Five days after WAAK began broadcasting, The Journal sponsored a program over the station. Loud-speakers were set up at three locations—in the old Schubert Theater, at the Journal building, and at Lake Park Lutheran Church. Among the performers were Lionel Barrymore, then playing at the Davidson Theatre, and the Sophia Brant Opera Company.

The second Milwaukee station was WCAY, sponsored by the Kesselman-O'Driscoll music store. It went on the air June 16, 1922, followed two weeks later by WHAD, Marquette University's station, which grew out of physics laboratory experiments. The fourth station was WIAO, run by the Milwaukee School of Engineering, which had also experimented with laboratory radio. This station was later changed to WSOE. All four stations operated at irregular periods.

Yet, despite broadcasting irregularities and other disappointments, public interest in radio grew steadily. The Milwaukee Journal's Consumer Analysis report for January, 1924, showed 12,471 receiving sets in the Milwaukee area. Most of them were tuned to outside stations. The need for more dependable, higher quality broadcasting in Milwaukee was obvious. Partly to fill this need, and partly to develop news broadcasts supplementary to the paper, The Journal decided to enter the radio field. It arranged with Marquette University, January 25, 1925, for the operation of WHAD, the university to handle the technical matters, the newspaper to take over the programs. The lounge of the new Journal building, at Fourth and State streets, became a studio for radio broadcasting. Additional facilities in the Wisconsin Theater, the Athletic Club, and the Badger Room of Hotel Wisconsin were set up.

At this time, radio was entering what has been called "the period of chaos." Broadcasting stations were jumping each other's wave lengths and taking each other's assigned hours. Soon many fine programs were ruined. In contrast, WHAD was dependable as to time and quality, so that most Milwaukee listeners cut off outside stations and tuned to local broadcasts. Equally important, the number of sets in Milwaukee doubled in a single year.

This favorable development was accelerated, also, by the fact that Walter Damm, program manager for WHAD, was constantly expanding the field. For example, in 1926, WHAD broadcast the Eucharistic Congress at Mundelein, Illinois. The cost for this remote control feature was $1,500, a large sum for programming in those days, but it was repaid many times over in the appreciation of thousands of listeners who had special interest in the event. A little later WHAD put Milwaukee Brewer baseball games on the air, with Sam Levy, Journal sports writer, at the microphone. Another step forward was taken when WHAD gave Wisconsin listeners the first radio show of the new National Broadcasting Company, featuring Mary Garden and Will Rogers. Fourteen thousand letters and telegrams poured in asking that Milwaukee be put on the NBC network.

Finding talent for local programs was not easy. Damm and Robert E. Knoff, radio editor of The Journal, who also acted as talent-booker, used Journal employes for some of the regular features or to fill in when a program hitch developed. Carl Skinrood, financial editor, conducted a period on business and markets. Floyd S. Van Vuren and F. Perry Olds gave reviews of new books. Van Vuren also had a program on Wisconsin birds. Faye McBeath conducted a program for children; Jessica Knowles talked to home gardeners; "Betty Ann" of the women's department gave the latest news on styles; Oliver Kuechle, Sam Levy, and Billy Sixty featured sports; John R. Wolfe discussed current events. Among The Journal's musically inclined employes who were called on for programs—sometimes for emergency duty—were Richard S. Davis, Jack Iverson, Albert Smack, Hildegarde Gloyer, Alice Phillips, Hazel Granzo, Gustav Schlaefli, and Ira Schnell.

While The Journal was learning how to run a broadcasting station, two important changes had occurred in radio. First, Congress had transferred control of the medium from the Department of Commerce to a newly created Federal Radio Commission. Second, it had become clear that the future of radio rested on private enterprise, with commercially sustained programs paying the costs. Since The Journal's contract with Marquette precluded commercial broadcasts on WHAD, new arrangements were necessary.

The Journal decided to have a station of its own. To obtain a frequency it bought WKAF, which had gone on the air in 1925 from the Antlers Hotel, following discontinuation of the broadcasts of WCAY. Old equipment was junked, and The Journal built a new broadcasting tower a few miles west of Milwaukee on the Bluemound Road. On July 25, 1927, WTMJ went on the air as the first fully equipped station in the Milwaukee area. It operated on the 1020 kilocycle frequency with 1,000 watts of power. Within a month it affiliated with the NBC network to share in nationwide radio then developing.

In 1928, the Federal Radio Commission, seeking to distribute broadcasting facilities more evenly over the nation, set up forty cleared channels, forty-four regional channels, and six local channels, and divided them among the five radio zones. It did not, however, do anything to equalize facilities within each zone, and it was there that the worst inequalities existed. For instance, in the fourth zone—Illinois, Missouri, Indiana, Wisconsin, Minnesota, Iowa, Kansas, Nebraska, North Dakota, and South Dakota—four and four-sevenths of the eight available channels were held by Illinois alone. Wisconsin, although the fourth most populous state in this zone, had no cleared channel facility.

The Milwaukee Journal belatedly challenged this inequality and made application for a cleared channel. That action was the opening of what came to be known as Wisconsin's "battle of the air." The Federal Radio Commission refused to disturb Illinois' channel assignment, but in an alternate proposal gave WTMJ the highly desirable 620 kilocycle regional channel, with the definite understanding that WTMJ's broadcasts were to be protected from interference.

WTMJ added more equipment and, with 2,500-watt power in the daytime and 1,000 at night, could be heard throughout Wisconsin, in upper Michigan, across Lake Michigan, and in northern Illinois and northern Indiana. Then, in April of 1929, the commission placed station WJAT of Cleveland on the 620 wave length for daytime broadcasting. Some interference was evident. On October 18, 1929, WLBZ of Bangor, Maine, a station already on 620, was allowed to increase its nighttime power, producing more interference. The really ruinous blow fell two weeks later when the commission allowed WFLA and WSUN, two poorly equipped stations at Clearwater, Florida, to use the 620 channel with 1,000 watts of power. Their signals came straight to Wisconsin. The result was chaos in much of the area that WTMJ had been serving. The interference disrupted programs altogether in central and upper Wisconsin. At times reception was upset within twenty-five miles of the WTMJ transmitter.

After collecting data on interference through the use of silent periods that permitted listeners to hear the call letters of the offending stations, WTMJ got a hearing before the radio commission. Hundreds of listeners' affidavits were offered, but the commission refused to change existing conditions. WTMJ then went to the District of Columbia Court of Appeals, which, in an historic decision, rebuked the commission and ordered it to restore WTMJ's channel protection to what it had been before the interference began.

During this long contest, WTMJ had kept before the commission its application for a cleared channel, offering to build a 50,000-watt station when such a channel was awarded. However, the commission decided that the change involved in correcting the inequity of the original cleared channel allotment was too drastic to be made now.

The station redoubled its efforts to improve programs and equipment. From the beginning WTMJ led the movement of independent local radio stations against network infringement. At a time when local stations in other cities were operating with a staff of two or three, WTMJ maintained a sixteen-man orchestra and broadened its local programs to include talks and panel discussions by political leaders, educators, scientists, and homemakers. The result was a steady growth—even in the Depression years—that taxed broadcasting capacity. In 1936, WTMJ installed a new 5,000-watt transmitter and erected a new tower on the Bluemound Road site. It also expanded and sound-proofed its studios in the Journal building.

As early as 1928, WTMJ had started a continuing program of research and planning for the future. In the 1930's two developments were shaping up which gave promise of playing vital roles.

150

One was frequency modulation (FM) broadcasting; the other was television. FM developed as a system which gave a static-free signal that was stronger and clearer than that of the standard amplified modulation (AM) system. Because of these qualities, FM held the possibility of a useful future, especially in a state like Wisconsin which had no all-clear channel. After experimenting, The Journal, on February 23, 1940, put an FM station on the air. It was W9XAO, later changed to WTMJ-FM, the first station of its kind west of the Allegheny Mountains.

Just as the FM station was getting under way, World War II brought a "freeze" on manufacture of radio sets. Television, which was to give "eyes" to radio, was a victim of the same freeze. In the 1930's The Journal had experimented continuously in television. A rayphoto which sent pictures through the air was set up; and an experimental closed circuit TV station was operated for seven years. Company executives were careful not to make the mistake in television which they, and Wisconsin as a whole, had made in radio in the early 1920's in passing up an opportunity for a cleared channel. On September 16, 1941, The Journal Company received a construction permit for a regular TV station. In June of that year land had been bought on Capitol Drive, at the Milwaukee River, as a site for Radio City. Because work had started before the Pearl Harbor attack, construction was permitted to go on. WTMJ and WTMJ-FM moved into the building in August of 1942.

An FM transmitter had been erected on a high hill at Richfield, northwest of Milwaukee. After the war The Journal Company bought a Wausau station (WSAU) and added FM to it. Plans were made for another FM station at Green Bay. But when the rapid rise of television overshadowed all broadcasting, Journal efforts in FM were discontinued in 1950. Several years later, however, there was a revival of interest in radio FM as a medium for high fidelity broadcasting of fine music. To meet this interest, WTMJ resumed in 1960 the FM broadcasting in which it had pioneered.

WTMJ-TV began broadcasting December 3, 1947, the eleventh television station in the United States. Sales of receiving sets in the Milwaukee area boomed. To extend the broadcasting radius a 1,035-foot tower was erected. When NBC offered its first network color program, December 20, 1953, WTMJ-TV was ready to receive it. And seven months later, on July 18, 1954, the station put on the air the first live color television program to originate in Wisconsin.

In the thirty-five–year development of Journal broadcasting, the names of two men stand out. One is Harry J. Grant, who as the paper's publisher in the 1920's, saw in radio "a service parallel to the newspaper," and loosened the purse strings to keep The Journal abreast of progress in the medium. The other is Walter J. Damm, who foresaw the possibilities of radio, urged the early experiments, and with an amazing driving power made the creation and development of Journal radio and television his lifework. He became nationally known for his defense of independent TV stations against network encroachments. Among Damm's important assistants were Lewis W. Herzog, Russell Winnie, Donald B. Abert, Robert Heiss, Philip B. Laeser, and George R. Comte. At Damm's retirement in 1958, Comte succeeded him as radio and television general manager.

25

Again We Go to War

Adolf Hitler had absorbed Austria, had taken the Sudetenland, and now, in 1939, had attacked Poland. World War II raged in Europe, but on this side of the Atlantic neutrality still seemed possible. The Journal supported Roosevelt's neutral policy, and at the same time took a strong stand for the elimination of the "bund" in Milwaukee.

Even before the war Nazi propagandists had attempted to spread their doctrines in America, largely through the German-American Volksbund, commonly known as the bund. They chose Milwaukee as their Midwest headquarters and brought organizers from Germany to open their drive. The Journal assigned reporters to cover the rallies and printed full accounts of the Nazi doctrines preached, the Nazi songs, and the presence of Storm Troopers who had instructions to throw out anyone who protested what went on.

When Chicago Communists picketed the bund's meeting at the Milwaukee Auditorium, The Journal said: "Milwaukee wants no 'isms'—either the Nazis inside the auditorium or the Communists and their sympathizers outside."

Faced with daily exposure from The Journal, the bundists took to secluded areas outside the city where they held their meetings, put on Nazi military drill, and conducted schools to indoctrinate children. These meetings were supposed to be secret, with no outsiders admitted. But after each meeting the bundists would find in The Journal a full account of what had taken place.* As a result the bund made little headway in Milwaukee.

When the Nazis tried to get control of the Wisconsin Federation of German-American Societies, of which Bernhard Hofmann, a foe of Nazism, was president, the movement met a resounding defeat. Old families of German descent, remembering how they were misled by the Kaiser's propagandists in World War I, refused to be drawn into the Hitler intrigue. Even at its peak in 1938, the Milwaukee bund had on its rolls only a few hundred families. Most of them were Germans who had arrived here after World War I.

While the bund fight was on, and while the government was trying to keep America out of the war, the presidential election of 1940 took place. The Republican convention platform condemned Roosevelt's New Deal spending and deplored the failure of several important Roosevelt plans to improve the economy. But the platform also accepted much of the New Deal program— farm aid, social security, labor's right to collective bargaining, and reciprocal trade agreements. Full national preparedness was endorsed.

Wendell Willkie was the Republican nominee for President; Oregon Senator Charles L. McNary, their nominee for Vice President. Willkie, a newcomer in national politics, had been head of the Commonwealth and Southern Utility system before its main properties were bought by the Tennessee Valley Authority in 1939. Indicting the New Deal for extravagance and too much experimenting, some of it dangerous, he said: "America must meet changing conditions in economic and social fields but at the same time hold to fundamentals of democracy."

The Democratic convention in Chicago defied an American tradition. It nominated Franklin D. Roosevelt for a third term.

* Three Journal reporters who broke through the bund's secrecy were Paul Ringler, later editorial editor; Harvey Schwandner, later assistant managing editor and, after the purchase of the *Sentinel,* executive editor of it; and Laurence C. Eklund, who became head of The Journal's Washington bureau. Editorials on the bund were written by F. Perry Olds, the translator who had exposed the pro-Germans in World War I days.

The Journal, faced with the dilemma of deciding between changing Presidents in a perilous time and changing American traditions, said firmly on the Sunday after the Democratic convention: "This country should not grant Franklin D. Roosevelt a third term." The paper supported Willkie not only on the basis of opposition to a third term, but also for his analysis of the American situation. After the court-packing battle of 1937, The Journal had never returned to its earlier enthusiasm for Roosevelt.

In the late summer and early autumn of 1940, when Hitler, from his bases in occupied France, was bombarding England daily, more and more Americans began to feel that the British Isles had become our own first line of defense. War was coming closer and closer. Voters, believing that this was no time for a change in the White House, re-elected Roosevelt. He carried Wisconsin by 35,000; in 1936 his Wisconsin plurality over Landon had been 420,000.

Shortly before his third inauguration, President Roosevelt proposed a program of aid to the Allied nations, to be known as lend-lease. Under this plan supplies could be sold, leased, or exchanged to any nation whose defense the President found to be vital to the security of America. At the end of the war these materials, if still in existence, were to be returned; if they had been used up or lost, they were to be paid for. Secretary of State Cordell Hull, in support of the lend-lease bill, told the House committee on foreign affairs that the only sensible course left for America was to yield the neutrality it had tried so hard to maintain and openly furnish supplies to those who were holding the line against Hitler. The Journal commented:

It is a solemn thing for this nation to be confronted with a policy which can, at almost any moment, carry it into total war. That is what the Hull statement comes down to. And for the most part the statement will be accepted as sound common sense. This country has supported defense without limit of expenditure. But it has hoped that defense meant the avoidance of armed conflict by land and sea. Now defense includes all we can give a belligerent.

The time for pretense and wishful thinking is over. What is left is to prepare with all the might we have to defeat the "organized, ruthless and implacable movement of steadily expanding conquest."

Since 1939 The Journal had supported neutrality, in the hope that America could stay out of a second world war. Now it faced the grim fact that our democracy would not be secure if left alone in a world dominated by Hitler.

Lend-lease proved effective. It was largely instrumental in keeping England alive as a barrier to Hitler. But it also brought us nearer to war. Our actual entry into the war came on Sunday, December 7, 1941, when a Japanese force attacked Pearl Harbor, where our Pacific fleet was stationed. Japan had begun to talk openly of war with America because this country opposed Japanese encroachments in Asia. By bringing us into the war now, Japan would force us to fight on two fronts.

President Roosevelt, going before Congress the day following Pearl Harbor, asked for a declaration of war against Japan and said: "No matter how long it may take us to overcome this premeditated invasion, the American people in their righteous might will win through to absolute victory." This pledge was supported and echoed all over America. The Journal's editorial was characteristic:

We are all in it today. Once again the message of war sounds as a new generation learns that it is not ours to say whether there shall be war or even peace. Even as Americans were reading of the direct appeal of President Roosevelt to the emperor of Japan [to prevent war between the two nations] the voice of radio brought them word that bombs had rained on Honolulu. . . .

Americans stand together today in determination. We pray that the struggle may not be long continued, nor the cost in life and human values too great. But long or short, we are all in it—to aid our government with material things, with counsel, with the unfailing assurance of support, whatever the price to be paid.

The Journal endorsed Roosevelt's requests for billions of dollars to expand the Navy for a two-ocean war, to equip the draftee divisions and get them to battlefields, to fill the air with fighter and bomber squadrons.

Throughout the war the paper helped keep Wisconsin families informed about their sons in the service. When General Douglas MacArthur, after a year of American reverses, started the long road from Australia back to Tokyo, The Journal sent reporter

Robert J. Doyle as war correspondent to the southwest Pacific. His assignment was to report the news about Wisconsin boys—to tell of their struggles, their longings, their joys and sorrows, as well as their battle-front maneuvers. In October, 1942, Doyle joined the Allied invasion forces in New Guinea. He flew from Australia over the Stanley Mountains in a "boxcar" transport and down to the Buna front.

"Anybody here from Wisconsin?" was Doyle's greeting as he came up to one unit. Everybody seemed to be from Wisconsin: this was Wisconsin's own Thirty-second Division. And every soldier was glad to see somebody from home. Doyle reassured them and in turn his dispatches reassured their families at home. He gave names of men and details of the meetings. The Thirty-second was participating in a campaign that was destined to be the first land reversal for the Japanese, and Doyle's account of the part Wisconsin troops played in the storming and capture of Buna was the most vividly personal war story to come out of the Pacific up to that time.

The year 1943 was brightened by MacArthur's victories in the Pacific, the defeat of the Nazis at Stalingrad, and General Eisenhower's campaign in the Mediterranean area to prepare the way for the invasion of western Europe. On the home front things were not so satisfactory. Farmers, industrialists, and labor unions were putting pressure on Washington in order to get more personal benefits out of the war. When some labor unions went on strike regardless of war needs, The Journal assailed them: "It is not right for millions of young Americans to risk their lives in battle while other Americans—the best paid workers in the world —can, and sometimes do, walk off the job if they feel like it."

When wounded and maimed service men began to arrive back in the states, The Journal sent a staff man, Frank Sinclair, to study and write about veteran rehabilitation. It was the first newspaper in America to explore this field for the men of World War II. Sinclair on his trips to Washington aroused interest with his searching questions, prompting other newspapermen there to take up the problem. He next went to Canada, which had worked out a rehabilitation plan, and reported his findings in special articles in The Journal. When Congress, early in 1944, enacted a GI bill of rights, providing hospitalization, rehabilitation, free education, and financial aid to returning veterans, the new law embodied much that Sinclair had cited as most needed.

The presidential election of 1944 came when America was deeply committed to an all-out war effort and when hopeful signs of victory were appearing on the battle fronts. The Republicans nominated Thomas E. Dewey of New York for President and John W. Bricker of Ohio for Vice President. The Democrats named President Roosevelt for a fourth term and for his running mate Senator Harry S Truman, who had come into national prominence as head of a committee investigating the war program on the home front.

In this wartime election, The Journal said, leadership should be put above party. Framing four questions for guidance, the paper shortly before election gave its own answers:

1. Roosevelt would be the surer choice for finishing the war in the shortest time. He was familiar with Allied strategy. There would be no break or interlude in support of that strategy, such as might come if a new man were put in the White House.

2. Roosevelt would be more likely to succeed in perfecting a world organization for peace and in gaining America's participation in this organization. Dewey, personally for international cooperation, might be hampered by the isolationists within his own party.

3. Dewey would make the better President to deal with postwar economic and administrative problems, assuming that he would hold fast to the liberal policies he had espoused in the campaign. His record as governor of New York indicated that he was a better administrator than Roosevelt.

4. Dewey would surely use his influence and direct his policy toward that balance of forces which is the essence of democracy. He would be much more likely to avoid government by groups or by edict.

"There it is—two and two," summed up The Journal. "The answer to this sequence of questions depends upon the relative

THE MILWAUKEE JOURNAL

Sixtieth Year

Circulation Yesterday ... 321,846
Circulation One Year Ago ... 308,713

Monday, December 8, 1941

Daily .... 3 Cents
Sunday .... 10 Cents

46 Pages—Final Markets

Japanese Blast at Manila;
1,500 Killed in Hawaii Raid

Congress Quickly Votes a Declaration of War

Roosevelt's Request Gets Speedy Action

Senate Vote Is 82 to 0, House Count Is 388-1; President Says Attack 'Will Live in Infamy'

Washington, D. C.—The United States, through its congress, declared war on Japan Monday.

Moving with unprecedented speed to answer the Japanese assault upon this country's Pacific possessions, both houses passed the war resolution within half an hour after President Roosevelt grimly asked for such action.

Congress acted with the greatest unity seen on Capitol Hill in years.

The senate vote, first to be recorded, was 82 to 0. In the house it was 388 to 1. The only opposition vote was cast by Representative Jeanette P. Rankin (Rep., Mont.). It was a dark...

Fires Raging After Attack, Radio Asserts

New York, N. Y.—Japanese bombers raided Manila early Tuesday morning and an NBC reporter said that "terrific damage" had been left, including the apparent destruction of the gasoline supply at Nichols air field.

There was a lull in the action some time after 3 a. m. Manila time, but at 3:41 a. m. the anti-aircraft fire reopened, and the radio reporter, from Bel Air, added that the fire had died down at Nichols field, in the southern part of Manila. He continued:

"Fires raging after attack, said the Japanese army air force says a brilliant red..."

Two U.S. Warships Down, White House Statement Admits

Japanese bombers struck at Manila, capital of the Philippines, for the first time early Tuesday, a few hours after the White House issued a statement saying that loss of life in Japan's Sunday raid on Hawaii — the attack that set off the war — would be around 1,500.

The attack on Hawaii, the White House said, resulted in the capsizing of an old battleship, the loss of a destroyer, damage to other vessels and destruction of a relatively large number of planes.

The official statement added that several Japanese planes and submarines had been accounted for, and said that active resistance was "still continuing" against the Japanese attacking force in the vicinity of Hawaii.

This statement, the first authentic government appraisal of the attack Sunday, said that total casualties at Oahu island of the United States naval base near Honolulu were expected to mount to about 3,000.

First Statement on Japanese War

Stephen T. Early, the president's secretary, read to reporters the official statement on the battle at Hawaii, saying the announcement had been approved by President Roosevelt. It said:

"American operations against the Japanese attacking force in the neighborhood of the Hawaiian islands are still continuing. A number of Japanese planes and submarines have been destroyed. The damage caused to our forces in Oahu in yesterday's attack appear more serious than at first believed.

"One destroyer was blown up. Several other small ships were seriously hit. Army and navy fields were bombed with the resulting destruction of several hangars and a large number of planes were put out of commission.

"A number of bombers arrived safely from San Francisco during the engagement—while it was under way.

"Re-enforcements of planes are being rushed and repair work is under way on ships, planes and ground facilities.

"Guam, Wake, the Midway islands and Hong Kong have been attacked. Details of these attacks are lacking.

"Two hundred marines—all that remained in China—have been interned by the Japanese near Tientsin.

"The total casualties on the island of Oahu are not yet definitely known but, in all probability, will amount to about 3,000. Nearly half of these are fatalities, the others being wounded.

"It seems clear from the reports that many bombs were dropped in the city of Honolulu, resulting in a small number of casualties."

Milwaukee Get Traffic Moving

Late War Bulletins

London, England.—Reuter's news agency said in a dispatch from Singapore Monday that a British communique declared "official warfare growing out of warfare disorder..."

New York, N. Y.—C.P.—The United Press listening post Monday heard the Vichy radio broadcast that Japan reports that a great air and sea battle was in progress off the Philippines.

San Francisco, Calif.—C.P.—The Singapore radio heard here Monday reported that two American built Hudson bombers operating off the northern Malayan coast had scored direct hits at the lost Japanese troop ships.

Washington, D. C.—C.P.—Federal Security Administrator Paul V. McNutt Monday ordered the government of all states urging them to make immediate preparations for the protection and relief of suffering growing out of warfare disorder.

Forced to Act, Says Emperor

Britain, U. S. Left Japan 'No Other Recourse,' Hirohito Asserts

Tokyo, Japan.—(From a broadcast).—Emperor Hirohito declared Monday that the action of the United States and Britain in the Pacific left Japan "no other recourse" but to resort to arms in self-defense.

Japan's Bombers Hit Hawaii Like Lightning and War Is On

Honolulu, H. I.—C.P.—War broke with lightning suddenness in the mid-Pacific Sunday when waves of Japanese bombers out of the United States Marine fleet with a blunder a big naval office...

California Schools Close as Safeguard

Oakland, Calif.—(P)—All schools in metropolitan Oakland were ordered closed Monday as an air raid precaution on reports that a Japanese airplane carrier may be off the Pacific coast.

In Tomorrow's Journal

Journal artists have prepared a full page color map of the entire Pacific area from the Aleutians to New Zealand and from Singapore to the coast of North and South America. This detailed map of the battlegrounds where Japan and the United States are now struggling is the kind you will want to save for future reference.

If There's Another Job to Do, We'll Do It

War declared, December 8, 1941.

A mallard duck—Gertie—in 1945 chose the busiest spot in Milwaukee to make her nest, and kept on the front page even on the day Germany surrendered.

Harry Grant and Nieman's niece, Miss Faye McBeath, admiring the model of
Mr. Grant's yacht given him by Journal employes in 1947 on the tenth anniversary of the stock ownership plan.

Editor Marvin H Creager, Harry J. Grant, and city editor T. Murray Reed at the celebration of Reed's fiftieth year in newspaper work.

President Truman, not supported by The Journal for the Presidency, nevertheless enjoyed visiting the Journal editors. He had just told an off-the-record political joke about Huey Long when a photographer snapped him and Journal President Ferguson in 1954.

Radio City, completed in 1942, on East Capitol Drive near the Milwaukee River, houses WTMJ, WTMJ-TV, and WTMJ-FM.

John Keating (*below, left*), vice president and mechanical superintendent at the time of his death in 1952.

Walter Damm (*below, right*), vice president and manager of radio and television, until his retirement in 1958.

Rayburn Dies Quietly After a 36 Hour Coma

He Just Stopped Breathing, Doctor Says; Mr. Sam Was Speaker Twice as Long as Any Other

Bonham, Tex., (AP) Sam Rayburn, who served longer as house speaker than any man, died Thursday in the home town he loved.

Cancer and its complications caused his death. He would have been 80 on Jan. 6.

"It was a very easy death for a very great man," Dr. Joseph A. Risser told reporters.

Asked about the immediate cause of death, Dr. Risser said simply, "He just quit breathing."

Then, in more formal language, he put it this way:

On, Wisconsin

Gov. Nelson's veto of a bill that would have allowed counties to keep more of the money from county forest timber has been sustained by the narrowest of margins—only three votes in the assembly.

One estimate is that 27 counties will get $250,000 less in the next two years as their share from timber sales, under the present law, than they would have under the vetoed bill. The state will get correspondingly more as repayment of money it has advanced to these counties.

There are even more important issues than how the timber proceeds are shared. Safeguarding the 2.2 million acres of county forests and using them to the greatest possible advantage of the counties and the state as a whole must be matters of greatest concern. Future resources, as the state population grows and both the forest timber and the recreational opportunities become more valuable, must take precedence over added income now from timber or land sales.

There's no question but that the 30 year old forest crop law, as applied to county forest, needs revision. It was a well conceived, far sighted measure in its time.

The state-county venture, under the law, in restoring forest wealth has been a marked success. Times and conditions have changed, though, and the law needs a thorough revision in light of all interests involved rather than patching in response to pressure tactics.

This is what the governor had in mind in promising that he would soon appoint a special committee, representing those diverse interests, to review the matter thoroughly. The committee is to make a report and recommendations for benefit of the next legislature.

This is a sound and fair way to approach the real and difficult problem here presented.

"At 6:20 this morning Mr. Sam passed away. He died quietly. His respirations stopped.

"The heart continued to beat for four minutes after the cessation of respiration. He showed no evidence of pain lines in the face. He seemed to be as one in sleep."

Rayburn had been unconscious for about 36 hours before his death.

Full Page of Pictures on Page 12

The doctor said Rayburn had spent two near sleepless nights at the hospital.

Rayburn had lost nearly 50 pounds in the months that cancer had ravaged his body. His normal weight was 176. Dr. Risser said he had dropped to about 120.

No immediate arrangements for funeral services

Turn to page 2 column 1

Tax Plan Gains GOP Supporters

Pommering and Alfonsi Describe Changes Felt Acceptable to Nelson

Journal Madison Bureau

MADISON, WIS.— Gov. Nelson's compromise tax bill survived a major test Wednesday in a two hour closed door caucus of Republican senators and assemblymen.

Two top Republicans laid their party futures on the line by backing the bill with amendments which they said Nelson would accept.

They were Assemblymen Pommering (Rep., Wauwatosa), the party's major spokesman on taxation, and Assemblyman Alfonsi (Rep., Minocqua), assistant GOP floor leader.

Pommering and Alfonsi told the caucus they were ready to back the bill with several new changes Nelson agreed to Wednesday. After long discussion, the caucus made these decisions:

Nelson's bill would be withdrawn Thursday from the legislature's joint finance committee and placed on the assembly calendar for action. It probably will not be taken up until next week, however.

Turn to page 14 col. 1

Samuel T. Rayburn, 1882—1961

—AP Wirephoto

Mailers Walk Off Job in Journal's First Strike

The Meter Keeps Right on Ticking for the Taxpayer

Snow, Sleet, Rain Slap at Wisconsin

Road Conditions Hazardous in Northern and Western Parts of the State

Snow, sleet and heavy rain covered Wisconsin Thursday. Hazardous road conditions were reported in the northern and western parts of the state.

The weather bureau in Milwaukee reported that five inches of snow had fallen by midmorning in the La Crosse area. Tomah reported four inches and Sparta three inches.

Weathermen' R. W. Harms said that up to six inches of snow was expected to fall in north central Wisconsin by Thursday night.

Turn to page 14 col. 1

Late Bulletins

Washington, D. C. (AP) — President Kennedy, saddened by the death of House Speaker Sam Rayburn, set out Thursday on a 4-day western trip. The trip will be partly political but probably will open with a major foreign policy talk. The schedule may be altered so that Mr. Kennedy can attend Rayburn's funeral.

Earlier, Vice-President Johnson, scheduled to attend a dinner in Seattle Thursday night along with the President, cancelled his trip to fly to Bonham, Tex., where Rayburn died Thursday.

Moscow, USSR (AP) — About 2,000 foreign students attacked the French embassy Thursday, breaking windows and throwing banners into the front hallway. They were demonstrating against the imprisonment in France of Mohammed Ben Bella and other Algerian Nationalist leaders.

Mutinous Congo Troops Slay 13 UN Italian Fliers

Bodies Are Dismembered and Thrown Into River in Kivu Province; Violence in Albertville

LEOPOLDVILLE, CONGO—(AP)— The United Nations announced that insurgent Congolese troops had brutally murdered 13 Italian UN airmen at the Kivu province town of Kindu.

A UN spokesman said the murdered fliers were sought by mutiny troops shortly after their arrest Saturday.

Some of their bodies were dismembered and hurled into the Lualaba river, the spokesman added, by soldiers who apparently suspected them of being enemy paratroopers.

For the spokesman, George Ivan Smith, said the UN command was protesting, "in specific proposals" to the central Congo government for forceful action to investigate and punish those responsible for the murder and to prevent a repetition.

If the government response never materialize...

to reinforce the UN can Katanga UN garrison in Elisabethville.

He did already had difficulties military action. If the rebellious soldiers were part of a disorderly command of more than 2,000 claiming allegiance to leftist Vice-Premier Antoine Gizenga—failed to give up the Italians.

The slaying of the Italians was announced after word that Congolese Gen. Victor Lundula was returned to Kindu for another attempt to secure the airmen' release and to quell what was desired as an open outcry against the authority of the central government. Diplomats in Leopoldville said that Gizenga should be responsible for the outcry.

The Italians had flown into Kindu in two transports on a routine mission. Congolese troops attacked the airmen in one UN Malayan officers' mess, beat them and sent them one after the one to his death.

Eyewitness reports to the UN said the men were sent across a river, then shot or clubbed after one reached the central Congolese for mutiny problems deplored a guarantee of the events.

Printers Honor Pickets; Other Unions Work

Negotiations Broken Off; Contract Expired in April; Company Reveals Plans to Continue Publishing

By Stanley A. Zuckerman
of The Journal Staff

Members of The Milwaukee mailers local 23 went on strike against The Milwaukee Journal at 3:20 p.m. Wednesday.

All but one member of the typographers local 23 affiliated with the mailers, refused to cross a picket line mounted by the strikers.

Enough members of the eight other unions involved in The Journal's production and maintenance operations crossed picket lines, at the instructions of their unions, to enable The Journal to publish.

A company spokesman said that The Journal planned to continue publishing its regular editions.

Printers and compositors, members of typographers local 23, continued to work Wednesday afternoon, but the next shift did not report for work at 6 p.m.

The strike was the first in The Journal's 79 years of publication. It occurred after negotiations on a new labor contract, under way since last February, were broken off by the union Wednesday. There are 57 members of the mailers union at The Journal, and about 240 members of the typographers union.

Members of building trade unions working on The Journal's new addition reported to work on schedule Thursday morning. A building trades spokesman said union members had been advised that the mailers had not applied to the Milwaukee county labor council for strike sanction, and that other unions were not bound to respect their picket line.

Engravers Wednesday night at first declined to cross the line, but returned to work after the international union president, Wilfrid T. Connell, telephoned from Boston, Mass., that the union's "no strike" agreement with The Journal should be honored. Thursday morning,

Turn to page 14 column 3

The Weather

Temperature range Wednesday, 42 at 9 p.m. and 32 at 5:30 a.m.; precipitation for 24 hours ending at 6 a.m. Thursday, .05 of an inch.

Temperature range a year ago Wednesday, 66 and 50; precipitation, 1.28 inches.

Humidity at 6 a.m. Thursday, 93%.

Sunrise Friday, 6:40; sunset, 4:27.

Moonrise, 2:11 p.m. Friday; moonset, 2:13 a.m. Saturday.

Satellite visible: Echo 1, west to overhead, 6:34 p.m.; 7:58 p.m.; 11 p.m.

Publisher Irwin Maier (*right*) became president in 1961.

Donald B. Abert (*below*), executive vice president and general manager.

The Journal building after completion of a $14 million addition in 1962.

Election night in the Journal newsroom, with candidate John F. Kennedy, political reporters, and television men receiving returns of the 1960 Wisconsin primary.

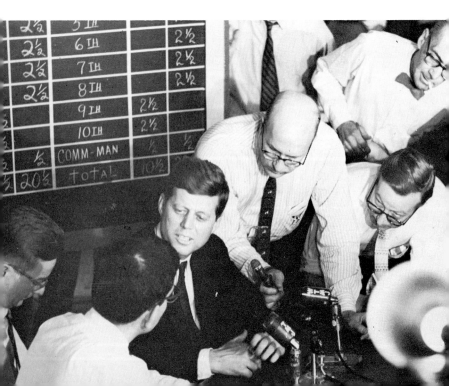

importance of the questions themselves. Such evaluation we leave to the voter. . . . In the final analysis each voter should make this analysis for himself, for it is his destiny that is at stake." The voters decided 25,600,000 to 22,000,000 that Roosevelt should finish the fight. (In Wisconsin, Dewey got 671,860 votes to Roosevelt's 647,472.) Three months after he entered his fourth term, however, Roosevelt died of a massive cerebral hemorrhage, and Vice President Truman became the nation's head.

Two great events came soon after. One was the convening in San Francisco of the long-planned international meeting to set up the United Nations. The other was the defeat of Hitler. When Germany surrendered, The Journal emphasized one point—that the occupation control must be effective enough to change the attitude of the German people and wipe out the conceptions of world conquest which had been held by the Kaiser and by Hitler. Germany must be given no opportunity to break its agreement with the Allies "as it broke the Treaty of Versailles almost before the ink was dry."

To report on the United Nations' organizational meeting, The Journal sent Lindsay Hoben, long a student of international problems, to San Francisco. For weeks he gave Journal readers reports of the struggles that went on there, especially the battles with Russia over Poland. When the final draft of the charter was signed by fifty nations on June 26, 1945, The Journal printed the complete text and hailed the signing as "one of the great moments of history."

All that remained now of the war was to finish the conquest of the Pacific. The way had been prepared through the capture of Okinawa, the last barrier to Japan. In connection with that victory, a unique experience had fallen to the lot of Journal war correspondent Robert Doyle. As Okinawa's invasion hour approached, the American commander authorized a novel experiment in press coverage—allowing one correspondent to fly over the actual scene of assault in a superfortress photo-reconnaissance plane to get an "eagle eye" view of the battle. Doyle, who had done outstanding work in the early days of the war in the Pacific, was chosen by lot to be the reporter, to represent the entire American press.

Sitting in his "flying press box," Doyle wrote his description of the early phases of the battle and handed it to the Army censor who was also aboard the superfortress. The censor passed it on to the radio operator, who sent it by short wave to San Francisco. Two hours later it was in The Journal and other newspapers. Here is the story, the first ever written and actually transmitted to the press from above a battlefield:

Aboard a B-29 over Okinawa—It is a strange thrill to sit up here over the gray-green island of Okinawa and see countless American ships of all types criss-crossing in the dark water off the invasion beaches of "D-Day plus."

We arrived over the invasion convoys shortly before dawn and circled until the sunrise highlighted the steep slopes and valleys of Okinawa, where American soldiers and marines are knocking boldly at the southern doorway to Japan. We watched dawn patrols from carriers climb up to look us over, and we saw warships lying offshore belching flames as they bombarded the Japanese. We watched flak rising from both our own and enemy guns, but we saw no enemy aircraft. Carriers and battleships moved majestically around the invasion perimeter as other craft move straight toward the beach.

We are fortunate to have perfect, clear weather over Okinawa as we made three runs in this superfort photo reconnaissance plane over the convoys and beaches. It is impossible to tell from this height what opposition ground troops are meeting, but it is clear that hundreds of our ships are moving toward the beaches to supply and reinforce the men ashore.

This beginning which Doyle saw developed into a struggle that took eighty-two days to win, but when it was completed Japan's position was perilous. Her sea lanes were closed, her cities were open to bombardment, invasion of her shores was possible. America, however, chose another way—a way which few then knew existed. On August 6, it was announced in Washington that an atom bomb, the world's first, had been dropped on Hiroshima. Three days later another bomb was dropped on Nagasaki. Faced with the alternative of making peace or being "literally blown from the face of the earth," to quote President Truman, Japan yielded.

On September 9, 1945, representatives of Japan surrendered

160

to General MacArthur aboard the battleship *Missouri,* ushering in what The Journal, expressing the feelings of all Americans, fervently hoped would be a permanent peace.

In the spring of this last year of the war, Milwaukee had found a delightful release from strained emotions, in the adventures of Gertie the Duck. She was only a little brown mallard hen, but her story packed drama beyond the fondest dreams of newspapermen the world over.

The Journal got the story first because Gordon MacQuarrie, freckled-faced, red-headed reporter, had a friend. Gordon always had a friend. That was one of his assets. Another was his talent for colorful writing on outdoor life. Thus it happened that when the bridge-tender at the Wisconsin Avenue bridge saw a duck laying eggs on top of a piling in the river at the busiest, noisiest spot in town, he told a city electrician, who called his friend Gordon MacQuarrie. MacQuarrie grabbed Harris Nowell, Journal staff expert on wildlife pictures, and rushed to the scene. Before the story which began then had been completed, The Journal was to print more than 30,000 words and 150 pictures. Even on the day of Germany's surrender Gertie was not crowded off the front page.

The reasons the story was so good are obvious. It had universal appeal. The Associated Press and United Press assigned reporters to cover it. Milwaukee families sent Journal reports to their men overseas. The Journal later published a 48-page illustrated booklet, *The Story of Gertie,* which subsequently inspired a network television show.

The story had suspense, as on the dreadful night of the storm when ducklings were falling into the river and Gertie, along with everyone else, was frantic. The "everyone else" included Larry Hautz, president of the Izaak Walton League, men from the humane society and the state conservation department, various reporters, bridge-tenders, and, of course, MacQuarrie and Nowell. It was a bad time for the bridge-tenders, who manned row boats and spent all night retrieving ducklings with dip nets.

The story had moral uplift: everyone was offering to help. The public works department had pumps going around the clock flushing 2.5 million gallons of water an hour to assure a clean, oil-free river should any little duck fall in. When the Memorial Day parade passed over the bridge, twelve feet from Gertie's nest, the bands stopped playing, everyone went *s-s-sh,* and the marchers walked softly. A construction company, ready to install new pilings for the bridge, delayed operations until Gertie should leave the nest. And when life for Gertie and her brood became too rough in the storm, Gimbel's department store, located at one end of the bridge, gave the use of a show window to house the wildlife family. Barriers were built to protect the glass from the pressure of the crowds.

The story was inspiring. The courageous little duck, having selected a decaying piling and made her nest, had sat it out for thirty-seven days while streetcars rumbled over the bridge, while an average of 87,000 men, women, and children walked over the bridge daily, and during the twenty-five times the bridge was opened to let ships pass through.

And the story had a happy ending. (How MacQuarrie and everyone on the inside had worried about that!) On a beautiful day in June, Gertie and her five healthy ducklings were put into cartons, taken to the lagoon on Lake Michigan, and released. Upon being set free, Gertie flew directly to the water, then returned and proudly led her five young hopefuls to their natural home. All were good swimmers.

26

McCarthyism at Its Peak

"The senator is either drunk or lying," said J. Donald Ferguson, editor of The Journal, referring to a speech Senator Joseph R. McCarthy made at a Republican political rally in June, 1952, at the Milwaukee Auditorium. Brave words to be printed by a responsible editor in a responsible newspaper! They showed the depth of contempt to which McCarthy had sunk in the opinion of The Journal. They also showed that the paper knew whereof it spoke. No paper deliberately invites a libel suit. McCarthy in his speech had charged that during one Senate investigation the "Communist" attorney of a witness had telephoned The Journal nine times. Ferguson, who announced that he had never met the attorney nor spoken to him on the telephone, investigated and concluded that McCarthy was "either drunk or deliberately lying."

On another occasion, following a speech by McCarthy, September 14, 1950, in which he accused the paper of being controlled by a New York attorney and urged Wauwatosa housewives to boycott its advertisers, The Journal printed in detail what he had said, then commented in an editorial headed, "McCarthy Grows Wilder": "This is in line with the senator's other irresponsible tactics. We wonder whether the senator's friends shouldn't persuade him to see a pyschiatrist."

By this time the paper had decided to add ridicule to its already powerful arsenal of weapons, regretting only that it had not joined battle against McCarthy when he made his first bid for national prominence. In 1946 the unknown McCarthy had defeated Senator Robert M. La Follette, Jr., for the Republican senatorial nomination. Neither The Journal nor the weak La Follette political organization had found out until after the primary about McCarthy's state income tax difficulties or his other irregularities, including the granting of "quickie" divorces, as a circuit judge. La Follette had sought Journal support against McCarthy, but the paper took no stand in that crucial primary. McCarthy won by 5,400 votes out of a total 410,000. In the November election The Journal considered the Democratic candidate, Howard McMurray, weak, and endorsed neither nominee. McCarthy's overwhelming victory ushered in the era of "McCarthyism," a form of hysteria resulting from the inordinate fear of communism which gripped many people in Wisconsin, and elsewhere, after World War II.

The indiscriminate labeling of innocent persons as Communists, The Journal pointed out, was undermining the United States' efforts to find and expose the real Communists and their subversive activities. In this stand the paper was in agreement with a group of prominent Wisconsin citizens that included Dr. Nathan Pusey, then president of Lawrence College in Appleton (which happened to be McCarthy's home town), and later president of Harvard University. Early in 1952 this group published a book, *The McCarthy Record,* which showed by citing congressional records, state records, court records, and direct quotations, the series of false charges and questionable financial dealings of McCarthy in his campaigns for office and in his conduct during his first term as senator. The Journal reprinted *The McCarthy Record* serially.

The paper also, in editorials, kept up its exposure of McCarthy and his devious practices, revealing his untruths and irresponsibility. An editorial, "The Man They Nominated," published September 10, 1952, was more frequently reprinted in other publications than any previous editorial the paper had run. It was also included in an anthology of outstanding editorials of American newspapers. It read:

164

An overwhelming majority of Wisconsin citizens who voted in the Republican primary Tuesday endorsed Senator McCarthy. Thus they nominated a man who:

Was censured by the Wisconsin supreme court for destroying evidence in an important case in which he was judge.

Was found by this same court to have violated his oath as a lawyer and as a judge.

Was charged by the board of state bar commissioners with "moral turpitude."

Tried to fool the people about his war record, claiming that he enlisted as a private when he actually entered the service as a commissioned officer; pretended to have been wounded when he actually injured his foot in a moment of horseplay on board a ship in peaceful waters.

Left the military service of his country while the war was still raging so that he could advance his own political fortunes.

Accepted a $10,000 fee from the Lustron Corporation while he, as a senator, was serving on a committee passing on policies of a federal agency lending millions of dollars to that corporation.

Had his bank note endorsed by a Washington lobbyist and immediately championed a sugar control measure of vital interest to that lobbyist.

Had to be required by the Wisconsin tax commission to pay more than $2,700 in delinquent income taxes and interest.

Charged that Gen. George C. Marshall was disloyal to the country.

Attempted to link Gen. Dwight D. Eisenhower with what he called the Marshall conspiracy—"a conspiracy so immense and an infamy so black as to dwarf any such venture in the history of man."

Was named by Washington newspaper correspondents as the "worst senator."

Was voted by the American Political Science association's legislative experts to be the "poorest" senator.

Loosed a campaign of character assassination against many American citizens and institutions while hiding behind his senatorial immunity.

Has been caught in dozens of lies, half truths and misstatements only to leap from one falsehood to another—always making charges, seldom answering them.

In his only primary speech, in Shorewood, chuckled cynically as his audience applauded statements that he deliberately falsified—implying that a plot of 24 years ago was a current statement of conditions in the state department.

This is the record of the man to whom voters in the Republican primary gave their approval on Tuesday.

To hide an appalling record of fraud and deceit from the voters of

Wisconsin—to make them forget his poor record in the senate—McCarthy came up in 1950 with his issue of "Communists in government." He had considered other possible issues he could exploit—an old age pension plan of fabulous proportions—all-out support of the St. Lawrence waterway—but decided they lacked the necessary "appeal."

He had never before paid much attention to communism anywhere. But now he began making sensational charges. As soon as one charge proved false, he made more. It was Hitler's big lie technique all over again and it was exploitation of the same basic fear of communism.

Certainly there have been Communists in our government. It is more than probable that there are some today. But the justice department, the FBI, the loyalty boards, the house un-American activities committee, other congressional committees, and senators like Richard Nixon and Karl Mundt, both Republicans, have worked to weed them out. This is still being done—by careful investigation, by legal processes and with respect for the rights of citizens.

These persons and boards did not depend on character assassination, on lies, on sensational charges. And they got results, something that Senator McCarthy has never got insofar as discovering and digging Communists out of the government.

A majority of those voting in the Republican primary Tuesday fell for this hoax.

This is not only appalling—it is frightening.

It betrays a dulled moral sense, a dimmed instinct for truth, for honor, decency and fairness.

It rewards falsehood, chicanery, deception, ruthlessness, the tactics of smear and fear, and contempt for the constitutional principles that safeguard American human and legal rights.

It will cause misgivings for the future across the land, for it evidences the dangers which confront our fundamental freedom.

And The Journal's efforts were rewarded. In 1946, Milwaukee County, the largest in the state, had voted for McCarthy, assuring him the election. By 1952, the year the quoted editorial was printed, Milwaukee County turned against him by 100,000 votes. Dane County also rejected McCarthy by 48,000 to 29,000 votes, largely due to the McCarthy exposure conducted by the Madison *Capital Times*. Nevertheless McCarthy was re-elected. He carried every county in the state where a majority of the newspapers supported him or stood silent. But he lost every county in the state in which either a daily paper or a labor weekly fought him with the facts.

Commenting on this election, the *Progressive* magazine, published at Madison, said: "We are convinced—and the events of the recent past strengthen that conviction—that the most effective weapon against McCarthyism, as indeed against Communism, or any other counterfeit philosophy, is the truth."

Senator McCarthy died in 1957, a discredited man, "condemned" by the United States Senate. Only twice before in 178 years of American history had the Senate thus rebuked any of its own members.

27

A City and a Paper Brighten Up

In the years following World War II Milwaukee experienced the greatest civic development in its history; and The Milwaukee Journal, its greatest expansion. Long before the war, The Journal had suggested and supported plans for improving the city. The Depression and the war had intervened; and streets and buildings were in a rundown condition.

Milwaukee citizens—merchants, industrialists, labor leaders, and professional men—all were agreed at the end of the war that work should start at once. Soon after the surrender of Japan, the 1948 Corporation was formed to promote civic improvement and to handle the three centennials that were approaching—Milwaukee's in 1946, and those of Wisconsin and the University of Wisconsin in 1948. Irwin Maier, Journal publisher and later president, was a director of the Corporation; and Donald B. Abert, at that time business manager of The Journal, was an active member.

To commemorate the centennials The Journal published two books, *The Milwaukee Story* and *The Wisconsin Story,* both by Journal writer H. Russell Austin, after running them serially in the Green Sheet. The centennial edition issued by the paper consisted of sixty-four pages, thirty-one of them in color, with a rotogravure section providing a pictorial history of Wisconsin.

In its civic development program, the 1948 Corporation was concerned with blight elimination, development of Maitland lakefront airstrip, off-street parking, housing, completion of the civic center, a new zoo, expressways, Mitchell Field airport enlargement, a sports arena, a county stadium, and a war memorial building to house Milwaukee's art institute. The war memorial was first suggested by three Milwaukee women's organizations—the Altrusa, the Zonta, and the Business and Professional Women's clubs. The suggestion was lauded by The Journal, as was the proposal to build more houses to meet the acute need expected with the return of servicemen. It was essential, The Journal said, to have a community-wide housing program, carried out by private effort where possible, but supported by public funds when necessary.

Once the centennial celebrations were over, the 1948 Corporation was dissolved and the Greater Milwaukee Committee for Community Development was formed, with expanded membership. Results of the Greater Milwaukee Committee's efforts were evident in the next decade, in the number of expressways completed or under construction; in the lakefront War Memorial, designed by Eero Saarinen, to house the Milwaukee Art Center; in the sports arena at the civic center; in County Stadium, with seats for 44,000 Braves baseball fans; and in the improved Mitchell Field airport. The Milwaukee skyline had been brightened by the seventeen-story YMCA building and the contemporary architecture of the city hall annex. Construction of the Marine Plaza and of the $14 million addition to the Journal building had been completed. A new county zoo, the envy of zoological garden planners everywhere, was being finished. It had, as a gift from The Journal, a miniature railroad which circled its grounds. One engine, named "Lucius W. Nieman," was numbered "1882" for the year Nieman started The Journal. Another engine, the "Harry J. Grant," was numbered "1916," the year Grant came to the newspaper.

In this postwar period The Journal expanded in both editorial and business departments, sending newsmen to trouble spots around the world, adding and enlarging features, modernizing the plant. Especially notable was expansion of the Sunday department, begun under Waldo R. Arnold, managing editor who died in 1946, and continued by Wallace Lomoe, his successor, who later became executive editor. By 1953 the Sunday paper was in twelve parts—the main news section, the state and local news section, sports, the men's and recreation section, the editorial section, the women's section, the home section, classified advertising, the magazine This Week, the Sunday Picture Journal, colored comics, and the TV-Screen tabloid. The size of the Sunday issues varied from 250 to 350 pages, depending on fluctuations in advertising.

Quality of editorial content was elevated far above that in Sunday supplements of the early-day sensational press. The Sunday editorial section, for instance, was enlarged from four pages to six to present more fully background articles on world affairs, American problems, state and community movements, as well as cultural arts. A page of music and theater news and a page on the fine arts were added. A book page and the editorial page had long since been regular features. By this time Literary Editor Leslie Cross was receiving more than 4,000 new books a year; often a book which was not treated among the reviews became the basis for an editorial page feature in the daily Journal.

The men's and recreation section, making its first appearance September 27, 1953, was an innovation in newspaper editing. It included features on outdoor life, travel, hobbies, boating and automotive activities, economics and business—in fact, almost anything which especially interests men. Don C. Trenary became its first editor. Women were also interested, surveys showed, especially in the travel pages, and Paul McMahon, editor of them, made frequent trips to Europe, Asia, South America, and Africa to obtain firsthand information for his readers.

The TV-Screen magazine, a colorful Journal-produced tabloid, mirrored the world of television, radio, movies, and records. It also printed the weekly broadcasting schedules. Donald Dornbrook, its editor, went regularly to Hollywood and New York to gather material on people and events in entertainment.

The Journal library, with a highly efficient filing system for clippings and research and biographical material, expanded to meet needs of the new pictorial journalism. A daily picture page, started in 1931, had increased the number of photographs used in the paper. By 1949 Journal photographers were taking 1,200 pictures a week, and even this figure grew when the photo staff was enlarged to seventeen men and each photographer's car was equipped with a two-way radio. Pictures poured into the library, not only from Journal photographers, but by mail from agencies and by wire from the Associated Press and the United Press International. Librarian William Schiela and his successor, Ruth DeVoy, were in charge of this expansion.

For use of reporters and feature writers, the library had, by 1961, upwards of three million newspaper clippings (with 400 more added daily), more than a million pictures, uncounted thousands of pamphlets, 5,000 reference books, and files of more than one hundred magazines. All this was supplemented in 1962 by the addition of the *Sentinel*'s large library when that newspaper was bought by The Journal. The library staff of twelve was doubled to serve both papers.

The Journal's expansions in the fifteen years after the end of World War II greatly increased the number of employes, and made necessary an addition to the building. The remainder of the block bounded by Kilbourn Avenue, State, Third, and Fourth streets was purchased, and on the quarter block at Third and State streets work started in 1959 on a multimillion dollar addition, which was completed in 1962. The new structure, designed by the architectural firm of Eschweiler and Eschweiler, was in contemporary style, of reinforced concrete faced with pink Kasota limestone, black granite, and gray brick. Its northern half was built three stories high, its southern half six stories. The building was erected on 1,111 steel H-piles, averaging 65 feet long and weighing 3,445 pounds. Such a foundation, needed to carry the heavy presses and other mechanical equipment, would bear a 42-story building.

The cornerstone was laid by Harry J. Grant on September 15, 1961, his eightieth birthday. The addition was the largest undertaking, in terms of expense and size, in the first eighty years of The Journal. The cost of the building, its equipment, and the remodeling of the old structure, was more than $14 million.* In equipment, two 8-unit presses with decks for ROP (run of paper) color printing, were installed, at a cost of $3 million. Each press had the capacity to print a 64-page section at a speed of 60,000 copies an hour. Room was provided for two more such presses should they be needed. The most advanced equipment for mailing, stereotyping, and the handling of paper and ink was provided.

Perhaps the most remarkable expansion in the years following World War II was in the area of advertising. The year the war ended—1945—The Journal claimed first place for advertising linage, but Media Records allowed the Chicago *Tribune*'s "split run" advertising claim and put the *Tribune* in the lead. The Journal's 22 million line total that year was considered a peak not likely to be reached again, but five years later the paper's linage was double that figure.

In the years 1950 through 1954 The Journal led the world in volume of newspaper advertising.† The peak year of the five was 1953, with a total of more than 51 million lines. The Chicago *Tribune* was in second place; Los Angeles *Times,* third; Miami *Herald,* fourth; and Washington *Star,* fifth. The peak year in The Journal's eighty-year history was 1956, with a linage of 58,132,817. In 1961, handicapped by a strike from November 15 to December 11, The Journal dropped to fifth place in newspaper advertising volume, with a linage of 51,219,412.

This linage leadership did not mean that the paper's revenue from advertising was the greatest in the world. Large dailies in New York, Chicago, and elsewhere commanded higher rates which brought in greater total revenue. The Journal's policy, as laid down by Grant, had been to keep its rates low enough to permit

* This figure may be compared to the $2.1 million spent in 1924 on building and equipment.

† Advertising linage was:

1950	44,649,859
1951	45,788,940
1952	49,457,702
1953	51,073,874
1954	49,370,297

small business firms to advertise, and the volume of ads was impressive.

This heavy advertising had been built up largely under Irwin Maier's regime as vice president and publisher. Maier was born in 1899 at Mellen, Wisconsin, of German and Irish ancestry. After graduation from the University of Wisconsin and a stint as advertising manager of the Madison *Capital Times,* he joined The Journal in 1924 as an advertising salesman. He rose steadily, becoming vice president and publisher in 1943, and president in 1961 when J. Donald Ferguson retired. As a Journal executive, he advocated more vigorous efforts to get national advertising, much of which was at that time going by default to magazines. In 1937–38 he was president of the Newspaper Advertising Executives' Association. Through the Bureau of Advertising and kindred organizations he fostered development of advertising research through which the advantages of daily newspaper linage could be proven to heads of large corporations.

Maier was elected to the board of the American Newspaper Publishers Association, an organization of 1,000 dailies, in 1955, and became its president in 1962. As a representative of the ANPA he attended the International Press Institute conference in Paris, in 1962, where the world movement for freedom of the press and higher journalistic standards was debated. At the same time he took part in the conference of the International Federation of Newspaper Publishers, a world-wide organization similar to the ANPA.

When Maier was elected Journal president he did not take the position of editor also, as his predecessors—Nieman, Grant, Creager, and Ferguson—had done. Instead he appointed Lindsay Hoben editor. Hoben, who began his career on The Journal in 1926, was born in Milwaukee in 1902, the son of Dr. Allan Hoben, a Baptist minister who later became president of Kalamazoo College, in Michigan. After graduating from Carleton College, Northfield, Minnesota, Hoben worked on The Journal for a year and then took time from his job as a reporter to visit Europe and Russia. A short time afterward, in 1929, he started on a year's trip around the world, going by land through China and Siberia. In Russia he traveled 10,000 miles, from Vladivostok to Archangel, then looped back through Soviet central Asia to the Caspian and Black Sea regions.

He saw more of communism in action than had been seen by any American correspondent up to that time. And his previous trip enabled him to evaluate changes made by the Soviets. En route he sent back a diary-like series, "Around the World with a Journal Man," which appeared on the editorial page; and when he got away from Russian censorship, he wrote three well-documented articles on the character of communism—its lies to its people, its play upon their fears, and its dictatorial power over them. He wrote, on the other hand, that the Soviets were providing more schools, more extensive electrification, and many minor improvements which had been undreamed of in old Russia. He also noted the development of a privileged class of Communist leaders. Reprints of his articles were distributed to many papers through the North American Newspaper Alliance.

Hoben later visited the Near East and wrote an accurate prediction of the trouble that was to develop between the new Zionist state of Israel and the Arab world.

In 1934, Hoben became the first editor of the newly created Sunday editorial section, which provided a history-in-the-making background for the news. He was made an editorial writer in 1938, chief editorial writer in 1949, and vice president of The Journal Company in 1955. At the retirement of Ferguson in 1961, Hoben became editor of The Journal, the paper's fifth in its seventy-eight years.

28

The Employes Become Owners

"It has been my desire and purpose in my lifetime to establish The Milwaukee Journal as a newspaper of independence and force, devoted to the maintenance of high ideals for the civic and moral life of the community, . . ." So Lucius Nieman had declared in his will. Before he died, on October 1, 1935, after fifty-three years as head of The Journal, he had given careful thought to the future of the paper. He had framed his will so as to insure that his successors would be able to follow his principles. The statement quoted just above continued ". . . and it is my wish and I authorize and direct [the] trustee to carry out such purpose in the management of the trust estate and in any disposition of the stock."

Nieman at his death owned 55 per cent of the paper's stock. The heirs of his former partner, L. T. Boyd, owned 25 per cent. Harry Grant owned 20 per cent. Nieman's will left one-half of his holding to his wife, Agnes Wahl Nieman, and one-half to his niece, Faye McBeath. The will had a mandatory provision that the stock be sold within five years after Nieman's death.

When the contents of the will were made known, an idea which Harry Grant had long had in mind began to take form. He had come to the paper as an employe and now owned one-fifth of its stock. This holding had been an incentive to him, an inspiration to do his job well. "If owning stock works for me," he reasoned, "it should work for others on the payroll." He explained to Mrs.

Nieman and Miss McBeath his plan for employe purchase of the stock.

Miss McBeath, who at the request of her uncle some years before had given up a teaching career to become a member of the Journal staff, and who had long identified herself with the paper's spirit, approved. Mrs. Nieman, eager to perpetuate the institution her husband had built up, was also cooperative. The trustees (Edwin S. Mack, the First Wisconsin National Bank, and Frederic Sammond) were cautious: some businesses had been wrecked by employe ownership. Grant contended that The Journal's staff was capable of taking the responsibility, and pointed out that this might be the only way to preserve The Journal in accordance with its principles and to save it from absentee ownership.

At Nieman's death, Moses L. Annenberg, owner of the Philadelphia *Inquirer* and of a racing wire service, tried to buy the Nieman stock. Several other newspaper owners and chains expressed interest in purchasing it at prices equal to or higher than the bid Grant made, but Annenberg's was the only firm cash offer. All of these prospective owners represented out-of-state groups which saw the paper chiefly as a profitable investment.

Grant could have made a bid on his own account. He was offered the financial backing with which to buy all the Nieman stock but turned it down with the statement that he would resign and leave The Journal unless his plan for employe participation could be realized. Mrs. Nieman herself was putting pressure on the trustees to accept Grant's offer as 1935 came to a close. Early in 1936, Mrs. Nieman's nephew, Cyril Gordon Weld, to whom she had intended leaving her estate, died in New York. Mrs. Nieman made a new will, bequeathing the proceeds of her 27.5 per cent of her late husband's holdings to Harvard University "to promote and elevate the standards of journalism in the United States and educate persons deemed especially qualified for journalism." This bequest, which amounted to $1.3 million after inheritance taxes were paid, was to become the basis for the Lucius W. Nieman Fellowships at Harvard, where each year a dozen or more chosen men and women, on leave from their newspapers, may attend any classes or pursue any studies they choose.

The wisdom of Mrs. Nieman's bequest to Harvard University has been borne out by the record of the more than 250 Fellows who have later gone on to more fruitful work in their profession.* Their presence was also good for the university, according to James Bryant Conant, president emeritus, who once spoke of the advantage to students and faculty of having in their midst mature, experienced men with the ability to ask "rude questions."

On February 5, 1936, Mrs. Nieman died, and there ensued further complications in settling the future of The Journal. The case for Grant's employe ownership proposal was saved by the clause in Nieman's will which provided that trustees "shall not be bound to sell [stock] to persons or corporations who may bid or be willing to offer the highest price, but may sell to such persons or corporations as in the judgment of said trustee or trustees will carry out the ideals and principles which I have always attempted to maintain and support during my lifetime in the conduct of The Milwaukee Journal."

Who could best fulfill that requirement of maintaining Nieman's standards? "Certainly no stranger," said Grant. "Certainly no chain newspaper owner. Not even a group of Milwaukeeans unacquainted with the institutional history of The Journal and its day to day work. I maintain that only the staff—those who have lived with The Journal and become a part of its spirit—can meet this test."

Harvard University, which now held Mrs. Nieman's 27.5 per cent of stock, was open-minded about the employe ownership plan, sending its treasurer, Henry Lee Shattuck, to Milwaukee for consultation. He was impressed by the soundness of Grant's proposal and agreed to the plan. Miss McBeath and the Boyd family, the latter represented by Elwyn Evans of Wilmington, Delaware, who had married Boyd's daughter, Mary, gave their endorsement. In

---

* Journal men who have been Nieman Fellows are Ralph Werner (1940–41), Robert H. Fleming (1949–50), Don Janson (1952–53), John D. Pomfret (1960–61), John W. Kole (1962–63).

1936, Grant, Miss McBeath, and The Journal Company offered to buy the Nieman stock at $3,500 a share. Trustees and County Judge Michael Sheridan approved the sale though the total purchase price was about $2.5 million less than Annenberg's bid. Then came a period of litigation resulting from the effort of three distant relatives of Mrs. Nieman to invalidate her will. Though the effort failed, the series of legal actions, carrying the case to the Wisconsin Supreme Court, meant more delays.

Finally, on December 28, 1936, The Journal Company in a preparatory step used $2.8 million of its reserve funds to purchase 800 shares of stock, which it placed in the company's treasury. Six hundred and fifty of these shares came from the Nieman estate, fifty from Miss McBeath, and one hundred from the Boyd family. This deal equalized the holdings of Grant, Miss McBeath, and the Boyd estate, with each owning one-third of the stock.

The next step was to split the stock into smaller units for convenience in distribution to employes. The number of shares was increased from 2,000 to 200,000. On May 25, 1937, each share was worth $35 instead of $3,500. The total value of all Journal stock was $7 million. Each of the three active owners agreed to make available 10,000 shares for the initial employe-ownership plan distribution. Lawyers were called in to create an instrument providing a workable means of employe participation, one that protected rights of all and would meet all future contingencies, and also would make sure that the stock would remain in the Journal "family," passing from old employes to new, and not into the hands of the outside public.

Under The Journal Employes' Stock Trust Agreement,* the actual shares of stock are placed in trust. What the employe buys is a "unit of beneficial interest." Each unit embodies all the rights of common stock with one exception: the owner cannot dispose of his units in any way that separates them permanently from the

---

* The original trust agreement was signed by Harry J. Grant; Faye McBeath; Susan A. Boyd, widow of L. T. Boyd; Katherine Boyd Morehead and Mary Boyd Evans, daughters; Elwyn Evans, representing the Wilmington Trust Company, which had charge of the Boyd estate; Leslie A. Webster, Journal publisher; John Donald Ferguson, chief editorial writer; Leonard L. Bowyer, business manager; and Marvin H Creager, managing editor.

stock trust. The units must be sold to the trustees when the owner ceases to be an employe. To fix a fair price for resale of stock to the trust fund a formula was set up, based on the book value, the earning power over a period of years, the increase in plant or institutional value, and the surplus in the treasury not declared as dividend. Because of the financial success of The Journal, the value of stock advanced steadily. In 1948 the stock was split five for one. On July 30, 1962, the price per unit, under the formula, was roughly seven times the 1937 cost.

To assure fair distribution of units to employes, a provision placed this responsibility with the president of the company, acting not in his official capacity but as an individual. One limitation was imposed upon him—he could not allot any stock to himself without specific authorization by the directors for each allotment. As president, Grant made the first allotment of 30,000 shares to employes in 1937. Every employe who had been with the company five years was given an opportunity to become a unit-holder. A company bonus plus the employe's one-fourth down payment enabled him to have these first units half paid for at the time they were received. Interest rates for the unpaid half were low.

After getting the new stock plan in operation, Grant became chairman of the board, and Marvin Creager, managing editor, succeeded him as president and editor. Creager made the second allotment of stock, in 1938, when Grant and Miss McBeath offered 18,000 more shares to employes. When Creager, due to failing health, retired from the presidency and editorship in 1943 to become vice president and editorial adviser, John Donald Ferguson, who succeeded him, allocated the stock units.

Gradually a definite formula was built up, based on wide distribution and on recognition of responsibilities of each employe's work. Employes who are under union contracts were included in the distribution. "The allotment of stock," said Ferguson, "has been such that no single group, and no possible combinations of two or three groups, including the executive group, could control the company."

To increase interest in actual operations of the paper, and to provide an orderly method for the election of employe-owner representatives to the board of directors, a unit-holders' council was created in 1943 at the request of Grant. This council, of twenty-four members, was made up of four representatives from each of six departmental divisions: (1) advertising and promotion, (2) circulation, (3) editorial, (4) business office, (5) mechanical, (6) radio and television. Council members were elected by unit-holders to a term of two years, with half of the terms expiring each year. Company executives could vote as unit-holders but were not eligible for council membership. In the nominations each unit-holder had one vote. In the election to choose six council members to serve on the board of directors of The Journal Company for one year, the unit-holder had one vote for each unit he owned.

The employe ownership plan worked so successfully that in May, 1947, at a banquet on its tenth anniversary, Grant and Miss McBeath announced that they were making available 18,000 more shares, which would give employes a majority control—55 per cent—in The Journal Company. In 1953 another step was taken to broaden employe ownership, when Grant arranged employe purchase of half of the shares owned by the Boyd family heirs. This stock was delivered over a five-year period—15,000 shares a year. The Boyd family agreed in 1960 to sell the remainder of its stock holdings to the trustees over another five-year period. This would bring employe ownership to 80 per cent by 1965. At mid-year, 1962, unit-holders numbered 1,039, controlled 72.5 per cent of The Journal stock, and were moving steadily to increase this percentage. President Ferguson could say of the ownership plan:

It has been successful even beyond our hopes in 1937, not only in the advantages to employes in sharing the earnings of the enterprise, but in the pride they take as sharing owners in turning out the best product and giving the best service of which they are capable. . . . Employe ownership has not only thus been of great benefit to the newspaper and the broadcasting operations, but likewise to the community which we serve and in which we live.

Of greater significance, perhaps, were remarks made at the banquet, in 1947, celebrating the tenth anniversary of employe participation in ownership. Harry Grant said then that the Journal plan was "in no sense a departure from the capitalistic system under a democratic form of government," that it was an adaptation of that system to the particular problems presented by the American newspaper, adding:

Our Unitholders' Stock Trust Agreement has attracted national attention. Its feature of actual stock ownership is something greater than profit sharing, annual bonuses or work guarantee plans, which may be dissolved at the discretion of the management. Owners of important newspapers are beginning to realize its broad advantages for perpetuating vital policies and for assuring the future of their institutions. No other plan has so much promise.

Employes recorded their opinion of the plan on scrolls which were presented to Grant, Miss McBeath, and Elwyn Evans:

. . . Employe ownership knits our lives together. We don't work FOR The Journal. We ARE The Journal, newspaper and radio. Above all we are grateful for the security which sharing ownership has brought into our lives. Now no bidder at the auction block can take the newspaper or radio from us. We stand on guard to preserve and perpetuate this institution in our time, and beyond. . . .

In addition to stock ownership, The Journal provides a liberal welfare program. In 1925, group life insurance was set up, with one-half of the premium paid by the company. First aid and health service were added in 1936 with a full-time nurse in charge. Hospital insurance was added in 1940, and surgical care in 1944, both paid by the company. A retirement and disability pension plan, integrated with social security, was set up in 1943, with costs paid by the company. Maximum pension for a thirty-five year employe was 52.5 per cent of his average pay received in the ten years prior to age sixty-five.

In addition to these welfare benefits, employes were offered invaluable help through the Journal Thrift Association, started in 1939. Under the guidance of Joseph Kopp, composing-room man who advanced to the position of mechanical coordinator, the association enabled many employes to acquire homes, to tide themselves over family crises, to build up investments for the future. The association's assets by the year 1962 were more than $3.8 million.

29

A Benevolent and Dynamic Leader

When Harry J. Grant relinquished active control of The Journal he was fifty-six years old, the paper was prosperous, and he was at the pinnacle of his power. Nieman had died in 1935, and Grant had become president and editor. Shortly thereafter he laid out his plan for employe ownership, and then in April, 1938, gave up both his titles and became chairman of the board. He insisted on being relieved of regular duties, but kept in daily touch with Journal executives whether he was in his apartment in Milwaukee, his home on Rivo Alto Island, Miami Beach, or on his 71-foot yacht, *High Tide,* in Florida waters.

"I have seen too many men become hard and stubborn as they grow old," he said. "Before I get that way—which God forbid—I am going to step out."

Grant appointed Marvin H Creager president and editor, and refrained from directing the editorial policy of the paper. Instead, he stressed character and high moral tone, and, while he seldom made public speeches, he occasionally addressed employes on their duties. Here are some of his thoughts:

"We stick by principles instead of to individuals."

"Character is what matters on a newspaper."

"We must have freedom . . . not to be willful, or bigoted, or swell headed . . . but so that The Journal can act entirely as it thinks best for the community. The Journal is above our frailties. The Journal's job is to serve the public. It can't be anything else."

"The editorial columns express Journal opinions and strive to win people by marshaling facts and appealing to minds through logic rather than prejudice, emotions and hysteria."

"I know we are right when both sides damn us. But whatever they say about us, they can't control us."

To his employes Grant was kindly. The pension plan he had established for the paper provided that while employes might retire at sixty-five years, they were not required to do so. Of men and women whose work was no longer adequate he would say, "They were loyal to us all these years. Now if they want to stay on, it's time for us to be loyal to them."

For infractions of the moral code, however, he showed no leniency. There was the Journal executive who was convicted of driving while intoxicated and fleeing from the scene of an accident. The story was printed on the front page of the paper and the executive resigned.

Police Chief John W. Polcyn once said: "The Journal watches officials like a hawk. God help you if you get out of line. They take the flesh right off your bones."

So sternly did Grant hold himself to his own code of ethics that he refused to make any public appearances. The governor of Wisconsin once invited him to a dinner in honor of Adolph Ochs, publisher of the *New York Times*. Grant wanted to meet Ochs, whom he greatly admired, and he liked the governor, but he declined the invitation because he felt that the head of a Wisconsin newspaper should not be the guest of a Wisconsin lawmaker.

In the confines of his office, however, this seemingly shy man was most frequently referred to as a dynamo. During discussions of a controversial subject he would rise from his chair and pace the floor, stopping at intervals to make his point with gestures. At times he would mimic the mannerisms or speech of the person he referred to, causing his audience to be convulsed with laughter. He could have been an actor, said his colleagues. In his home he was a gracious host. His conversation was enjoyable and when the occasion was right, he could entertain delightfully on his guitar.

Grant received many honors that were gratifying to him and the paper. In 1949, the University of Wisconsin awarded him an honorary doctor of laws degree, citing particularly his part in the employe ownership plan. In 1956, he received from Marquette University an honorary degree of doctor of letters, the citation stating, in part, that "his superior performance of numberless tasks before him has fostered a great newspaper."

Northwestern University, celebrating its centennial in 1951, chose Grant as one of a group of men and women from six states of the old Northwest Territory to receive their "distinguished service to society" award. The citation for Grant read in part: "Under his direction The Journal has become recognized as one of the country's leading publications, independent and honest, avoiding the sensational."

The University of Minnesota awarded a medal and certificate to Grant in 1950 "for unusual distinction in the newspaper profession." This award is sponsored by the *Inland Daily Press,* and the recipient is selected by the Minnesota journalism faculty. All citations on these awards emphasize the importance of Grant's plan for employe ownership of the paper. In 1933, however, before the beginning of the ownership plan, the University of Missouri gave him a medal and certificate "for unusual distinction in the newspaper business."

Grant was made a professional member of the University of Wisconsin chapter of Sigma Delta Chi in 1948, one of the first three ever elected fellow in that honorary journalistic organization.

One honor of which Grant was particularly proud was a life membership card in the International Printing, Pressmen, and Assistants Union of North America (AFL). The citation, in part, read that the Journal pension fund "established a challenging precedent for all those who hold managerial positions with newspapers, magazines and printing offices."

Shortly after establishment of the employe ownership plan, a committee of rank-and-file Journal men and women decided to have a portrait of Grant painted by a leading American artist. No executives knew of the project until pledges for payment had been collected. When the committee called on Grant to ask him to sit for the portrait he was delighted but said that he would pay for the painting.

"Mr. Grant," said the chairman, "This is to be our portrait. This is one time when you are not running the show."

The portrait, by Leopold Seyffert of New York City, hangs in the lobby of the Journal building at Fourth and State streets where Harry Grant had his office and directed the paper for so many years. It makes a fitting companion piece to the painting by Carl von Marr of Lucius W. Nieman, founder of the paper, which also hangs in the lobby.

30

Get the Paper to the Readers

A newspaper's lifeblood depends, aptly enough, on its circulation. Without satisfactory circulation no advertiser would advertise. A basic principle is that if a paper is a good one it will sell. Journal Circulation Manager Elmer Schroeder contended that if a paper is good the reader will continue to subscribe to it, but that he must first be introduced. The job of the circulation department is to make the paper readily available. When reporters have met the deadline with their stories, when the city editor and rewrite men have put the stories in readable form in next to no time, when copy editors and headline writers have passed them along with chain-belt rapidity, when they have gone through the composing room and the pressroom—then it is a matter of pride with the circulation department to "get that newspaper on the front porch."

By 1962, the eightieth year of The Journal, the circulation department each day of the week delivered 325,800 papers to Milwaukee area homes in four hours, and 33,000 more within a radius of two hundred miles in six hours. On Sunday, in time for breakfast, it delivered more than 550,000 Journals. These papers added up to 90,000 tons of newsprint a year, costing more than $12 million, a sum roughly equivalent to the total payroll of the paper. Delivery was performed by 150 full-time employes, 500 part-time employes, and 7,000 independent carriers. To transport the papers to distribution centers required more than 100 Journal-owned trucks rolling twenty-one hours a day, 150 relay trucks and passenger cars, and 25 to 35 rented trucks. The total annual run of this fleet was the equivalent of 145 times around the world.

These modern delivery figures are amazing to old-timers who remember the days when The Journal rented a horse and wagon or borrowed L. W. Nieman's white coach horse to haul papers to the railroad station. The first truck was purchased in 1911. Nowadays, so precise is the timing and so smooth is the operation that in fair weather the trucking task seems simple. It is heavy Wisconsin snows, ice-coated streets, or torrential rains that tax the ingenuity of circulation men. In emergencies, boats, planes, trains, and helicopters are brought into play.

One Saturday night in 1956 the newsroom received word from the weather bureau of a flash snowfall in a band across the middle of the state. Circulation Manager Schroeder held back his trucks, telephoned the Milwaukee Road to put on an extra baggage car, asked some trains to wait at junction points, alerted district circulation managers in the state to meet the trains, and so got The Journal through. Deliveries of rival Sunday papers bogged down, with trucks stuck in the snow. On another occasion, when the Mississippi River flooded at La Crosse, Journals were delivered by boat. Several Wisconsin lakes regularly have marine delivery of the paper to summer visitors. When Mellen, Wisconsin, was isolated by floods, papers were flown in by chartered plane and dropped to the town. When a gang of robbers with machine guns held up a Green Bay bank and shot several policemen one morning at 9 o'clock, The Journal rented a plane and had 1,000 papers in that city by 3 P.M.

The Journal has always prided itself on being a home-delivered rather than a street-sale newspaper. The year of its eightieth anniversary 90 per cent of the total number of daily Journals and 92 per cent of the Sunday Journals were delivered to homes.

Each Journal carrier owns his paper route, having paid to a previous carrier 32.4 cents for each daily subscriber and 19 cents for each Sunday subscriber. The boy makes 1.9 cents on a daily paper and 5 cents on a Sunday. An average route includes about eighty-five customers. When a boy decides to go out of business he sells his route to the next carrier. Though he looks to the district manager for guidance in his job, the boy is not an employe of the paper. And while no concessions such as reduced prices* are offered to the subscriber, The Journal conducts contests among the newspaper boys to encourage them to get more customers.

There was a time, strangely enough, when all personnel of the circulation department, trained exclusively to sell, had to reverse their procedure and try to get rid of subscribers. This was during World War II when a great increase in persons wanting the paper was accompanied by a shortage of newsprint. Beginning in November, 1942, the paper went through a period of discontinuing contests among carriers for new subscribers, of removing want ads and local display advertisements from state editions, and of dropping out-of-state subscribers except for men in the service. In 1944, the paper was "happy" to announce that it had cut down 10 per cent of its circulation. At one time there was a small added amount of newsprint available and restrictions were eased a bit, but subscriptions poured in so fast that by November, 1944, circulation was cut off in most of the upper peninsula of Michigan and many northern Wisconsin counties. As the shortage continued, circulation in Milwaukee County and eventually in the city of Milwaukee was "frozen." If a Milwaukeean wanted the paper delivered to his home, the circulation department took a copy off a downtown newsstand quota to supply him.

In its effort to obtain newsprint The Journal bought 40 per cent interest in the Peavey paper mill at Ladysmith, Wisconsin, but even this additional supply did not meet the need. It was not until September, 1948, that all newsprint restrictions were removed and the paper was able to invite its old subscribers to come back. The circulation department's wartime "retreat" had lasted six years. Renewed efforts brought subscribers back. By 1962, The Journal ranked ninth in circulation among afternoon dailies of the United States.†

* The price of The Journal does not equal the cost of the paper it is printed on. Newsprint in 1962 cost 6¾ cents a pound. The daily paper, priced at 7 cents, averages more than a pound, and the Sunday paper, at 20 cents, weighs about three pounds.

† By mid-1962, Journal circulation figures had passed 371,000 daily and 511,000 Sunday.

The life of a newspaper, by its nature, is closely involved with the public. Readers agree or disagree with what the paper prints, subscribers are pleased or disgruntled with the delivery service, advertisers are concerned with the effectiveness of their ads. Beyond the task of improving to the best of its ability the editorial content, the circulation facilities, and the advertising service, a paper must strive for the good will of its community if it is to succeed. Obtaining this good will is the function of the promotion department.

Perhaps "Brownie" Rowland was the first promoter on The Journal. Certainly his activities in providing touring information gave motorists of the 1920's a kindly feeling toward the paper. But since those days, newspaper promotion has expanded into a broader field, one that includes service not only to readers but also to advertisers. In 1922, Walter J. Damm, later of Journal radio and television, was put in charge of a fact-finding bureau, called merchandising service, and told to get from merchants information on the buying habits of Milwaukee housewives.

"Why not get this information from the consumers themselves?" Damm asked. And he launched into consumer analysis. Hundreds of housewives in all parts of the city were mailed questionnaires asking, "How many bars of laundry soap do you use in a week? What brand?" and similar inquiries covering purchase of the packaged, canned, or bottled goods a housewife normally buys. Then, if the housewife took the properly filled-out questionnaire to The Journal, she received a large shopping bag of samples that had been gladly contributed by manufacturers. The idea caught on like fire, and the manufacturers were amazed at the accuracy of the market information that the Journal analysis gave them. This consumer analysis was continued yearly by The Journal, and the idea has been copied by more than twenty newspapers from Maine to Hawaii. In 1960, Milwaukee housewives claimed 6,459 bags, each containing forty items; this represented an 80 per cent response to the questionnaires.

The survey is one of many activities of the promotion department, headed by Courtland R. Conlee, who succeeded Walter Damm in 1927. The annual student art calendar competition, put on by the department, has been an inspiration to talented students from the seventh through the twelfth grades in Wisconsin public, parochial, and private schools. Begun in 1943, the contest had grown, by 1960, to 2,262 entries from 132 communities in the state. Each of the six students winning top honors in painting that year received a $100 United States savings bond. Thirty silver palettes and fifty bronze palettes were awarded for other paintings of merit. The six best pictures of the show were reproduced in color—and thirty others in black and white—in The Journal's Christmas calendar, distributed by the newspaper boys. A selection of several hundred pictures was hung in an exhibition for three weeks in the Journal building.

In 1961 the paper sent three Milwaukee area high school students who aspired to newspaper careers to the University of Wisconsin journalism workship at Madison. The following year there were so many applicants for this opportunity that the number was increased to five outstanding pupils from city and suburban public and parochial high schools.

In a contest in 1936, The Journal had asked school teachers to write on their use of newspapers in classrooms. A book based on the teachers' reports was prepared by Luvella and Alfred Reschke, widely known Milwaukee teachers. Their newspaper consultant was Will C. Conrad of The Journal, who revised the edition in 1951. The book was then the basis of a year's experiment in Sauk County schools, in which the daily paper was supplied for supplementary reading and study. Following this example, several years later, the Texas Daily Newspaper Association launched a statewide program on similar lines. In other states, summer workshops have been established to instruct teachers in correlating education and the news of the day.

Two Wisconsin high school teachers have been sent each year since 1959, at Journal expense, to the American Newspaper Publishers Association's "Newspaper in the Classrooms" workshop at the University of Iowa. A Milwaukee workshop for 580 interested high school students and advisors was conducted in 1961 at West Division High School by members of The Journal's editorial, advertising, and photographic departments. Another 275 attended a workshop held later in the paper's cafeteria.

An effective device in encouraging students to make intelligent use of the newspaper has been the distribution of The Sunday Journal's editorial section each Tuesday or Wednesday to schools throughout Wisconsin. In 1962 more than 12,000 of these supplements were sent out, to 400 schools.

"Learn-a-Language" records, recommended by the state Department of Public Education and the University of Wisconsin, were put on sale by The Journal at a nominal cost in 1962. More than 130,000 were sold in the first few months.

The promotion department builds good will for The Journal through the many public events sponsored annually. These include the junior tennis tournament, the chess tournament, marble tournament, snapshot contests, ski school, Four-H farm safety program, all-star football dinner, shotgun hunters' clinic, Boy Scout journalism seminar, youth review, science fair, silver skates races, power boat regatta, indoor track games, track clinic, and an exhibition of elementary school art in addition to the Journal calendar art competition show.

The department also has a service which prepares advertising copy for business firms too small to have their own ad writers, and for organizations wishing to advertise as a group.

The program of events has been flexible over the years. When a project has been successfully launched it is frequently taken over by an organization. The Food Show, begun by the paper, was continued by the Retail Growers' Organization. The Journal's radio show in the Auditorium became the Builders' Home Show. The Journal conducted the city's first automobile show.

Throughout the years The Journal has been a publisher of books. *The Milwaukee Story* and *The Wisconsin Story,* mentioned earlier, filled a need for popular histories of the city and state. To aid servicemen who had been injured in World War II, The Journal published a book on veterans' rehabilitation, containing reprints of a detailed series that had appeared in the paper. Five annual volumes of *As The Journal Told It,* containing reprints of the best articles of the year, have been widely used in schools as examples of good writing. Booklets, varying in subject matter from Wisconsin trees and Wisconsin fish to radio news-writing, occupational therapy, the newspaper in the classroom, golf, and a fashion art notebook, have been published and widely read.

31

Integrity Commands Respect

To be held in esteem by a jury of one's peers is a gratifying experience in any profession. In 1960, a poll of 335 daily newspaper editors in the United States ranked The Journal third in their list of the country's ten best papers, with the *New York Times* and the *Christian Science Monitor* ranking first and second. In similar polls, in 1961, 311 publishers voted The Journal fourth place among all dailies, and 125 deans and professors of journalism ranked it fifth.*

These editors, publishers, and university men placed independence and reliability high among their criteria of quality in a newspaper. Continuity of purpose, or the paper's role in raising social,

* The following tables show the results of the three polls:

Journalism Deans and Professors—1961	Editors of Daily Newspapers—1960	Publishers of Daily Newspapers—1961
1. New York Times	1. New York Times	1. New York Times
2. Christian Science Monitor	2. Christian Science Monitor	2. St. Louis Post-Dispatch
3. Wall Street Journal	3. Milwaukee Journal	3. Christian Science Monitor
4. St. Louis Post-Dispatch	4. St. Louis Post-Dispatch	4. Milwaukee Journal
5. Milwaukee Journal	5. Washington Post	5. Louisville Courier-Journal
6. Washington Post	6. Louisville Courier-Journal	6. New York Herald-Tribune
7. New York Herald-Tribune	7. Wall Street Journal	7. Washington Post
8. Louisville Courier-Journal	8. Atlanta Constitution	8. Los Angeles Times
9. Chicago Tribune	9. Chicago Tribune	9. Chicago Tribune
10. Chicago Daily News	10. Des Moines Register	10. Kansas City Star

cultural, and political standards in its community, was also a factor in determining their choice. Another was the paper's achievement in recording and reflecting the history of its day.

During the ten years prior to 1960, The Journal had greatly increased staff coverage of world news and conditions behind the news. Following World War II, in response to growing public interest in foreign affairs, the paper sent its writers to Europe, Asia, Africa, South America, and Cuba. Articles written on the spot gave significant information to readers, and the correspondents returned better qualified to interpret developments in the countries visited.

When Poland agreed, in September, 1945, to admit the American press, a Journal reporter who spoke the Polish language, Edward S. Kerstein, was sent there. His articles telling of the suffering that Poland was enduring because of broken promises of the Soviet Union were the first direct reports from postwar Poland to any American newspaper.

At the invitation of the War Department in 1946, a group of newspapermen including J. Donald Ferguson, editor of The Journal, went to the occupied zones of Germany and Austria. Ferguson's articles brilliantly expounded the problems America, Britain, and France faced in these areas. He also learned from occupation forces detailed facts about what went on in Hitler's Germany that had not been previously revealed.

In 1947, The Journal established a Washington bureau. Laurence C. Eklund, who was put in charge, held this position for many years, with an office in the National Press Building. He kept in close touch with congressmen from Wisconsin and watched particularly any developments that might affect the state. In 1949 he was one of twelve American newspapermen invited to go to Norway, Sweden, and Denmark to report on postwar conditions there. Later, in 1960, Eklund flew to Antarctica and wrote detailed stories on America's activities in Operation Deep Freeze as part of the International Geophysical Year.

Austin C. Wehrwein made an intensive study of Canada, interviewed Canadian political, industrial, and agricultural leaders, and wrote a series on Canada's advancement which The Journal later published as a booklet, *Canada's New Century*. For Wehrwein's work he was awarded the 1953 Pulitzer prize in international reporting.

In 1954, Paul Ringler, editorial writer on political and international subjects, visited France, Germany, Austria, Italy, Yugoslavia, Greece, Turkey, Lebanon, Israel, Iran, and Egypt. He interviewed many leaders, including Abdel Nasser in Egypt. Early in 1957, John N. Reddin, also an editorial writer on international and political affairs, went to Afghanistan, Pakistan, Nepal, India, Ceylon, Burma, Thailand, Cambodia, South Vietnam, Singapore, Indonesia, the Philippines, Formosa, Japan, and Korea. He had long talks with Prime Minister Nehru of India, President Garcia of the Philippines, and General Chiang Kai-shek in Formosa. Reddin, in his three and a half months of traveling, wrote sixty articles.

Lindsay Hoben, as editorial editor, became an active leader in the International Press Institute (IPI), a world organization devoted to the free flow of reliable news among nations and to the improvement of journalism. In 1957 at the Institute's general assembly in Paris, attended by editors from Great Britain, France, and the United States, Hoben and Jenkin Lloyd Jones of the Tulsa *Tribune* analyzed in speeches American editorial attitudes toward Britain and France. A week later, at the Amsterdam conference of the Institute, Hoben talked on the use of color in newspapers, explaining The Journal's experiments and progress. In the 1960 meeting of the Institute in Tokyo, Hoben was moderator for the session on "The Mass Press, East and West." The following year, in Tel Aviv, Hoben spoke negatively on "Is the Press Falling into Disrepute?"

In October of 1958, Harry S. Pease went to Russia, and in thousands of miles of travel got a revealing view of Soviet life. He wrote thirty-six articles giving Journal readers his observations of cities, villages, collective farms, schools, and homes. When he returned home he put together ten newspaper pages of photographs to round out the picture of Communist life.

When the Cuban revolt was climaxed by the overthrow of Fulgencio Batista, in 1958, William Normyle flew to Havana. In twenty-six articles he reported in detail on the significance of the Fidel Castro movement.

Early in 1959, Edwin Bayley, a Journal political writer, went to Europe on an exchange fellowship awarded by the International Press Institute, one of four American newspapermen so honored. For four months he toured Great Britain, France, and Germany, reporting on conditions that affect the vitality of freedom and democracy. In the same year, Don C. Trenary, editor of the men's and recreation section, traveled widely in Africa, to observe and report on reactions of people in the new nations as colonialism gave way to independence. He visited Liberia, the Ivory Coast, Ghana, Nigeria, the Republic of the Congo, the Belgian Congo, Uganda, the Sudan, and other areas. Two years later he retraced his steps to observe changes that had taken place.

As mentioned earlier, The Journal's high rating among American newspapers depended partly on the role it played in raising standards in its community. In 1956, when he was editor of the Journal editorial page, Lindsay Hoben said in a speech:

> Because of the intense partisanship with which the average American takes his politics, too many persons seem to be under the impression that a newspaper's support or opposition to any political party or to any particular candidate is the most important function of editorials.
>
> Far more important is the usually quiet, year after year hammering for needed reforms and improvements.

Over the years the primary goal of Journal editorials has been to foster a better community and to eliminate injustices. As examples, in the year mentioned—1956—The Journal pleaded for a modern criminal code in Wisconsin, for creation of a state traffic patrol, for the integration of the University of Wisconsin with state colleges, and for needed changes in the conservation department. It opposed pensions for state legislators, it was against laws that it believed would cripple housing projects, it was opposed to the loyalty oath bill, and it fought to expose any secrecy in government.

"On the national scene," said Hoben, in the same speech quoted above,

The Journal probably printed more information on the Tennessee Valley Authority controversy over the Dixon-Yates deal than any other paper in the country. The Dixon-Yates case involved a private utility's effort to poach on TVA territory at Memphis, Tenn. President Eisenhower cancelled the contract when a government consultant was shown to be financially interested through a Boston bank. The president's decision supported our dim view of the whole mess.

We were among the first to point out the deterioration in the food and drug administration, and the importance of FDA to good health.

In the field of foreign affairs we continued to explain the complexities of the problems, to tell why conditions in Cyprus, Jordan, South Africa and the Sudan—though far away—were important to Americans, who should be concerned about them.

The Journal sought to reveal the twists and turns of Soviet policy, the changes since Stalin's death, the worthlessness of Soviet pledges based on historical record, the Soviet dependence on falsehood and misrepresentation. We voiced skepticism about the "Geneva Spirit" from the start—and were very soon justified.

As early as 1943, when hope of Allied victory in the war was growing, The Journal had raised the question of whether Russian Communists would ever join with the Western powers in building a durable peace. An editorial said: "The only hope for a stable world is the cooperation of the great powers. Will Russia go along? It is a grave question." After the Teheran conference and the Yalta meeting, the disturbing answer came. "Not only is Russia failing to do her share in building collective peace and security," an editorial commented on July 16, 1946, "she is actually obstructing such efforts."

The hottest differences of opinion on The Journal's editorial stands usually arose over political matters—local, state, national, and international—as Hoben remarked in the speech in 1956. "The Journal does not support a person on the basis of whether he will win or not. It supports a man because it believes him to be the better qualified practical candidate for a particular office at a particular time. We are sometimes accused of being politically partisan. Actually The Journal has long been, and is, an independent newspaper."*

* *Time Magazine,* February 1, 1954, said: "The paper calls itself independent as

In state politics, the paper backed a Republican, Walter Kohler, for governor in 1930 and again in the 1932 primary when his opponent was Phillip La Follette, a Progressive. However, in the November election that year no clear-cut endorsement of either Kohler or Albert G. Schmedeman, the Democrat, was printed. Schmedeman won in the Roosevelt landslide. In 1934 Journal support went to Schmedeman; and in 1936 to another Democrat, Arthur W. Lueck, in a three-way race with Phillip La Follette and Republican Alexander Wiley. La Follette won.

It is worth noting that The Journal never had the enthusiasm for Senator Robert La Follette, Jr. and Governor Phillip La Follette that it had for their father, "Old Bob," in his early days. Young Bob was considered a conscientious senator and was sometimes commended, sometimes criticized. Editorials were more friendly toward him than toward his brother Phil. As governor, Phil was praised for many things, among them the "roller coaster" highways which eliminated numerous railroad grade crossings, but was vigorously denounced when he brought politics into selection of a University of Wisconsin president and when he attempted to form a political organization with overtones of Hitlerism. Phil never forgave the newspaper for its denunciation. He once said that he would rather have his children grow up illiterate than have them read The Milwaukee Journal.*

In 1938 and 1940 the paper endorsed Julius Heil, a Republican, against La Follette, but in 1942 backed Orland S. Loomis,

---

many other dailies do, but for The Journal the term is an understatement. In a single election the paper once supported a Socialist, a Republican, a Democrat, and a Wisconsin Progressive. Grant's independent attitude is to go to the truth wherever you find it, and to hell with left or right." The four endorsements *Time* referred to were probably these, in 1932: Hoan, the Socialist, for mayor, and Mudrock, the Wisconsin Progressive, for city treasurer, in the Milwaukee spring primary; Kohler, the Republican, for governor in the September state primary; and Roosevelt, the Democrat, for President in the November election.

* Many other persons have expressed almost the same feeling. Commenting on this fact, the *British Weekly* of London, for January 12, 1956, said: "The city reads The Milwaukee Journal (which has been rated in the top 10 in the United States) that is so fearless and fair in any controversy as to be usually respected but rarely loved."

a Progressive, because it felt that Heil had not lived up to expectations. In 1944 and 1946 support went to Walter Goodland, a Republican, against Daniel W. Hoan, Milwaukee's Socialist mayor who was running as a Democrat. In 1948 only mild backing was given to Oscar Rennebohm, a Republican, but before his term was up the paper felt that he was one of the state's better governors. In 1950 no preference was expressed, but both Carl W. Thompson, a Democrat, and Walter J. Kohler, Jr., a Republican, were considered well qualified. In 1952 and in 1954 no endorsement was given to either Kohler or William Proxmire, Democrat. In 1956 the paper favored Proxmire but did not declare for him; nor did it endorse Gaylord Nelson, Democrat, in 1958, though it favored him. It supported him in 1960 when he was re-elected. In 1962 it backed John W. Reynolds, Democrat.

The Journal has seldom endorsed a candidate for United States senator, though it did back Leonard Schmitt in 1952 in his fight to unseat McCarthy.

The Journal's stand in presidential elections before 1948 has already been recorded in earlier chapters. In the presidential campaign of 1948 the Republicans nominated Governor Thomas E. Dewey of New York for President, and Governor Earl Warren of California for Vice President. The Democrats nominated President Truman and Senator Alben W. Barkley of Kentucky. The Journal praised the Republican platform as "an encouragingly good document" and criticized Truman. He had created confusion in the country through his handling of domestic issues, an editorial said, and had let a bad situation develop in Washington by his coddling of political cronies. The paper's endorsement went to Dewey.

Four years later the presidential contest was between Republican General Dwight D. Eisenhower and Democratic Governor Adlai Stevenson of Illinois. The Journal said of Stevenson that he showed "a broad understanding of the nation's problems" and that he talked "plainly to the American people, taking unpopular positions and telling voters things they did not want to hear." Toward the end of the campaign the paper endorsed Stevenson, saying it believed that he would make a good President, and "possibly a great president."

In the 1956 campaign President Eisenhower and Vice President Richard M. Nixon ran against Stevenson and Senator Estes Kefauver of Tennessee. Criticizing Eisenhower for his lack of leadership in his first term, The Journal supported Stevenson in this his second unsuccessful try.

The Democratic primaries of 1960 preceding the national convention were dramatic. The Wisconsin primary was crucial for John F. Kennedy. To start his campaign rolling he needed a spring victory over his chief opponent, Senator Hubert Humphrey of Minnesota; Kennedy and the Kennedys swarmed over the state. The Journal noted that the religious issue was "smoldering" and deplored it as having "sinster roots." "Religious prejudice," said The Journal, "has no proper place in American life." It is a transgression of a "constitutional principle." To vote either against Kennedy or for him solely because he was a Catholic would be wrong. The Journal had said the same thing in the 1928 campaign of Al Smith. It called upon Wisconsin voters to repudiate prejudice. Kennedy won the primary by a 100,000 vote margin.

The Journal backed Kennedy for the Presidency, over his Republican opponent Nixon. In assessing the two men it found many similarities. Both were called "young and vigorous . . . intelligent, confident, poised and trained for leadership." Both were seen as professional politicians who "do their home work." But The Journal believed that Nixon was concerned basically with his image, while Kennedy's major interest was in ideas. Nixon professed to be satisfied with America's direction and progress, while Kennedy showed deep dissatisfaction and determination to greatly improve our rate of progress—which coincided with the way The Journal had been feeling.

Foreign policy was the main issue, The Journal believed. It also believed that Kennedy was right in saying that our power had been dissipated and our prestige diminished, a charge which Nixon denied. In a long, detailed editorial The Journal summed up: "In the best judgment of The Journal, John F. Kennedy is the clear choice in this year of 1960."

In the eight presidential races following the crash of 1929, The Journal had endorsed the Democratic nominee in five elections, the Republican in two, and had expressed no choice in one. The paper had been for Roosevelt in two of his four races, Dewey in one of his two, and Stevenson in both of his tries. It had declined to choose between Dewey and Roosevelt in 1944. It had been for Willkie in 1940 and for Kennedy in 1960.

32

A Strike, a New Paper, a New Day

"We do not work FOR The Journal. We ARE The Journal. . . . We stand on guard to preserve and perpetuate this institution in our time and beyond." So Journal employes had said in 1947, on the tenth anniversary of the employe ownership plan.

Were these idle words, written by makers of fine phrases and subscribed to unreflectingly? Men and women of the paper had opportunity late in 1961 to prove that they meant what they had said. On November 15, that year, occurred the first strike in The Journal's seventy-nine years. In mid-afternoon fifty-seven mailers walked off their jobs, followed by printers, who had a joint contract with the mailers. Other union crafts refused to cross the picket lines. The strike lasted twenty-six days, but the paper did not miss publication a single day.

An inspired force of reporters, editors, advertising men, bookkeepers, truck drivers, radio and TV workers, artists, promotion writers, and typists stepped into the breach. For most of these men and women, acquaintance with the mechanical side of the paper had been limited to an occasional glance into the pressroom at those huge mysterious machines so nimbly operated by experts. The forty-hour week was forgotten. A large staff was on duty at 5:30 A.M., and quitting time for many was midnight.

The typists were of prime importance in getting out the first papers. News stories and other editorial matter were typed, photographed, and then made into etched plates which were printed.

But these typists had not learned to justify their lines to newspaper column widths, and the results were sometimes strange to behold. In the final paste-up by news editors and men in the art department, articles too long were left out or were ended abruptly. The paper that had been 136 pages the day before the strike dropped to eight. On three days all advertising was omitted; on another day editorials and editorial features shared a page with pictures. There was no Green Sheet those first few days.

Then the process began to improve. The women quickly acquired skill in a tape-perforating method for automatic operation of the typesetting machines, and the paper was issued with practically no printers other than foremen. A few editorial and business-office men were found who had started their careers in country printing offices. There was one newsman who had worked his way through college as a printer; an upstate circulation man had once been a Linotype operator. Other employes found themselves doing their regular work plus mechanical jobs they had never heard of. There was no hint of weakening by any of these men and women, although some said later that they did not know how much longer they could have held up under the grueling hours. During the strike their determination that "the paper must come out" kept them going.

These employes did not belong to a union though they had had an opportunity to join. In 1943 the American Newspaper Guild attempted to organize the editorial department, but the effort met with so little success that the Guild's petition for an election was dropped. Grant, much disturbed at the time, told his executives, "It's a choice between me and the Guild. If the American Newspaper Guild comes in I leave."

In retrospect the 1961 strike had its amusing aspects. How to keep in order the hundreds and hundreds of yards of perforated tape that were pouring in from the telegraph machines was one problem. A news editor solved it by buying a clothesline and clothespins. The line was strung in the plant which prides itself on having the latest in equipment. Another incongruous sight was that of a striker leaving the picket line to attend the meeting of the Journal board of directors called to vote the semiannual dividend for himself and the 1,038 other employe-owners. In striking, these employes raised the interesting question of whether a man could sensibly strike against an institution in which he himself was part owner.

Pickets were avid to buy copies of the paper when it was put on the street—not for the news, but to see how it looked. They found plenty of errors, especially at first. In reproducing by the photo-engraving process an advertisement that the rival *Sentinel* had used, the inexperienced Journal men had neglected to delete the line below the ad that read, "Sentinel Want Ads Get Best Results." Then there was the Sunday TV-Screen magazine which came off the presses with the colored cover on the back page, and the back page advertisement where the cover should have been.

The 350-page Sunday Journal, a creditable job, which appeared after eighteen days, was thought by many to have broken the back of the strike. On December 11, twenty-six days from the time it had begun, the trouble ended.* The major demand of the mailers for a "status quo" clause in the use of improved equipment was not granted. The mailers accepted the terms, which included job guarantees to men then employed. The Journal had offered that assurance before the walkout occurred.

Nearly six months later, on May 27, 1962, another strike, one that was never to be settled, began at the Milwaukee *Sentinel,* that paper's first in 125 years. This strike was called by the Milwaukee Newspaper Guild, representing about 350 employes in the editorial, advertising, business, and circulation departments. The *Sentinel,* which had 650 employes, ceased publication, leaving Milwaukee without a morning newspaper.

Six weeks later the Hearst Corporation, owners of the *Sentinel,* offered to sell it to The Journal. Twenty-five years before, when Hearst had proposed sale of the *Sentinel* and the *Wisconsin News* to The Journal, the offer was not accepted. Would a different decision be wise now? After an intensive study of the question, The

* Journal advertising for the 26 days of the 1961 strike totaled 2,826,555 lines, a loss of little over two million lines from the total of the same 26 days in 1960. On the other hand the *Sentinel,* not on strike, gained almost a million lines over its 1960 total for the period.

Journal decided on July 14 to consider Hearst's proposal. Final terms for the sale—$3 million and assumption of the Sentinel building lease—were agreed upon July 18 at the New York offices of the Hearst Corporation. On the next day the board of directors of The Journal Company ratified the agreement. Two members of the board came great distances to attend the historic meeting. Editor Lindsay Hoben, on a round-the-world vacation, was reached by telephone at Perth, Australia, at 4 A.M. on Monday, July 16. Managing Editor Arville Schaleben was notified in Moscow, Tuesday night. Both men were on hand when the meeting opened Thursday at 9 A.M.

The Hearst announcement of the *Sentinel* sale was brief. "The paper has suffered substantial losses over a long period," it read. "Prohibitive operating costs and labor demands have forced us to leave the Milwaukee newspaper field, which we have been privileged to serve for 38 years." The Journal Company's statement read, in part:

It was the sincere hope of The Journal Company that the Sentinel would resume publication as a Hearst enterprise. This hope was not realized.

An offer of sale was made recently by the Hearst Corporation. It was considered reluctantly by The Journal Company. This organization has never wanted to acquire the Sentinel or any other paper. . . . In its 80 years The Journal has never bought or acquired another newspaper. It has grown on its own.

However, The Journal has an obligation to the people of this city and this state. Permanent passing of a morning newspaper in Milwaukee would result in a serious loss of reader and advertiser service. . . .

The Milwaukee Journal has acquired assets of the Milwaukee Sentinel with the purpose of publishing the best possible morning newspaper in the city and state and maintaining the Sentinel as a vital part of American journalism and as a significant contribution to the life, progress and history of Milwaukee and Wisconsin.

The Sunday *Sentinel* was discontinued. The new daily *Sentinel*, directed by a group of key Journal executives who were transferred for the task, began publication July 23, in the recently vacated annex of the Journal building. Harvey Schwandner, Journal assistant managing editor, became executive editor of the

Sentinel; Harry Sonneborn, Journal city editor, was made *Sentinel* managing editor; and Robert Wills, assistant city editor of The Journal, became *Sentinel* city editor. Many *Sentinel* newsmen were hired, and six Journal writers were transferred to the *Sentinel*.

Outside of the news department and mechanical departments, operation of the two papers required no major increase in personnel. The addition to the Journal building and the installation of new equipment having been completed just prior to purchase of the *Sentinel,* adequate physical facilities were assured.

At midyear, 1962, The Journal Company had more than 2,500 employes, of whom 1,600 worked full time and 900 part time. Circulation figures for The Journal had passed 371,000 daily and 511,000 Sunday. Executives of the company at the end of 1962 were Harry J. Grant, chairman of the board; Irwin Maier, president and publisher; Donald B. Abert, executive vice president and general manager; and the following eight vice presidents: Lindsay Hoben, editor; Arville Schaleben, executive editor; Robert K. Drew, business manager; Harold E. Daniels, advertising manager; Elmer H. Schroeder, circulation manager; Courtland R. Conlee, promotion manager; Robert J. Dumke, production manager; and George Comte, manager of radio and television. Treasurer of the company was Thomas J. McCollow; secretary, Francis D. Kelly; editorial editor, Paul Ringler; and managing editor, Richard Leonard. Other departmental editors included: city editor, Harry Hill; news editor, Fred Remick; feature editor, William Radloff; picture editor, Charles Scott. The art director was William Westerman and the photography manager was Elmer Staab.

Led by Irwin Maier and Lindsay Hoben, the management was steadfast in its resolve to maintain the principles laid down in 1882 by Lucius W. Nieman and implemented by Harry J. Grant. The challenge was great. A relay satellite in the sky held the promise of instantaneous communications. America's Midwest was no longer an area apart. What happened anywhere in the world could be of immediate concern to all men. Would the future show The Journal rising to the challenge?

Nieman in his day had met his challenge: from a 10 by 10 foot cubbyhole and borrowed presses in 1882, he had led the paper through fifty-three years of growth and widening influence. Then Grant had forged ahead to achieve further expansion and new prestige for the paper. During these years Milwaukee had grown from a community of 120,000 to a metropolitan area of more than a million. And The Journal had grown with it. Principles, alone, had not changed. Nieman said that the paper must be independent, it must endeavor to give the facts, to do injustice to no one, to serve the people. Grant fostered this independence in a complex and changing world. The paper, he believed, should steer its own course, always oblivious of outside influence.

In 1962, the men at the helm recognized the greater responsibility that went with ownership of the two major papers serving Milwaukee and Wisconsin. But they and the thousand or more employe-owners could look ahead with the confidence that comes from following a well-charted course—the course of independence, fairness, vigilance, and dedication to the truth.

Appendix · Index

Appendix

CHRONOLOGY

Dec. 11, 1882	L. W. Nieman, at 25, became editor and half-owner of the three-week-old Daily Journal.
Jan. 10, 1883	Eighty lives lost in Newhall House fire; exposure of owners' negligence "made The Journal a newspaper."
Jan. 29, 1883	Moved to 433 Broadway; incorporated as The Journal Company; announced circulation was growing by about 300 copies a week.
Jan. 1, 1884	At end of first year, circulation in the city was largest of any English-language newspaper.
May 11, 1885	Moved to larger plant at 92 Mason Street, changed masthead to "The Milwaukee Journal," and two days later printed its first page-one illustration.
Oct. 14, 1889	Frustrated by Republican abuses in state treasury graft, removed "independent newspaper" from masthead; two years later became "official state paper" under Democratic regime.
1890	Opposed Bennett law which required that schools conduct classes in the English language.
Nov., 1890	Supported Democrat George W. Peck for governor on platform for repeal of Bennett law.
Jan. 5, 1891	First known use of color printing in The Journal.
1892	Circulation 14,000, "largest in Wisconsin."
May, 1892	Moved to Montgomery Building, at Milwaukee and Michigan streets.
1893	State supreme court upheld conviction of state treasurers who had pocketed state fund interest, a Journal victory in a 10-year fight.
July 22, 1893	Open house for public to see eight Linotypes, the first

	in Wisconsin, and to see press which would print 48,000 small papers an hour.
Sept., 1896	Bolted Democratic party, repudiated Bryan and free silver policy, and permanently became "an independent newspaper"; lost half of circulation in three weeks.
Nov. 7, 1904	Won U. S. Supreme Court decision in conspiracy case in which three rival papers had plotted to undermine The Journal through advertisers.
1906	Edna Ferber began her three years as Journal reporter; later used "Brownie" Rowland as prototype in her novel *Dawn O'Hara*.
Apr. 8, 1907	Moved to new building, 734 N. Fourth Street; financial statement for 1907 showed $6,220 loss, the only year "in the red" since earliest days of the paper; earnings for 1908 were $10,231.
1908	Carl Sandburg joined staff and became city hall reporter.
1911	First motor truck rented by circulation department; bought own trucks in 1917.
Nov. 19, 1911	Sunday edition started.
May 6, 1912	State nonpartisan election law enacted as result of Journal's "test election" which united political parties and defeated Socialists in Milwaukee.
Apr. 10, 1915	Hoisted "Over 100,000 Circulation" pennant. Year's earnings passed $50,000 for first time.
June, 1916	Harry J. Grant joined Journal as advertising manager.
Oct. 14, 1916	Printed first documentary exposure of Milwaukee pro-Germanism.
June 2, 1919	Received Pulitzer prize for stand against wartime anti-Americanism in Wisconsin.
Nov. 22, 1919	Admitted "grievous error" in its stand in 1890 against the Bennett school law which required that classes be conducted in the English language.
Mar. 13, 1921	First issue of Journal Sunday magazine.
Oct. 26, 1924	Moved to new $1 million building at Fourth and State streets.
Jan. 25, 1925	Joined Marquette University in operating radio station WHAD; no commercials.
July 25, 1927	Started radio station on its own—WTMJ.
Dec. 11, 1927	First colorgravure paid advertisement in Journal.
Sept. 8, 1931	Daily picture page started.
1935	Cartoonist Ross A. Lewis was awarded Pulitzer prize for 1934 cartoon on labor-industry violence.
Jan. 2, 1935	Wirephoto for transmitting pictures began operation.

Feb. 1, 1935	Death of Lucius W. Nieman, president and editor for 53 years; succeeded by Harry J. Grant.
Feb. 24, 1935	Became charter member of Sunday newspaper group originating *This Week* magazine.
Sept. 22, 1935	First issue of Screen and Radio magazine.
1936	Grant and Miss Faye McBeath, with court approval, bought Nieman's Journal stock for redistribution to employes.
May 16, 1937	First full color ROP process advertisement in Journal.
May 25, 1937	Employee ownership plan started, with allotment of 30,000 units of stock to five-year employes.
Apr. 16, 1938	Marvin H Creager became president and editor; Grant became chairman of the board.
Sept., 1938	Lucius W. Nieman fellowships set up at Harvard University through bequest of Agnes Wahl Nieman.
Feb. 3, 1940	First frequency modulation broadcasting station west of the Alleghenies—WTMJ-FM—went on the air.
Aug., 1942	Radio City, 720 E. Capitol Drive, completed.
July 12, 1943	John Donald Ferguson became president and editor when Creager's health failed.
May 10, 1945	First newspaper color photograph of a news event printed.
May, 1947	Employes' holdings of Journal stock increased to 55 per cent.
Dec. 3, 1947	Television broadcasting started on WTMJ-TV.
1947	Led world in volume of newspaper color advertising from 1947 through 1960.
1950	Advertising volume—44,649,859 lines—was world's largest. Journal was also first in 1951, '52, '53, and '54.
Sept. 10, 1952	Printed anti-McCarthy editorial, the most widely quoted editorial in Journal's first 80 years.
1953	Austin Wehrwein was awarded Pulitzer prize for international reporting on "Canada's New Century."
Dec. 20, 1953	First network television program over WTMJ-TV.
July 18, 1954	First color television program originating in Wisconsin.
Apr. 13, 1960	Construction started on $14 million addition to Journal building.
June 5, 1960	Lucius W. Nieman chair of journalism established at Marquette University through $300,000 gift of Miss Faye McBeath.
Dec. 1, 1960	Employes' holding of Journal stock increased to 70 per cent with purchase of additional shares from Boyd heirs.

Jan. 1, 1961	Irwin Maier became president and Lindsay Hoben became editor upon retirement of President-Editor Ferguson. Donald B. Abert became executive vice president and general manager.
Sept. 15, 1961	Cornerstone for addition to Journal building laid by Harry J. Grant on his 80th birthday.
Nov. 15 to Dec. 11, 1961	Journal had its first strike, caused by walkout of 57 mailers who had joint contract with typographical union. Foremen and non-union employes issued paper until strike was settled.
July 19, 1962	Journal Company purchased Milwaukee *Sentinel*, which had suspended publication because of Newspaper Guild strike since May 27.
July 23, 1962	First issue of "new" *Sentinel* under Journal ownership.
July 12, 1963	Death of Harry J. Grant.

JOURNAL STAND IN PRESIDENTIAL RACES, 1884–1960

Year	*Journal Supported*	*Elected*
1884	Cleveland (D)	Cleveland
1888	Cleveland	Harrison (R)
1892	Cleveland	Cleveland
1896	Palmer*	McKinley (R)
1900	(No choice)†	McKinley
1904	Parker (D)	T. Roosevelt (R)
1908	(No choice)†	Taft (R)
1912	Wilson (D)	Wilson
1916	Wilson	Wilson
1920	Cox (D)	Harding (R)
1924	Davis (D)	Coolidge (R)
1928	Smith (D)	Hoover (R)
1932	F. Roosevelt (D)	Roosevelt
1936	Roosevelt	Roosevelt
1940	Willkie (R)	Roosevelt
1944	(No choice)‡	Roosevelt
1948	Dewey (R)	Truman (D)
1952	Stevenson (D)	Eisenhower (R)
1956	Stevenson	Eisenhower
1960	Kennedy (D)	Kennedy

* Gold Standard Democrat.
† Bryan was Democratic candidate.
‡ Dewey was Republican candidate.

MILWAUKEE JOURNAL CIRCULATION

(Figures taken from September 30, 1913* through 1962, ABC Publisher's Statements)

Year	Daily	Sunday	Year	Daily	Sunday
1913	74,275	46,957	1938	210,588	243,284
1914	82,503	57,667	1939	243,825	259,667
1915	93,358	72,399	1940	251,373	277,953
1916	103,918	88,677	1941	262,257	295,596
1917	112,247	100,515	1942	280,378	314,087
1918	119,386	92,447	1943	282,509	314,548
1919	101,320	93,847	1944	278,521	311,418
1920	107,564	95,074	1945	281,467	314,298
1921	111,862	87,593	1946	299,998	352,912
1922	114,755	90,043	1947	308,818	368,042
1923	118,555	103,107	1948	309,414	378,048
1924	126,988	121,548	1949	318,681	413,087
1925	132,748	125,421	1950	324,268	435,939
1926	148,314	148,798	1951	327,944	446,307
1927	158,115	167,611	1952	333,171	449,778
1928	165,378	198,043	1953	339,532	463,613
1929	171,793	217,334	1954	346,364	471,833
1930	167,839	216,819	1955	345,684	477,285
1931	156,040	212,225	1956	348,393	484,956
1932	149,901	186,170	1957	352,566	494,619
1933	146,037	175,472	1958	361,856	497,598
1934	155,817	184,892	1959	369,418	503,059
1935	169,921	199,542	1960	370,989	507,270
1936	187,041	221,119	1961	372,276	513,696
1937	203,439	236,662	1962	373,657	561,118

* 1913 earliest year available in tabulated form.

Index

workshops of, 190–91; national rating of, 193–94; establishes Washington bureau, 194; on national affairs, 197; political independence of, 198 ff.; on anti-Catholicism, 200; strike against, 202–4, 214. *See also Daily Journal; Nieman, Lucius W.*
Milwaukee Journal (German), 43–44
Milwaukee Journal Consumer Analysis report, 147, 189
Milwaukee *Leader,* 68, 72, 94, 95
Milwaukee Newspaper Guild, 204
Milwaukee Road, 19, 187
Milwaukee School of Engineering, 147
Milwaukee *Sentinel:* early days of, 4; Nieman reporter for, 6; Nieman managing editor of, 7, 8; and Newhall/House fire, 12–14; on improvement of Milwaukee fire protection, 17; and state treasury scandal, 39; expansion of, 42; for nonpartisan elections, 72; conspires against *Journal,* 74–76; purchased by *Journal,* 154n, 171, 204–6, 214
Milwaukee Story, The (Austin), 168, 191
Milwaukee War Memorial, 169
Minnesota, 58, 143, 149, 200
Mississippi River, 189
Miss Lulu Bett (Gale), 78
Missouri, 19, 149
Missouri (battleship), 161
Mitchell Field (Milwaukee), 169
Moffett, Elizabeth B., 115–16
Moffett, Fred D., 115n
Monfried, Walter, 115
Morehead, Katherine Boyd, 178n
Morehouse, Frederic C., 71
Morris, Mrs. Howard, 50–51n
Moscow, 103
Moses, Mrs. Charles, 50–51n
Most, Johann, 26
Mukwonago, Wis., 5, 6
Mundelein, Ill., 148
Mundt, Karl, 166
My Four Years in Germany (Gerard), 96

N. W. Ayer and Son, 107
Nagasaki, 160
Napoleon (drama), 53
Nash, Mrs. George, 50–51n
Nasser, Abdel, 195
National Broadcasting Company, 148, 149, 152
National Council of Women, 51
National Recovery Act, 140–41, 143–44
Nazis, 153, 154, 157
Neacy, T. J., 71n
Nebraska, 135, 149
Neelen, Neele B., 75
Nehru, Jawaharlal, 195
Nelson, Gaylord, 199
Nepal, 195
Nevada, Clarice Rowlands, 116
New Deal, 143, 154
New Guinea, 157
Newhall, Daniel, 11
Newhall House, 10–17, 211
Newman, A. W., 40, 41
New Orleans *Item,* 99
Newspaper Advertising Executives Association, 173
Newspapers. *See Daily Journal;* Milwaukee; *Milwaukee Journal;* names of individual newspapers
New York City, 51, 52, 65, 107, 108, 112, 116, 158, 199
New York *Herald,* 72
New York *Herald-Tribune,* 193
New York State, 130, 138
New York *Sun,* 96
New York Times, 52, 96, 99, 183, 193
New York *World,* 49n, 96
Nieman, Agnes Wahl, 175–78, 213
Nieman, Conrad, 5
Nieman, Lucius William: founder of *Journal,* 3; as editior of *Daily Journal,* 5, 211; childhood, 5–6; trained as printer, 5–6; as reporter, 6–7; as editor in St. Paul, 7; as editor of *Sentinel,* 7, 8; purchases *Daily Journal,* 8; as editor of *Daily Journal,* 9, 11–16, 31; and Newhall House

fire, 11–16; on election of 1884 and Cleveland, 22–24; opposes spoils system, 25; as Democrat, 31 ff.; belief of in individual liberty, 33; on independent press, 36; and state treasury scandal, 37 ff.; and fight for honest government, 41; as stockholder in *Daily Journal*, 44; as organizer, 45; personality of, 46; makes paper independent of Democratic party, 47–49; opposes free silver, 48–49; and Charity edition of *Journal*, 50; and La Follette, 54 ff.; on Sunday edition of *Journal*, 78; marriage of, 79–80; and Woodrow Wilson, 85–86; to Europe, 98–99; illness, 108, 109; hires Grant, 109; as political forecaster, 112; on *Journal's* policy, 121; as editor and publisher of *Journal*, 173; as stockholder, 175; death of, 175, 203; management of paper, 206–7. *See also Milwaukee Journal*

Nieman, Violette, 5

Nigeria, 196

1948 Corporation, 168–69

Nixon, Richard M., 166, 200

Nonpartisan elections, 70 ff., 212

Normyle, William, 195–96

Norris, George, 82

North American Newspaper Alliance, 174

Northcliffe, Lord, 88

North Dakota, 149

Northern Hospital for Insane, 17, 18

Northfield, Minn., 173

Northwestern University, 184

Norway, 194

Nowell, Harris, 161

Oconomowoc, Wis., 19, 38, 40, 183

Ohio, 105, 135, 158

Okinawa, 159–60

Olds, F. Perry, 87, 94, 148, 154*n*

Oliver, Mrs. J. B., 50–51*n*

O'Mara and Ormsbee, 108

"On, Wisconsin," 128

Operation Deep Freeze, 194

Oshkosh, Wis., 17, 18, 32

Oshkosh *Northwestern,* 123

Otjen, Theobold, 71

Oulahan, R. V., 99

Oyster Bay, N.Y., 65

Pabst Theater (Milwaukee), 65

Pacific Ocean, 157, 159

Pageant, 117

Pahlke, Alfred H., 115

Pakistan, 195

Palmer, John M., 48, 49*n*, 214

Paris, 52, 173, 195

Parker, Alton B., 214

Paschen, Sheriff, 27

Patton, Constance Mariner, 53

Paul, George H., 25

Pawling, Alonzo, 71*n*

Payne, Henry C., 25, 54

Payne-Aldrich tariff, 82

Pearl Harbor, 151, 156

Pearse, Carroll G., 71*n*

Pease, Harry S., 195

Peavey paper mill, 188

Peck, George W., 34, 37, 38, 40, 55, 71, 211

Peck, Mrs. George W., Jr., 51*n*

Peckham, Mrs. George W., 50–51*n*

Peck's Bad Boy, 34

Peck's Sun, 34*n*

Peculiar Treasure, A (Ferber), 78

Pennsylvania, 58, 108

People's Council of America, 95

Pereles, Mrs. J. H., 50–51*n*

Petrograd, 98

Pfister, Charles F., 64

Philadelphia *Inquirer,* 176

Philipp, Emanuel L., 71, 102

Philippine Islands, 195

Phillips, Alice, 148

Photographers Association of America, 124

Photography in *The Journal*, 124, 125, 170–71, 212

"Picture Journal, The," 120

Pieplow, William E., 71